THE DAWN BOOK

INFORMATION FROM THE MASTER GUIDES

A SPIRITUAL GUIDE BOOK

by

Annie Stillwater Gray

working with her Spirit Guide, Darcimon Stillwater

For permission, serialization, condensation, adaptions, or for our catalog of other publications, write to Ozark Mountain Publishing, LLC., P.O. box 754, Huntsville, AR 72740, ATTN: Permissions Department.

Library of Congress Cataloging-in-Publication Data

Gray, Annie Stillwater -1946

The Dawn Book by Annie Stillwater Gray

At this time in the evolution of the Earth, much information is being made available to humanity through psychic and spiritual means. Channeled information has presented itself throughout history, but never as frequently or as forcefully as today. It is time for humanity to possess knowledge which has been, for the most part, unavailable until now. This sacred knowledge is entering the Earth plane in many places, in many ways.

1. Angels 2. Spirit Guides 3. Metaphysics 4. Master Guides

1. Gray, Annie Stillwater, 1946 II. Master Guides III. Title

Library of Congress Catalog Card Number: 2015943522

ISBN: 9781940265131

Cover Design: noir33.com

Book set in: Gentium Book Basic, Deneane

Book Design: Tab Pillar

Published by:

PO Box 754

Huntsville, AR 72740

800-935-0045 or 479-738-2348 fax: 479-738-2448

WWW.OZARKMT.COM

Printed in the United States of America

From the authors:

We believe that fostering conscious connections with Spirit Guides is the most important work humans can do in this time of transition. Every human can consciously connect with his or her primary Spirit Guide or Life Guide. Since this book was telepathically transcribed, we have been working together: speaking and teaching classes, workshops, and seminars. Contact the author at Annie@WelcomeRadio.com.

Annie and Darci have also written *Education of a Guardian Angel* published by Ozark Mountain Publishing in 2014.

∞ ∞ ∞

To all who walk with us into the new time

∞ ∞ ∞

Contents

∞ ∞ ∞

Illustrations

Introduction

At this time in the evolution of the earth, much information is being made available to humanity through psychic and spiritual means. Channeled information has presented itself throughout history, but never as frequently or as forcefully as today. It is time for humanity to possess knowledge which has been, for the most part, unavailable until now. This sacred knowledge is entering the earth plane in many places, in many ways.

The information in this book has been carefully prepared by the master guides who are in charge of disseminating this knowledge. These master guides have taken great care that this information be presented in a very simple straightforward manner so that all humans incarnated now on earth may have access to it. We who have written this book have exercised great diligence in channeling this information. We have, from the beginning, been aware of the significance and the importance of this material. This project remains a priority for us because it is time for this knowledge to become available to everyone. The very survival of the human species depends greatly on this information being accepted and put to use. It is our responsibility and our pleasure to show in the following pages that not only can humanity survive, but it can evolve to a state of being many never thought possible. This process of evolution takes attention, serious but joyful application, perseverance, and sincerity. All the basic information humans need to make this transformation is included in this text.

This book is a gift to humanity more precious than any jewel. The ramifications of this information may affect future generations for hundreds upon hundreds of years. We have been handed here an opportunity to become what we can become, to fulfill ourselves in the eyes of the universe. Every individual who reads this book is blessed. Every individual who takes this information to heart and allows it to begin to change his or her life is blessed and protected.

There are no gifts more sacred in this time of great change on earth than the guidance, the knowledge, and the love that are offered to us by our spirit helpers. We must rejoice and be glad of heart, for although we humans face tremendous challenges as we face a new millennium, we are given all the information, all the knowledge, all the guidance we need to make a great evolutionary leap.

We must pay attention and see ourselves, our lives, and the world around us with a new universal perspective. This book is here to help us do exactly that and more.

(Note: Breathing exercise information, helpful to the reader using this workbook, is available in the Appendix.)

Section One

Beginning Information

Every day each human being awakes, takes the first conscious breath, thinks the first conscious thought, feels the first conscious feeling of the day. The universe provides an extra burst of joy for that first conscious moment for each human being. All we humans have to do is be aware that it exists, and that joy is present for all of us.

The knowledge of the love and joy that pervades the universe makes all worries seem small. The material plane provides many tests, challenges, and worries, it is true. The earthly plane, however, is only one small manifestation of all of creation. The love and joy present in the universe is very much greater than any earthly problem, no matter how huge and troublesome this problem may appear. Our vision as humans has often gone only so far. We cannot see past the challenges and rewards presented to us on earth.

There is a barrier or veil which surrounds earthly consciousness. This barrier often acts as a reflector, bouncing our troubles back at us, sometimes even increasing their importance in the scheme of daily living. The veil, of course, is an illusion, but one that has been ingrained in human consciousness since humans first manifested on this plane. It is part of the challenge of living a human lifetime, for it is through the veil we pass at birth, and through the veil we pass at death. Both birth and death have always to this point in time been surrounded with mystery and often fear.

There have been those throughout history who have been gifted with the ability to communicate through this barrier between our realm and others. This gift is not an accident or random chance. Such a gift must always have been earned, because vision and contact through the veil are major challenges for earthlings. One can earn this psychic gift in many ways. In the past, there have been instances of trauma which forced the individual's consciousness to expand and pierce the illusion. Edgar Cayce was a well-known extremely gifted psychic who, in a former life, was wounded and left to die on the battlefield. He learned to move his consciousness out of his body as a way of alleviating his pain and suffering. This took an incredible force of will. When he reentered the earth plane years later, he carried with him this ability to see and move beyond the ordinary human consciousness. Kay Mora is another person whose psychic talents manifested only after she was involved in a critical auto crash. Trauma and near-death situations are not the only way to obtain psychic gifts. There has always been a gentle way for humans to achieve contact through the barrier. This path, however, takes perseverance. Daily meditation, prayer, and sincerity of heart are the keys to the gentle path.

Contact from guides and helpers from beyond the barriers that surround earthly consciousness is available to all. Just imagine the change in life perspective that contact through the veil brings! Now we see that there is so much more than birth, life, and death on this small planet. Here is the joyous news: the illusion is to be stripped away! The new millenium brings a new perspective to life on earth. There has been made, for all humans, an opening in the barrier through which the love, joy, and compassion abundant in the universe can flow. This opening right now is a small moment, the first conscious moment, the first waking moment each of us experiences.

Now that we know this, how can we begin our days with worry or fear? Let our first conscious breath, our first conscious thought, our first conscious feeling of each day from this time on be filled with joy and love. This opening in the veil floods human existence with new hope. It is up to each human to make use of this opening. We can start by being aware of it, and by experiencing the joy and love pouring upon us and surrounding us as we awake each day.

∞ ∞ ∞

The subject is now realms other than the earth plane. We humans might wonder what these other planes are like. There is an infinite variety of realms, most of them of no consequence to those incarnate on earth. There are, however, a few planes that are closely linked with human existence, and there are some facts about these "nearby" realms that it is now helpful for humans to know.

There is a plane which is a holding area or waiting space. This is where the spirit or soul is prepared for entry into a human body before birth on earth. This is also where humans are welcomed when they die, and where a review of their lives takes place. There is also a realm where spirit helpers dwell. Guides operate on this plane when making contact with humans on earth through the veil or when helping humans in any way. These realms are not like earth in that they are nonmaterial. Beings exist only as energy or spirits in these realms, yet beings do retain their integrity, their sense of who they are.

Few humans realize that much can be passed between the earth and these "nearby" planes. No physical or material items can be passed beyond the barrier surrounding our earthly existence (thus the saying "you can't take it with you") for this type of physical manifestation (gross matter) is unique unto this planet. What can be passed? What moves through the veil? Thoughts and emotions can not only move through the gate between realms, they actually possess an energy-shape in these nearby planes. This is why it is indeed helpful to send love and prayers to those who have recently died. The love and compassion take energy-shapes which surround them and comfort them as they undergo their life review. Other types of emotions also can take shape in these other realms. Anger is a forceful energy with a jagged shape.

Grief, sadness, resentment, etc., all actually take energy shapes or forms on these close-by planes. It is also appropriate, but rarely done, to pray for and send love to the souls who are about to incarnate. When love energy surrounds a soul about to enter the earth plane, the passage is easier and more joyous. In the same way, resentment or fear can make the passage more difficult.

We humans do not realize how powerful our emotions can be on earth, certainly, but beyond on these associated realms also. The most useful and helpful emotion to send to any soul is love. Love passes easily through the gate between realms and literally blossoms into beautiful light energy. Sending love is the finest way anyone can help a soul in transition, that is, a soul entering or leaving earth existence. It helps the passage become a joyous occasion for the soul in transit.

Now is the time for all humans to understand that whenever we feel a strong emotion of any kind, it has a shape, an energy form, a life of its own on another plane, and if the emotion is strong enough or if it is reinforced often enough, it can retain this energy-shape for a while. Much information like this has been withheld from human consciousness. Only now are humans ready to receive and use this new knowledge. The transformation of human consciousness that the turn of the millennium brings is opening the way for much new information. This book is a simple, straightforward guide to this information.

Once humans realize how powerful and far-reaching our emotions truly are, we can undertake much work with visualization. If we humans begin to see, to visualize our emotions in our own minds here on earth, we are then, of course, very much in touch with what we are feeling. More than this, we can learn to channel these feelings, processing out anger, jealousy, revenge, and other hurtful emotions. This is not to say that these emotions are not felt, but we can learn to process them, that is to acknowledge them and then use visualization to put them at rest. Techniques for doing this are outlined later in this book.

The most splendid emotion is love. Love and compassion are healing and helpful to all. One of the most constructive ways we can help humanity and the earth is to gather in groups and generate love energy. How quickly we could heal the problems on earth if many humans gathered with such an awareness and purpose! If we flood the earth and nearby planes with love, the transformation of human consciousness is swift and joyous.

The knowledge that our emotions materialize or take an energy-shape and have an existence unto themselves hopefully tunes all humans to what we are feeling and instills a sense of responsibility for these emotions. We can use our emotions to bring peace, love, understanding, and compassion to the earth and its associated planes. We can use our emotions to bring a significant change in human consciousness on this planet. Those who are discarnate are aware of how powerful human emotions can be. Humans to some extent are aware of emotions, and once in a while we catch a glimpse of the power of these feelings. Often in the material earth plane such emotions are held as useless and undesirable. It is time for this to change. It is time for a new perspective and a new approach to human emotions. Using feelings and visualizations together, the human species can bring a much-needed transformation to the earth.

∞ ∞ ∞

Perhaps it is best to clarify that, when we speak of other realms nearby the earth plane, we speak of realms that are particularly tied into existence on earth. There a multitude of other realms that have nothing whatsoever to do with earth life, but there are a few that do. Humans are, for the most part, unaware of these few other planes that are linked to the material earth plane. It is now time not only to learn of them, but to make use of these nearby realms to better life on earth.

We have recently spoken of how emotions take an energy form in these realms, so what humans do on earth definitely affects these realms. These planes are a part of earth's existence, and what manifests in these nearby realms affects life on earth as well. The first step for humans is to recognize the existence of these nearby realms and the barrier between them and earth consciousness. Once this is seen, ways to move consciously through the barrier are found. Thoughts and feelings pass on a regular basis from humans on earth through the veil to these nearby spheres, but humans are not aware of this. It is time to become aware.

We can change the condition of life on earth by changing the energy existing in these related realms. Our thoughts and feelings are that powerful! Emotions become much more valued than they have ever been in the past, for it is seen that they can transform life on earth. One person's emotions, even the most passionate human, can produce only so much energy. The transformation comes when many people feel a similar emotion. Such a transformation occurred in Eastern Europe. For twenty years, people in the Eastern bloc countries desired freedom of expression and freedom to move. Their emotions amassed in the nearby realm, gathering and strengthening until the tide turned here on earth. Their desire for freedom collected, as it were, on the nearby plane until the energy was great enough to change the course of events on earth. Most of these people did not openly fight their controllers, their leaders, through those long years of domination. Yet their hearts cried out. Their emotions took an energy form and amassed until the vibration was strong enough to affect a change on the material earth plane.

The next amassing of energy needs to be love and compassion for the planet. If enough humans feel love for the earth and distress at her present state of pollution, these feelings then collect on the nearby plane, the vibration there changes, and this change then manifests on earth. We are getting there, but more *emotions* need to be directed to this end. Once a great number of people *feel* for the planet and continue to emote, we surely see change. This is not to say we do not participate. Actions are valuable. Individual actions help spread the word, communicate the problems, evoke the feelings necessary for a change en masse. We must work on all levels to address this problem. It is simply time to be aware of this new way, for great change can be affected in this manner.

Now that this knowledge is available, we see how valuable our emotions can be. We see how a large number of people, whether they are physically together or not, can create a great form of energy by channeling their emotions in one specific direction. This energy mass then exists unto itself. If we keep adding to it (as the people in the Eastern bloc countries have done), the emotional energy mass eventually affects significant change on this material earth plane.

∞ ∞ ∞

Very young children (age five and under) maintain a connection through the barrier between realms. In the past, children lose this thread to other worlds as they begin school and grow to adulthood. In the upcoming century, humans learn to keep and in fact nurture this connection. In this way, psychic gifts can be explored and developed from childhood along with other skills now taught and valued on earth.

Psychic awareness and growth are the keys to the transformation of human consciousness. The teaching of the psychic arts comes into its own in the twenty-first century. In the new millennium, learning psychic arts is considered every bit as important as learning math or geography.

Care of the human energy field is another area that gains tremendous importance. Already many healers work with more than just the physical body when dealing with illness or injury. In the new century, it is seen that working with the energy field of a person is just as important as examining and treating the physical body. Many at this time are ill, not from gross physical causes, but because their energy fields are askew. With the development of psychic awareness and psychic skills, many are able to see the layers of the aura, the energy field surrounding each human. Much can be learned about a person's condition by the shape, color, and vibratory rate of the aura. It becomes standard practice to examine and heal the aura as part of natural healing. Up to now, this side of healing has been neglected for the most part, but this is now changing.

True health is also related to the energy present in the spine and head. The chakras (energy centers along the spine and head) receive much attention and study. This must occur for true health to exist on planet earth. By neglecting the energy present in each human, the gross material side of existence on earth has been overemphasized. It is true that medical technology in the latter half of the twentieth century has saved lives and prolonged life in general. Yet these practices are not only expensive, they are often risky or downright dangerous. Some even make matters worse in the long run.

It is time for the realization that working with and changing a person's energy field affects the physical body. In fact, we are looking to a time when most healing is accomplished within the energy pattern of humans. With the development and acceptance of skilled psychic healers, there occurs an entirely new approach to treatment of illness and injury.

It is time for humans to learn how much we can do for ourselves as far as healing and maintaining health are concerned. Working with our energy fields is every bit as important as eating healthy meals or getting proper exercise. Visualization and breathing techniques are the keys to maintaining a healthy energy field. This information has been available on earth for a very long time. It is now coming into the spotlight and is becoming widely accepted.

There are now, all around the globe, psychic healers and teachers in training, ready to lead humanity on a huge leap of consciousness. In the past, humans have been willing to place themselves in the hands of medical doctors for surgery, transplants, radiation, and the like. Now it is time to look to the psychic avenues for healing. Now it is time to seek out the psychic teachers and healers. It is time to look forward. There is no need to look back.

∞ ∞ ∞

The leaders of the transformation of human consciousness are the psychic healers and teachers. Each of these healers and teachers is undergoing extensive training specifically for the purpose of aiding humankind in this great transformation.

The trust that people have in the past placed in their doctors, professors, and priests can now be placed in themselves. Each person can now experience a personal link to healing and knowledge. Training in yoga, breathing, meditation, and visualization has been available on earth for many years. Now, through an opening in the veil between realms, humankind as a whole can incorporate these practices into daily life for the greater good of all.

This book is offered as a guide for use by psychic teachers and by individuals. In this text, we explore the basic steps that humankind is undergoing in this great transformation. The information regarding this metamorphosis which has before been esoteric and available to only a few is now available to humanity as a whole.

∞ ∞ ∞

The universe moves as a whole to balance itself. This is the meaning of karma. The scientific, the technological, the intellectual side has been greatly developed on earth throughout the past century. Now equal spiritual gains are called for to balance the vibrations on the planet. The movement to this end is nearly automatic, though it is being aided through the veil.

The basic task of the psychic teachers is to show that we humans can discover the truth of this movement, this transformation, within ourselves. The truth lies within. This message has been communicated to humanity since the beginning, yet it has been greatly overshadowed by outer material concerns. To be in touch with the truth of our own spirits, we must be in a quiet space with no distractions. The vision, the words, the knowledge are there and available to all. Once we reach a place of inner calm and tranquility, we see a door open inside us, and the love, knowledge, understanding, and wisdom from beyond the veil floods through us. Everyone can do this. The key is our spirits, our souls. Once we tune to that essence, that life force inside us, we find the way is easily opened.

Many all over the earth are now meditating. Many are reaching a place of inner calm and tranquility. Many are turning the key that unlocks boundless knowledge, security, love, and joy. The opening between the realms is there. It does exist. It remains only for each individual to find quiet, go within and seek it. No longer need we rely on others for the truth. The truth lies within each of us. The psychic teachers are available all over the globe to help teach individuals how to find that quiet place within. Individuals can do this by themselves as well. There are many ways to reach this place of inner peace, which then unlocks a universe of truth. It is time for every individual to experience this inner peace, this universal truth, this all-pervading love.

There is a unique energy surrounding the planet at this time. It is the infectious energy of expanding light and love. The time is now for great changes within and without. This book is here to make it easy for everyone. In basic simple language, we outline what is coming to pass and how each individual can tune in to make the very best of it.

There is sure to be a comfortable and, in fact, a joyful way for each human to incorporate these changes into his or her own life. There is a quiet space in every day for each of us to turn inward, to touch the truth which the universe offers us. It takes only a little time, a little quiet, and trust that going within touches the very core of universal peace and love.

∞ ∞ ∞

There are many skeptics on this planet, and many who cling to the pursuit of material gain. There is, however, a new energy, a new tide flowing. Many, even those who have very little, are beginning to see the emptiness and the fruitlessness of operating solely to obtain physical comforts. This change brings new hope. For the first time on earth, there is the possibility of eliminating poverty and hunger, but much must first be done.

This transformation of human consciousness can happen much more swiftly than people have heretofore imagined. This uplifting transformation can come just as quickly as the changes in Eastern Europe. It may be confusing to some, but for those who operate through the feelings, there is no mistake! The love and joy which are already beginning to pour through the opening between worlds pervades every-thing on earth. It remains only for humans to tune to this energy, enjoy it, and let it transform us.

It must be widely recognized that gathering in groups for the purpose of amassing an emotional vibration has a great effect on events on earth. It is in this way we can save the planet from hopeless pollution and ruin. Already many have begun this work, gathering together to send love and healing energy to the earth. The earth is an entity unto herself, and needs nurturing and care so she can, in turn, care for us. Sending love energy to the earth, especially in large amounts such as a group can generate, is one of the most powerful ways we can turn the situation around. It must be done all over the globe, so that the love and healing energy that is amassed can reach every spot, indeed, every molecule on earth.

The psychic healers and teachers are leaders in this movement. It is for them to teach the environmentalists the transforming power of such practices. The environmentalists can then organize large-scale gatherings for just this purpose. The results amaze many and bring joy to all who love the earth.

Another role the psychic healers and teachers are taking is working with those who are pregnant. A new practice is beginning. When a woman is about to bring a soul onto the earth plane, in the seventh to eighth month of pregnancy, the future mother, along with family and close friends, and possibly the midwife and a psychic teacher, hosts a ceremony for the soul that is about to enter. This ceremony we can liken to a funeral or wake in that prayers and love are sent to the entity in transition. Remember, the emotions present at such a gathering take an energy-shape which is sensed or known by the soul who is to be born. It is important that fear, worry, resentment, and any anger be eliminated, and that the ceremony be bathed in joy and love. Flowers and gentle music are appropriate, and love, much love, must be generated, for then the passage and the lifetime of the soul are much more joyful and true to the path. The ceremony can take many forms. It is suggested that visualization of color and light be used. The group that has gathered must be surrounded with golden light. Place the mother-to-be in a pyramid of shimmering white light. Singing, chanting, and praying are all appropriate. The most important part of the gathering is generating joy and love for the arriving soul. A moving song or prayer that evokes love in the hearts of everyone present is needed. The sweet smell of flowers and incense, the soothing sounds of soft music and song, the warm light, the love and joy generated by the group affect the incoming soul.

We must attract and make way for more evolved souls to come and help and heal on planet earth in the new century. This welcome ensures that those we need so much now enter this plane.

In a similar way, the ceremony known as a funeral or wake is changing. Once it is generally known and accepted that the emotional energy we generate on earth affects those who have recently passed, a new view is taken on these ceremonies. Joy replaces grief. Love replaces sorrow. The purpose of the gathering, instead of remembrance only, includes generating love and joy to send to the recently departed as a helpful gift. The more people present at the funeral who can sincerely generate love for the one who has passed, the more love energy the deceased has to carry him or her on from the holding plane to the next phase.

Generating love, especially in large groups, is one of the biggest steps humanity can make as we enter a new century and a new age. Once this is recognized as effective, it becomes standard practice. Comings and goings from earth improve in that they become easier and much more filled with love and joy.

∞ ∞ ∞

For the first two years of life, babies have a soft spot on the top of their heads called the fontanel. This area is the opening of the crown chakra, the very top of the energy centers of the body. This is the major passageway for the body's energy. One of the changes occurring with the transformation of human consciousness is a change in the energy flow of the human body. Whereas before the major flow was horizontal, now the emphasis is on vertical flow along the spine and out and in through the top of the head. The horizontal orientation has kept us trapped in the survival struggles, the sex and power struggles of the material world. This change in orientation of the major energy flow of the human body is *the primary factor* in the transformation of human consciousness. It is opening people to an entirely new way of existing on earth.

This vertical energy flow is one of the keys to communication through the veil. Once a person's energy orientation is changed from horizontal, that is, being preoccupied by daily material concerns, to vertical, that person enjoys an entirely different perspective on life on earth. The vertical flow of energy in the human body clears the way for many things. Once the energy orientation is vertical, heaven to earth and earth to heaven, the link between the conscious and the superconscious is made. The path to understanding is cleared. We can then pierce the illusion that the earth plane exists unto itself. We can then communicate through the veil between earth life and other realms. We can then see how much more there is to human existence than material gain. The new opening in the veil which has arrived for the new century is the major force in changing the magnetic fields and the energy orientation of humans.

Each morning when we awake there is an instant when joy floods through us. This is the energy of unconditional love flowing through the new opening in the veil. There is a magnetism associated with this flow. This magnetism pulls our individual energy fields upward. For that moment, our major energy orientation is vertical.

Of course, horizontal energy flow is natural and necessary to life on earth. Survival, sexual activity, material achievement are all a part of earth existence. What is taking place is the quality of the horizontal flow is changing as we humans experience more and more of the vertical energy flow in our own bodies. This vertical flow of energy through the top of the head and up and down the spine is becoming the major energy orientation for humans for the new century. The vertical flow then feeds the horizontal flow which moves out onto the earth plane through each human.

Once we humans have changed over so that our major orientation is to a vertical energy flow, the quality of life on earth becomes markedly different. We are then operating on the energy of love and compassion straight through us from the creative force rather than from our personal power drives, fears, loves and hates, neurotic reactions, and motivations. Let us picture a shaft of luminescent white light running from the base of our spines out through the top of our heads. This shaft of light vibrates and glows with blinding white light. From this center of vertical energy we operate, sending light out horizontally onto the earth. The light we send out horizontally can be many-colored and can be for many purposes, but its source is the vertical flow. This is how we must operate in the new century: tuned through our superconscious to a higher source of light and love.

SEE ILLUSTRATION 1:

Vertical Energy Flow as Contrasts with the Horizontal Flow

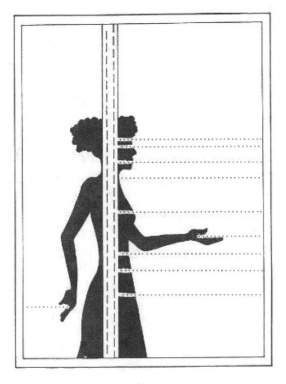

∞ ∞ ∞

One of the most marvelous structures of ancient times is still standing on earth, the great pyramid at Giza. This structure was divinely inspired. The information used to build it came from spirit guide sources. This pyramid was meant to be a map or picture of the evolution of humankind. The pyramid form was chosen because it is most conducive to spiritual attunement. The base of four equal sides stands rooted firmly on earth, whereas the apex literally soars toward heaven. Both these attributes are necessary for the spiritual evolvement of humans. Grounding in earthly reality is just as important as aspiring toward heaven.

People have been studying the great pyramid for many centuries. Its mysteries are at last being unlocked. Much important information concerning the pyramid was revealed in the Edgar Cayce readings, but there are a few essential facts which now are coming to be known by every human. The location of the pyramid itself is a pivotal point on the earth's surface. This location was not affected by the last set of major earth changes when there was much flooding and the great continent now called Atlantis disappeared into the sea. During the next set of earth changes, the pyramid continues to stand but actually rotates, or appears to rotate. The entire orientation of the earth at this time is different. The north and south poles are in different locations. This is the physical manifestation of the change in human consciousness. There takes place a thorough revamping of the energy on earth. The rotation of the great pyramid represents the turning of the human mind and spirit. This shift in the earth's orientation may sound catastrophic, but many survive, and this is when new values, new leaders, and new structures make our entry into the new millennium complete. These shifts come when humanity is ready, most likely early in the twenty-first century.

Humanity is coming to understand that all major spiritual events manifesting on earth are represented in the great pyramid at Giza. This includes all religions. Whenever a major spiritual uplifting comes to pass, it is represented in the structure of the great pyramid. This is a sacred structure. It is meant to show that spiritual evolvement is the major purpose for existence on earth. Those who built the great pyramid understood this and were divinely inspired to build this colossal structure as a message to the generations to come.

The pyramid is an excellent symbol. It is tangible. It is real. People all over the earth know of its existence as one of the seven wonders. Now its purpose also comes to be known. The discovery of the purpose of the great pyramid is coming to light by both psychic and scientific means. This event shows that there is not so much distance between the psychic and the scientific.

It is not long before these major changes come to pass. They have been spoken of for centuries, and now we are very close to experiencing them. For those who wish to tune in to the psychic changes and prepare for the transformation of consciousness, many things can be done, many tools used. One of the most useful tools is the psychic pyramid. Let each human who wishes to be ready construct a personal psychic pyramid. Groups can do this as well. This psychic pyramid is to be the same shape as the great pyramid at Giza, that is, having a base of four equal sides. Construct each of these psychic pyramids out of brilliant luminescent light, white or gold is best. Envision the psychic pyramid before sleeping, upon awakening, and upon entering meditation and prayer. In this way, our consciousness is tuned and blessed.

∞ ∞ ∞

This has been said before in many languages, in many religions, many times: love is the ultimate force in the universe. Love is the great transformative power that heals and moves us onward. Love is an emotion. We *feel* love. When our heart centers are open and flowing freely, much changes in our lives and on this planet. Love is also very cleansing. Love can clear us of petty thoughts and feelings such as jealousy, resentment, and bitterness. Love can even transform anger and hate. It is essential that we humans learn more about love and what it can do, and apply this knowledge in our lives. Love's transformative and healing powers are available to us every hour of every day.

What we are going to learn today is how to transform any emotion, no matter how violent, into love. It is not an easy technique in that we humans most often view our emotions as uncontrollable, or at the very least unmanageable. First, it is important that we be in touch with our own feelings and be honest about what we feel. We recognize that we feel a certain way, and we are truthful with ourselves in the face of the universe concerning what these feelings are. As an emotional surge wells up and surfaces, the first step is to consciously acknowledge that we are experiencing strong emotions.

Next, a bit of detachment is in order. We need to stand back or detach ourselves just enough to call the emotion by name. "I am angry." "I feel hurt and rejected." "I feel lonely." "I feel depressed." "I am jealous and feel resentful." We need to detach ourselves enough to name that feeling.

Now, put a shape and color to the feeling. Anger, for instance, is often pictured as jagged and red. Fear, loneliness, depression, and sadness could be seen as floating discs of various shades of gray. Emotions are, of course, very personal. We generate them within each of ourselves. Therefore, the visualization process is personal, also. We choose our own colors and shapes. We need to be open and inventive. This helps us get more in touch with the strong emotions we feel.

Let's take frustration and powerlessness as an example. We picture the frustration as a rusty wheel or gear, and we see its powerlessness as it rotates around connected to nothing, affecting nothing. We put our frustrated feelings into that image. We acknowledge our frustration fully and see it take shape as that rusty gear. Perhaps we can even hear it as it squeaks and scrapes slowly around. If the frustration has resulted from a particular situation, place the rusty wheel in the environment from whic' the problem emotion stems. If we are frustrated at work or with the boss, picture that rusty wheel creaking and groaning right over the bosses head. This step of visualizing our feelings is very important. We begin to have some control of our feelings when we do this. Remember, our emotions do take energy-shapes on a nearby plane whether we put form on them in our own minds or not. If we put shapes and colors on the emotions as we experience them, we begin to have control.

This next step is the salvation of the human consciousness. Once this practice becomes widely used, violence and hatred quietly die away. Take the visualized emotion, in this case our creaking rusty gear wheel, and surround it in a sphere of light. Surround the gear and the boss with a sphere of light if this seems appropriate. This color must be bright and luminescent, and, again, of our own choosing. Let us use our intuitions when choosing. Bright blue and emerald green are healing. Sparkling gold light is protective. Shimmering pink is gentle and loving. Let us completely surround the visualized emotion with whatever luminescent colored light we choose. We make a sphere of light around the image until it is completely incased.

Visualizing the emotion insists we acknowledge it. Putting form on it is a way to name it. Surrounding the image with light protects us and others from harmful effects. Now we can transform the emotional energy into love. This may not be easy to do at first, especially if the feeling is one of strong anger which has in the past led to violent outbursts.

It is time for humans to realize how powerful and far-reaching our emotions are. Once we truly recognize this, we must also acknowledge our responsibility for the emotional energy forms we are producing. The technique described here has not surfaced before because of fear of its misuse. This planet needs no more hatred, anger, or violence. These are already too often portrayed in books, films, and on television. Those who use this technique must take responsibility and approach this work with selflessness and with high-minded sincerity of purpose. We can eliminate violence and fear when this procedure is widely understood and used.

We have surrounded our rusty gear with a sphere of brilliant golden light. We see that powerful golden light begin to affect the wheel. The rust is flaking away as the golden light permeates the wheel. The gear wheel itself becomes bright gold. This process continues until we see every centimeter, every molecule of the gear as shiny solid gold. Then the wheel begins to turn smoothly and effortlessly, perhaps with a comforting hum. The wheel then turns faster and faster until it rotates so fast that it becomes a pulsating sphere of brilliant golden light.

If we had chosen another color in this visualization, say bright green, we find it appropriate at this time to surround the green sphere with another of gold. See the two of them pulse and whirl together, the green inside the gold. Gold is the color associated with unconditional love. Pink is also useful when transforming emotions into love energy. When in doubt, use white. White light purifies any emotion.

Now we have emotional energy transformed from a potentially harmful or hurtful state to a form which can only help the human who is experiencing the strong feeling, and can also help the earth's existence as a whole. We have this transformed emotional energy, and we can send it into the ether to be added to the love that is collecting in the nearby realms. We can send it to the boss, the object of our original frustration. We can take it back into ourselves. Now, wherever this transformed energy goes, it is love, and love is what we need more than ever all over the earth.

∞ ∞ ∞

Everyone at some time in life wonders about the reason or reasons for life on earth, for incarnate existence. With this transformation of human consciousness, people on this planet have a clearer picture of the purpose of this realm.

Earth is a learning place; many understand that fact. Let us add more to this picture. Life on earth is only one slice of the pizza of a spirit's total evolvement. The other slices have similar ingredients but exist on levels other than the earth realm. The slices are basically of equal size or value. The slice that is earth incarnation is no more or less important than the other slices, or levels of learning and evolvement. The other slices contain challenges to stimulate growth and evolvement of the soul, but these challenges are much different from those that exist here on earth. It is important for each of us to ingest the experience of each slice, to chew and assimilate thoroughly, to enjoy all the tastes and sensations, to experience each slice as completely as possible.

This image of the pizza, though much oversimplified, puts earth life in perspective. It shows that an incarnation on earth is but one phase (or one slice) in a larger cycle of evolvement. An earth life is not an end-all situation, only a step, a phase, a slice of the whole cycle. If we are going to liken the divine cycle of soul evolvement to a humble pizza, then let us at least picture the pie as loaded. There are many, many ingredients on the pie of spirit evolvement, many tastes, many sensations, sometimes a little heartburn and indigestion. As we ingest our slice of the pie in an earth incarnation, let us chew it slowly and thoroughly, enjoying all the flavors and experiences. If we gulp it down, we do not digest it properly, and what we have taken in is not utilized properly in soul development. (Pardon this unpleasant image, but we are dealing with gross matter here), we might even regurgitate the ingested material in some way, which could be seen as a setback on the cycle.

Just as it is important not to overemphasize the significance of earth life by thinking that this is the *only* realm, it is also essential to view life on earth as a necessary piece of the pie. Spirit evolvement is not complete without the earth experience. Being incarnated in a physical body and making our way in this material realm bring multiple challenges. All these challenges promote soul evolvement. With the transformation of human consciousness, individuals can grasp the truth of life on earth: that each challenge is an opportunity to learn, to grow, to thoroughly ingest the earth experience, so that we may move on to taste the next piece of pie.

∞ ∞ ∞

We are in the midst of a very great spiritual transition, one of the greatest ever to occur on the earth. It is a joyful time for the human race, although not everyone sees it as so. Old ways die hard, but it is very difficult for people to hold onto the old ways, old thought structures, old values in the face of what is taking place now on this planet. This book is a helper. It is here to help each individual understand and make the most of this transition.

It does not matter how tuned we are to our subconscious minds. The subconscious mind of each human is linked, as if by a shimmering thread, to the superconscious mind which is an energy form existing in one of the nearby realms associated with the earth plane. It is difficult to describe the superconscious mind in earth terms because it exists in an entirely different reality. Yet this superconscious mind is intimately entwined into human existence. When we light up that connecting thread between our subconscious and the superconscious, we experience our place in the universe. We see ourselves connected to everything, a part of everything, at one with everything.

The superconscious is now sending energy to the subconscious of each human being to help each of us tune to this spiritual transition. The energy is gentle and subtle, but persistent. This spiritual transition is a gift to every human on earth. The superconscious is awakening every human, through the individual's subconscious, to the possibilities of the time. No one is left out!

The leaders of this spiritual transformation are those who are tuned with both their subconscious and their conscious minds to the energy coming from the superconscious. These leaders are receiving conscious messages from the superconscious that are helping themselves and others prepare for this great transition. This book is a part of the flow of conscious messages.

So even though people hold stubbornly to old habit patterns, they possess within their own subconscious a new energy that is there to help each person tune to, accept, and, in fact, make the most of the transition. For many, it is a joy to let go of the old outmoded forms, for many are realizing that these forms do not work. Those that are seekers, those that have long sought new ways, are the ones who lead and aid all of humanity in this transformation.

The knowledge that the seed for this spiritual transition has been planted in the subconscious of every human is very important. There is no discrimination whatsoever when it comes to this transformation. It is for everyone. It is for the whole of planet earth. It is an experience we *all* share as we begin the new millennium. No one is left out. All are elevated in light and love.

∞ ∞ ∞

As each of us lives each day, we go through many changes in our energy. In sleep, our energies balance, that is, they become more evenly distributed throughout the body. This is, in fact, one of the major reasons the human body needs sleep each day, to restore this balance of energies.

As we rise from sleep and begin our day, the energy within our bodies begins to move around. The energy collects in some areas and increases, and, of course, decreases in other areas. Our daily activities, our thoughts, our feelings, our will, all affect the way our bodily energy moves. Let's say that a person is a vice president of a huge corporation. The day begins with thoughts of the upcoming board meeting, or the possible acquisition of another company. As soon as those thoughts flow, so does this executive's energy. The balanced state achieved in sleep immediately shifts, and energy is drawn to the power center of the body located just above the navel, also called the third chakra. If a person sings first thing after rising from sleep, the energy center at the base of the throat, the fifth chakra, attracts energy. The flow continues to change throughout the day as activities and concerns vary.

When we have days where we are particularly clumsy or out of sync with the flow of activity, we are somehow unbalanced. There is too much energy gathered in one part of the body and not enough in another. Of course it is impossible to maintain complete energy balance in the body every moment of every day. The energies flow and change constantly. However, the awareness of this phenomenon can help us all understand how we can be better balanced and more in tune with what we are dealing with around us.

Daily meditation is one way to maintain a generally balanced energy flow in the body. Taking a few minutes to meditate partway through the day provides a refreshment of the body, a calming of the mind, and a balancing of the energy within the body. Meditation is being practiced in many forms all over the world. It is time for meditation to become a part of everyday life for humans on earth. Meditation is much different from sleep. It does provide similar benefits as far as balancing the energies of a person and refreshing the physical body are concerned. People often feel more rested and revitalized after twenty minutes of meditation than after eight hours of sleep.

The human body needs sleep to rebuild tissue and manufacture new cells. These processes deal with gross matter and take time, and are best done when the body is asleep. The maintenance of the physical body is mainly addressed during sleep. Once we are awake and moving around, our bodies are called into action, and rebuilding is put on the shelf until we sleep again. Adding meditation to our day relieves the body of some of the work usually done in sleep; namely, the balancing of the energy of the body. Some people find they need less sleep once they begin regular meditation.

When the energy is continually drawn to one area of the body and continually sucked away from the other areas, it causes an imbalance which can become chronic. We do not, then, rebalance well in sleep. This unbalanced state then promotes disease and illness. In meditation there is a *conscious* rebalancing of the person's energy field, which then helps maintain good health and resilience. Meditation also promotes peace of mind, good humor, and a generally joyous approach to life. There are many styles, many forms of meditation, and these are widely available all over the world.

It remains now to say that meditation is playing a significant part in this transformation of human consciousness. A body that is unbalanced energy-wise may not accept the new higher vibratory energy rate that is infiltrating the planet. This higher vibration permeating the earth is helping to raise and transform the consciousness of each human. Through daily meditation and prayer, we each can make the most of this time. Those who try to ignore it and continue to operate on earth with chronically unbalanced energies are bound to suffer illness, deformity, and pain. Death then comes much more quickly. It is in this way the transformation becomes complete. Those who do not tune their energies pass away from the earth plane. We humans who use daily meditation to balance our energies and tune to this higher earthly vibration are flourishing. We then experience this transformation with excitement, gladness, and joy.

25

∞ ∞ ∞

The human race has used prayer extensively throughout the centuries. Prayer takes as many different forms as there are individual humans. Group prayer varies with the different religious structures. All in all, prayer has, in the past, been the salvation of humanity, and prayer continues to play an important part in the spiritual transition which is upon us.

Even though prayer takes a myriad of forms, the basis of it is the same: humans talking directly to God, the Creator, the Great Spirit, the Universal Mind. All these names refer to the same entity, the ONE. Speaking directly to the Creator involves asking and thanking. This may seem elementary to many who read this because prayer has been so widely used for so long. Because of humanity's familiarity with it, prayer is an important link between the old order and the new consciousness. In any transition there needs to be something constant that helps carry humans through. Prayer is this constant. Prayer is this link. Prayer, of course, evolves as the transformation of human consciousness becomes complete, but the basic form of the individual beseeching the Creator remains.

Prayer is much more effective than most humans realize. Our prayers for others are especially powerful, for unselfishness and compassion are blessed attributes indeed. Our prayers for ourselves and our own needs are heard and tended to, although we may not get what we ask for when we ask for it. Often it is the case that we are not in tune with what we really need at the time for our own evolvement. Sometimes hardships and challenges are just what are called for. At any rate, a simple prayer asking for what we need at the time to move us forward is very effective. When we ask for help for others, we are heard and our prayers are heeded. Praying for those who are ill does indeed relieve some of the suffering, though it sometimes moves the ill person closer to passing if it is time for them to die.

Thanking the Creator is every bit as important as asking. Offering thanks brings blessings upon us. Heartfelt gratitude is desirable in all prayers. The words of the prayer are not nearly as important as the emotion, the sincerity with which it is said. What would seem to be the simplest most commonplace prayer, were it written out, might be elevated to magnificent if the feelings behind it are strong, pure, and sincere. Daily prayer, like daily meditation, is very important as we undertake this transformation of human consciousness.

Prayer is very much an individual offering. Yet there are certain components that each prayer needs to include. The first and most important is sincerity in the heart of the one who prays. Repeating a memorized prayer, as if by rote, has little value. It is the emotion that is sent forth in prayer that is of primary importance. Next, a prayer is best when it includes gratitude, or giving thanks for the blessings we all enjoy. Sometimes it is difficult for us to think of our blessings when we are grieving or suffering in some way, but if we take a deep breath and pause for a moment, we can always find something to say thank you for. For instance, no matter what we are undergoing in our personal lives, we can always offer up thanks for the earth and her intrinsic beauty. If prayer includes the two above-mentioned elements, it is fine and complete. Often we want to add more, such as asking for something for ourselves or for others. The unselfish element of asking for help for others is an excellent addition to any prayer. It is certainly fine to pray for something we feel we need ourselves. Again, the content is up to the individual.

All prayers are heard. What is asked for is tended to in due time. Of course, we do not get everything we pray for, but we do get those things we pray for that we really do need. Sending love and compassion to another in prayer is extremely helpful to that person, even if that person has passed on. The vibration of the earth plane would raise considerably if, once a day, we all would send love in a prayer to someone else.

∞ ∞ ∞

The use of the colors gold and white is very important in visualization because these colors help raise the vibratory level. What we are talking about here is raising the rate at which humanity vibrates. As a new millennium begins, the universe is demanding that the earth respond by vibrating at a higher rate. This increase in the rate of vibration is easily seen in the acceleration of events on earth. Rapid change is everywhere. Those who use daily meditation and prayer are best able to respond to this metamorphosis of energy. Visualization is also a useful, in fact, a necessary tool. As events whirl faster and faster, as the vibrational level on earth increases, humans must adapt or pass from the earth plane to another realm where they are better able to handle the energy present. Those who wish to adapt have all the knowledge and tools necessary to do so. No one is left out. This transformation is for everyone.

Working with visualization can help us raise our personal vibrations so we can better prepare and better tune to the changes on earth. No matter what sequence of visualizations we choose to use, we accomplish the most toward the goal of raising our personal vibratory rates if we end the visualizations using gold and/or white.

Here is a simple visualization process that can be used by each person to help prepare. This is best done standing. It can be done anywhere, anytime, and is most effective if we are somewhere beautiful, somewhere we love to be, somewhere breathtaking. Stand with feet spread slightly apart for stability, arms at the sides, palms up. Ground by sending rods deep into the earth from the arches in the bottoms of the feet, and send a third rod from the base of the spine way down into the earth, at least eighty feet down. Make the rods out of a favorite substance. Gold is recommended. Now envision a pyramid, the base of four equal sides below, the sides rising to the apex way above the head. This huge pyramid must be seen as shimmering luminescent gold or white. Be sure to picture it as sparkling. Next feel the energy rising up from deep in the earth, rising up the spine, rising up through the top of the head and out the apex of the pyramid. Again color this energy gold or white. Breathe with the energy as it surges up from the earth, surges through the spine, out the top of the head, out the top of the pyramid. If we spend a few minutes visualizing this each day, we all tune to the changing energies on earth. We are able to adjust and tune to this higher vibrational level which has already begun to permeate all life on earth.

SEE ILLUSTRATION 2:

Visualization with a Human Standing in the Psychic Pyramid

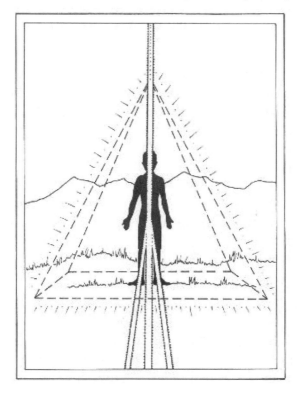

The pyramid shape has always been an important shape on earth, but now the pyramid has new significance. The stable base of four equal sides represents the earth plane. The point or apex centered directly above represents the Creator, the Universal Mind, the God-force. We humans are meant to exist and live our lives balanced between the two. We need a stable material base in the earth realm, and we need to be aware of and in touch with the Universal Mind.

As we mentioned, the pyramid at Giza is a divinely inspired structure that was built at the time the earth was going through another great transition. This pyramid is a marker on this planet. It represents the place where the major energy lines on the earth cross. There is a wellspring of earth energy at the Great Pyramid. We do not need to go to the Great Pyramid to tap into this wellspring of energy. Each of us can align ourselves with the pyramid and draw from its inspired source.

The Great Pyramid is but one of a series of markers placed around the planet. The others are not now available. These pyramids are symbols of the spiritual attunement of ancient civilizations. These peoples recognized their link to the Creator, the spark of the God-force within each of them. They understood the veil better than it is understood today. They knew how to reach through the veil for help and spiritual guidance. Inspiration through the veil guided these peoples to build these pyramids as markers of spiritual energy around the planet. There were originally four, but two have been destroyed and one remains undiscovered.

Much as these peoples were moved in ancient times in a period of great transition for earth, we are inspired today. We are being moved to mark this spiritual transition for the earth and the human race. People are being guided to new points of energy on the surface of the earth. These are spots where group energy can be powerfully generated to help this transformation be one of love rather than one of violence.

Once the poles realign themselves, these spots are the new energy crossings for the planet.

One of these new spots is a beautiful canyon in Russia. Another is in eastern Africa at the center of a breathtaking range of hills. The third is a magnificent waterfall in the upper Appalachian Mountains in the state of Maine. The major center of these new energy centers is in Peru, and is already very involved in spiritual awareness and activity. There is a lake in southern Peru. This entire basin is an energy high point for the planet.

There are other important energy spots. People who are attuned to the new vibrations on this planet instinctively gravitate to them. Once the transformation of human consciousness is complete, amazing new structures can be built to mark these spots and others. The earth is then ringed with new energy, with a new spiritual dimension.

The Great Pyramid at Giza can be seen as a giant marker of the energy laid in place at the time of the last human spiritual transformation. This upcoming transition is even more significant for the human race, for the vibrational rate of the earth is increasing immensely. With this transformation of consciousness, humans can grasp how to use the spiritual energy present in the body to affect physical change, both in the individual body and on earth. The ramifications are incredible. A significant time is upon us.

∞ ∞ ∞

There are points all over the surface of the human body that trigger energy flow. Acupuncture and acupressure are based on these points. When a person's energy is unbalanced, it can be brought back into a balanced state and the energy flow realigned by stimulation of the appropriate points on the body.

The earth has similar points on its surface. Stimulating these points can help bring a balanced state to the planet. By stimulating we do not, in this case, mean pressure. Psychic needles are called for. We can create psychic needles by gathering and focusing our thoughts and emotions, and by using visualization.

The following is an outline for such a ceremony. The gathering can be two people or two hundred. What is important is that all who are present cooperate in creating the same visualization. Leaders must prepare in advance. Collect in a circle, preferably right on the point on the earth's surface. Set up a harmonious vibration among all who are present. Chanting and song are useful to this end. Take time enough to ensure that all present are included in this feeling of harmony and all know the purpose of the ceremony. Once this state has been established, begin the visualization. If there is more than one leader, have them placed equidistant from each other around the circle. Have all present visualize brilliant white light moving around the circle counter-clockwise. Get the participants to feel it swirling. Begin slowly, then accelerate. Once this whirling white light is visualized, envision it swirling up toward the sky and boring down into the earth simultaneously, making a huge shaft or needle of whirling luminescent white light. Continue until the needle of white light has plunged deep into the earth and has risen high up into the sky. Then see the whirling pause. There is the needle, positioned on the energy point, still and shining with blinding white light. Now have all the participants pull sparkling golden energy from the sky or heaven down through the needle into the earth. Keep this energy flowing for a few minutes. Complete the ceremony by sending love to the planet. A prayer for the recovery of the earth and its return to a balanced state is appropriate here also. The visualized needle can be left in place. Visualize a protective shield over and around it so that no unwanted energy can filter into the needle and into this sensitive point. The needles in the acupuncture process are left in the human body for a few minutes. The earth is millions of times larger and has a slower vibratory rate, so the visualized needle can remain inserted for a much longer time. Once a balanced state has returned to the planet, the earth herself shakes off these shafts of energy, these visualized needles.

When many participate in such a ceremony, the energy drawn down into the earth is strong and plentiful. Even two people can have an effect on these points on earth, because, like in the human body, these points trigger energy flow and are very sensitive to stimulation. This process has a balancing and harmonizing effect. People are being led to these stimulation points for the purpose of healing the planet.

∞ ∞ ∞

The change that is here, the transformation of human consciousness, has been prophesied for centuries. It is now time for every human to feel the truth of these prophecies within him or herself. The truth lies within. The truth is always within. For those who are sensitive to energy flow and vibratory rates, this truth has already become conscious knowledge. It is time for all of us to be aware of this transition.

This transformation comes at a time of great trouble on the planet. Great change is called for, but the details of what this change entails are up to us. This transition has, indeed, been predestined, but the form that it takes has not. Of course, there cannot help but be some turbulence and some destruction, but we can keep the violence to a minimum. This book is a guide to help us understand the changes that are occurring and help us make this transformation the best it can be.

What can we do? We can do much on a personal level, and we can accomplish even more in groups. Each of us can pray for this change to be a blessing to the earth and its inhabitants. Each of us can meditate daily to tune our individual energy to the changing vibration of the planet so that we are each better prepared. Each of us can use daily visualization to help make this transition joyful for all. The keys are selflessness and sincerity of heart. If we wish to improve the conditions on this planet, we must approach this in a selfless way and be very sincere about it. The improvements must include all of humanity. There are to be no distinctions. All humans are experiencing the increase in vibratory rate. All humans feel the transformation coming from within themselves. All humans see this transition reflected in events and situations on earth. We must improve conditions on the planet for all. If this is not our approach, then much may go awry and disaster is unavoidable.

This is no time for fear. Although in the past many have feared major change, now many more long for it. The time is now. Change is now. It is here whether we wish it to be or not. It is up to us to shape this change for the greater good of the planet.

Love is the most powerful tool we have toward this end. We can accomplish much by gathering in groups and generating love energy for the transition, for the planet, for every living creature present on earth. For the sick, the injured, the malcontents, the surge of energy that accompanies this transition can bring renewed vigor and joy. For all of us it is a new beginning, a new century, a new age. It is of utmost importance that we generate love energy for this change. It is in this way we make the most of the potential offered to us here and now.

There has been much written about the upcoming earth changes, but the entire picture has not been presented. The physical changes on earth are but one part of the total phenomenon. Any true metamorphosis occurs on every level, and so it is with the transformation that welcomes the new millennium. Every being on the planet feels the increase in the energy level. Every cell, every molecule, every atom on earth is vibrating at a higher rate. Earth herself is a sentient being, and all of gross physical matter is responding to the new energy permeating the planet. There is no resisting this change to a higher vibratory rate. Our very cells are responding.

Many may become confused because old structures and former ways fall away. There is much help for those who wish to understand. This book, for instance, is a handbook or guide to this transformation. There are many other sources of assistance. We need only desire help and understanding, and we find it.

Of course, any major transformation is destructive in that the old ways, the old forms are destroyed. This is needed now on earth. It is time to let go of the former structures and their problems, and welcome the new millennium with its limitless potential. The increase in vibratory rate is only the beginning. The shift of the poles and the land masses are just the start of a new way of viewing the earth. Many survive the earth changes. It is up to all of us to see that this new path is entered upon correctly and followed diligently. Again, there is much assistance available to help us do this.

The main message of this chapter is: please do not grieve over the loss of the old forms, even those sections of the earth that are lost to the sea. Let go with joy. Welcome the new and surround this beginning with light and love. It is time for a new gentleness to be known on earth. Welcome the age of psychic connectedness and gentleness. It is time to be thankful for this cleansing and to be amazed at what the new energy brings to all on the planet. It is time for joy.

Instead of grieving for what is passing away, send the past away with honor and light. Surround those who pass during the transition with light and love. Send love through the veil to the many souls who choose to leave rather than stay and take part in the new ways on earth. There is danger in any great metamorphosis that anguish and grieving for what is lost overcome the populace. Let us replace the anguish with free-flowing love, and replace the grieving with joy! It is the time of great healing on the planet and a time of celebration. Those who choose to stay have much to do, first orienting themselves to the new energy levels present on the planet, helping others adjust, and forming structures for the new millennium. All is done with gentleness, light, and love.

Humans can accept that everything changes. Acceptance of major change is more difficult for most. That is why preparations are being made, information distributed, and techniques suggested to help tune and strengthen us. We need to be ready with loving acceptance, even joyful anticipation. Some things may seem very difficult when we are in the throes of major change. Be assured that there is a gentle solution to every problem, and assistance is everywhere. We need only ask for it. There are many who are now being trained to lead and to help guide us through this transition. We need to take a deep breath, and let everything that is ready to go pass away. If we envision a cleansing and uplifting of the energies of the planet, then we know true joy!

∞ ∞ ∞

The magnetic poles are easily measured as centers of energy for the earth. There are several other points on the planet that are important psychic energy centers. These points, as do the north and south poles, attract and gather energy. These points are wellsprings to those psychic healers and teachers who are being trained to help all humankind with this transition. These energy centers are places where strength can be renewed, where guidance can be received, where healing can take place. Gatherings at these centers generate important and much-needed awareness. Those that are aware of the new vibrational level and are tuned to it can then go out and help others. People have been specially chosen as caretakers for these spots of regenerative energy. They officiate the comings and goings of all who travel there to seek solace and help. They are the leaders who train leaders. These centers are open to all who seek strength, healing, knowledge, and love.

Those wishing to make a pilgrimage to one of the energy locations must be sincere of purpose. When people come to one of these centers, they place themselves in a field of energy which raises their personal vibration. Each visitor must be prepared, for illness can result if the individual is not ready for this increase in vibratory rate. Preparation consists of daily meditation and prayer, and sincerity of heart. True healing and strengthening can occur at these centers, again guided by the centers' caretakers. At first only a few are willing to commit to this work, but soon many are attracted.

Rather than list these centers which might mean an onslaught of visitors who are not prepared, we offer the following instruction: ask in prayer to be guided to the center that might be of the best service. Meditate upon this request, and guidance to the very spot then comes. The psychic healers and teachers are awaiting the arrival of those who are guided by their inner voice to seek these centers. Sincerity and persistence leads those who are ready to these centers. If direction to one of these centers does not come right away, continue to use prayer and meditation. When all is ready, information comes as to when and where to go.

The work at these centers is the most important work on the planet at this time. The major preparations for the monumental transformation of human consciousness are being made now at these centers.

∞ ∞ ∞

It is time for humans to receive much information that we have not had access to in the past. This book outlines the major part of this information. More details on any of this information are available by seeking the truth within. All of what is written here can be validated by turning inward to the quiet space, meditating, and listening to the inner voice within each of us which connects us to the Universal Mind.

There is a new opening in the barrier or veil surrounding existence on earth. This opening is within the consciousness of each individual human. The light and love energy which newly flows through this opening contains much new information. This book is meant as a guide to what each human can know deep within her or himself. The basics are given here. The details can be filled in by each person. This new information may apply differently to each individual. We encourage everyone to go within and seek the details which apply.

For instance, there are new power spots on earth which rejuvenate and strengthen, heal and tune humans for this transformation. However, it is up to each person to seek the spot which best serves his or her needs. As we enter this time of intense transformation, our individual needs differ. It is the responsibility of each of us to tend to our own personal needs, to make whatever attunements or adjustments that are necessary. This can only be done by turning within. Be assured all the information that is needed is available there. Let us offer a prayer that we may be given the information we need. Let us meditate and find that quiet space within. Our inner voice then tells us specifically what we need and how we can obtain it. Many already know this to be true. Many have used this technique for years.

This new information that is flooding human consciousness is very important, for it is the key to assuring that the upcoming transition is one of joy and love. It is time now to rid the planet of much that is hurtful and undesirable. This can be done, and done thoroughly, but only if we all listen to our inner voice, our connection to the universal truth.

For those who have never meditated or have difficulty finding the quiet place within so they can hear or feel this new connection, there are many helpers and teachers available. Guided group meditations are often very useful to those who are unfamiliar with listening to the inner voice. Psychic teachers are present all around the globe to help with this process. If assistance is needed, seek through prayer and someone is there to help. It is time for us all to turn inward and tune in. The truth lies within.

∞ ∞ ∞

We have been speaking of how the energy level on the planet is increasing. This affects every cell, every molecule on earth. This increase in vibratory rate affects animal and plant life as well as humans. It is time for the entire planet to evolve to another state of being.

What is happening? Many want to know as they see the earth change before their eyes. This book is here as an aid to help increase everyone's understanding. It is the sincere hope of those who write this book that it help alleviate panic and fear, and help promote understanding, love, and joy.

There is much more detail in many areas that can be given. The purpose of this book is an overview of this major transformation for the planet earth. Some of this information has been available on earth for centuries. Some of it is new. All of it pertains to this great transition.

∞ ∞ ∞

Conscious understanding of this great transition into the new millennium is the best tool we can use to prevent total chaos and panic. The new age is ushered in. The vibration of the planet increases rapidly. Everyone feels different. Everyone perceives differently. Disorientation and confusion are likely once the higher vibratory rate has permeated the planet. Preparation is, of course, another key to experiencing this transformation of human consciousness with a minimum of fear and a maximum of joy. Preparation includes daily prayer, daily meditation, use of visualization, and altered breathing. All of these forms of preparation align the individual with the increased vibrations which are now making their way to every molecule on earth. Many are already using these forms of preparation and are sensing the joy, the light, the love which this transformation can bring to humanity.

Here is how each of these forms of preparation can help. Prayer is one of the most ancient ways that humans relate to the divine. Most humans are comfortable with some form of prayer. Here prayer can be used to ask for understanding and guidance in this time of great transition. Meditation is visiting that quiet space deep within us. It is through meditation we hear the truth from our inner voice and receive understanding and guidance. Visualization is a powerful tool which is now beginning to be honored and widely used. We must use visualization to guide our own energies and the energy of the planet through this great transition. The truths and the understanding that come through meditation can be put into practice, can be made real through individual and group visualization. Breathing techniques have been used by yogis for centuries to raise their vibratory rates. It is time for us all to learn and practice yogic breathing so that we can tune our physical bodies to the new vibratory rate permeating the earth. The yogic breath helps clear us of fear and disorientation, thus eliminating the possibility of illness and discomfort.

This book offers a section on each of these preparations, providing the basics for their use. Further details can be gained from a variety of texts. Psychic teachers can also be helpful.

These preparations are extremely important for everyone on earth. Ignoring this transformation is, of course, impossible, for it affects every molecule on the planet. Ignoring preparatory measures is dangerous for the health and well-being of the individual and the planet.

This book is not written to promote sensationalism or to warn of impending doom. This book is here to promote joy and light and love. This book's purpose is to show that this great earth transformation can be a magnificent uplifting of the human spirit if we wish it to be and work together to make it so.

The technological achievements of the twentieth century have been very great. As always, the universe demands balance. In the twenty-first century, we need to balance these technological achievements with advancements of the spirit. The movement to do this has begun, but it is at its very beginning. The twenty-first century is bringing much spiritual progress to this planet.

Humankind must overlook the prejudices and mistakes of the past. Forgiveness is all-important if spiritual advancement is to be made. Forgiveness is the key which opens the door to compassion and understanding. Once we are in the throes of the great spiritual transition of the twenty-first century, we may find ourselves looking back in shame at past deeds and attitudes. Shame is useful only in that it leads to forgiveness and compassion.

Once the vibratory rate of the earth has increased to the point where all of us acknowledge that we are in major transition, many aspects of our lives undergo scrutiny and review. These periods of review are for recognition, perspective, forgiveness, and letting go. This must be done quickly and without hesitation. This process especially applies to our emotions. We may look and recognize that we have operated with anger or perhaps jealousy as the primary emotion in our lives. The increase in vibratory rate brings a new perspective showing how useless this was for us. It is important that we forgive ourselves for past actions and move swiftly to let go of them in the face of the new level of energy present on the planet.

Forgiveness toward others has always been important to the spirit, and it continues to be so. We are ready to move to a new higher level of feeling. Our emotional vibrations are increasing. We can leave much behind us now, but we must do so with forgiveness and love.

∞ ∞ ∞

In the centuries to come, our descendants will build an entirely new order on earth. It is up to us to lay a solid foundation beginning with the transition. The importance of this work cannot be overemphasized. Generations upon generations depend on it for their well-being. This book is a guide to the areas that must be tended to as we undergo the transition. Our spiritual growth takes the highest priority, for it is now that we can make a tremendous leap in consciousness.

New energy and new information are being made available to all earth-life. It is our responsibility as humans incarnated in this time to tune to and make the most of this new energy. We must open our hearts and minds to the new information, and apply it to life on earth as best we can. We have much help available to us now. We need only ask for assistance in these transitional times, and we receive it. There are many who are not presently incarnated on earth who wish to help in any way they can to make this transition joyful and complete.

In our prayers we can ask for guidance and assistance. We are always heard. Help comes in whatever way is appropriate for the situation. Patience is important. Many *hear* advice, instructions, or comforting assurances. This is called clairaudience. These people can further develop this psychic talent to the point of making daily contact with spirit guides. There are those all over the planet who are at this time making daily use of this gift of clairaudience. Many *see* pictures in their minds which bring guidance. This is clairvoyance. This psychic gift can also be developed. Both clairaudience and clairvoyance are ways to receive telepathic communications from beyond the veil. As we mentioned, many on the other side of the veil are ready and willing to help us. Because these helpers are discarnate, they have a different perspective than we do. They have different talents as well as access to different information which they gladly share. They can communicate helpful advice or needed information to us using telepathic means. Because we are incarnated, the equipment provided to us by the human body necessitates that we use our senses to receive these telepathic communications. Hearing and seeing are the most commonly activated senses, although there are some instances of the other senses being activated also. We may also receive help and guidance in our dreams. Many use the technique of asking for advice on a situation before going to sleep. Asking for several nights in a row is appropriate. If there is no answer, review what is being asked.

Be assured that assistance and guidance are widely available to all at this time. Each of us must be open to receiving this aid in whatever way is most appropriate. If we are sincere in asking in our prayers for help in our daily life, we receive all the guidance we ask for. Our hearts and minds need only be open to receive it.

∞ ∞ ∞

We are in transition; we are in transition, beginning a new century; we are in transition, beginning a new millennium; we are in transition to a new state of being. Our entire world is changing rapidly. Many things are not easy in such times of rapid change. It is often difficult to let go of old habits, old patterns, old ways of thinking and reacting. In these times of transition, it is very important for us to detach ourselves from our former patterns, for they no longer apply. In fact, insistence on clinging to them brings disorientation, confusion, even illness and disease. The old forms are crumbling. It is time for us to look ahead to new ways to order our lives.

If we are having trouble letting go of what has been so comfortable and familiar over these last many years, let us try this exercise. First, we see the old pattern that we are clinging to. We make a picture of it. This old pattern could be a condescending attitude toward women, prejudice against a certain racial group, or perhaps automatic violent outbursts triggered by a certain subject. Whatever the old way, we see it in a scene. We see the action. We see ourselves feeling the emotion, thinking the thought, acting and reacting. Now we put a frame around it, be it a picture frame or a video screen, and hang it on the wall. We step back and view it. We see the picture in a museum along with other memorabilia. In this way, we can recognize the old patterns that are tough to let go of, put them in the past, and walk away from them into the future.

There is no choice in that the transition is here. Our choices lie in how we deal with this rapid and dramatic change. This book is written for those who wish to understand the energies of this great transformation and work with these forces so that the earth and the people of the earth come through these changes joyfully and successfully.

∞ ∞ ∞

The types of visualizations we can do using our emotions are endless. By being creative and colorful, we can learn to work with our emotions in new ways. Any time we wish to change the way we feel, we can use visualization to do so. The use of visualization in this way is a big step for humanity. Now we humans have no reason to repress emotions, but instead we can transform them into positive feelings.

Emotions are unseen on this plane, but they do have a vibration. The lower the vibratory rate, the worse we feel. Conversely, the higher the vibratory rate of the emotion, the better we feel. Love has the highest vibration of all emotions experienced on earth. Compassion and forgiveness are also high vibrations.

It is detrimental to use visualization techniques to change an emotion to a lower vibration. The purpose of the exercise is always to raise the vibratory rates of the emotions we are experiencing. The entire planet is increasing in vibratory rate. There is no place on earth for the low vibrations. It is to our advantage always to raise the rate of vibration of ourselves and our emotions. Learning to transform our emotions is one of the basic ways we can prepare for this spiritual transition. Some emotions with low vibrations include greed, self-pity, resentment, jealousy, envy, and anger.

Transforming our emotions does take some discipline and the ability to detach ourselves from what we feel. Many find detachment easier by using the following visualization process:

1. Recognition: Let's say we are very angry at someone. The first step is to channel all that anger into a picture, that is, to put shape and color on the anger. We see our anger as a huge burning barn. We let all our anger flow into the visualization. The picture becomes stronger as we pour our anger into the fire engulfing the barn. Once we feel we have emptied our anger into the picture we hold in our mind of the burning barn, then we are ready for the next step.

2. Detachment: Step number two is to step back. In our minds we move a little away from the visualization so that we can see it clearly, but it is at a bit of a distance from us. This helps us gain perspective on what we are feeling and why.

3. Transformation: Now it is time to change the picture, to transform the visualization and with it the emotion it represents. Again it must be stated that this technique has not been taught before now because of fear that it would be misused. It is essential that emotions be transformed into the higher vibrations of love, compassion, and forgiveness. This is in line with the increasing vibratory rate of the earth. Transformation to a lower vibration would spell disaster for the person

using the technique, for the earth, and for all life forms upon the earth. In our mind's eye, we take the picture of the angry burning barn and begin to spin it, slowly at first, then faster until the image is a whirl of fire. Now the color gold begins to emerge in the whirling mass of light, and the fiery reds and oranges subside. Luminous gold light now spins and becomes brighter than before. We slow the spinning gold light until we see a golden sphere of beautiful unconditional love.

4. Dispersion: Now the transformation of anger to love has taken place, we have the pleasure of deciding what to do with this transformed emotion. We can always take it back into ourselves for strengthening and self-nourishment. To do this, we just picture the sphere of brilliant golden light floating toward us and enveloping us. We can send it out to the earth or to the universe to help with the general healing and the spiritual transition now occurring.

This exercise can take many forms. Let us use our imaginations. We must always use this exercise to transform emotions to a higher state of love for the good of the planet and all who dwell upon her.

∞ ∞ ∞

During times of rapid change, it is often difficult to maintain perspective. Preparation is necessary so that events are not viewed in a distorted way. Disasters have a way of being blown out of proportion at the time they occur. When tumultuous change is expected and prepared for, it is met with appropriate reactions.

For many years, earth changes have been forecast for this planet. These changes are natural and necessary. At this time of evolution on earth, such changes in the earth's mass can help bring an end to the continued poisoning and pollution.

We must prepare for a massive shutdown of commerce. The flow of goods and commodities cease as industries shut down for repair and revaluation. The shift of the land mass necessitates losing some areas. Such global movement can be viewed as disastrous, and for some it is so. Others see this as a healing phase for the planet and an opportunity to change our approach to life on earth.

Although material preparations are necessary to some extent, the major preparations need to be spiritual. It is through meditation and prayer that we are each guided to the correct circumstances and to correct action. Material needs are easily met when spiritual preparations have been thorough and sincere. In prayer we can ask that whatever changes and healing are necessary for the earth may come to pass. We can ask that we be in the right place at the right time so that we can help with the earth's healing. We can ask that any preparations we need to make be shown to us. In meditation we need only settle into the quiet place inside our mind-body, and we can receive answers, directions, or visions on how to proceed and prepare.

We cannot ignore such a massive transformation facing the human race. Rational means of preparation are not adequate. We cannot logically plan when we do not know what forms these earth shifts may take. There is much speculation and some prophecy, but the reality is that the earth changes when she needs to and where she needs to, and those needs may change from moment to moment.

If we view the earth as a being unto herself, we can get more of a feel for what is happening. The earth needs to heal herself from the scars of greed. Only the earth herself knows what may heal her. We humans cannot know or decide this. All we can do is prepare and be ready to help.

We also must be prepared to change as the earth changes. We must be open and adaptable, responsive and resourceful. The more we help others, the more comfort and solace we find in these changes. Now, before the change, already people are trying to slow the raping and desecration of the planet. These attempts have seemed feeble in the face of powerful big business and industry. Some projects, like recycling, are gaining momentum. This is seed energy which we must carry through the transition.

Once the earth has moved and shaken herself, we must approach her with new respect. We must clean up what needs to be cleaned up, and begin rebuilding with reverence. This is our opportunity to build a society based on love for our planet and respect for all living things. Greed must be viewed as undesirable. It must be widely recognized that when a single human profits at the expense of the earth or another human, there is only the illusion of material gain. In actuality, a loss is taking place on all fronts. The person who is being taken advantage of may be losing something material, but the one who profits suffers a far greater spiritual loss. This is the meaning of karma. This is seen with greater clarity during and especially after the transition. This new awareness can change the attitude of people and their approach to living. The potential for important and lasting changes on this planet is real. It exists before us as the transformation begins. Let us prepare. Let us be ready to help.

∞ ∞ ∞

The dawn of the new age brings many curious things. For one, we feel different within our own bodies. This is due mainly to the shifting and increasing rate of vibration on the planet. This new feeling inside our own skins takes some getting used to. Many who are uneducated about this great transition may think that they are ill. Illness is indeed a possibility for some during this time. Attempting to reject the transformation and resist the changes does bring friction and with it possible illness. Those who expect and prepare for this great transition greet these new feelings with reverence and joy. Such changes within are subtle at first, but become more and more apparent as the vibratory rate increases until the earth literally shakes. It is then that the greatest changes occur.

The most important preparations for this transformation are spiritual. Any preparations that need to be made on the material plane come through directions from within. In other words, if we prepare spiritually, our material needs are met. The key here is listening to the inner voice. Any preparations we need to make for relocating, readying our homes, stocking provisions, and so on can all come through the inner voice as divinely directed information. This information can be incredibly specific. Miserly stockpiling, barricading our homes, and arming ourselves with weapons are useless responses to this transition. This type of response is the type of low vibration that is fading away. We must turn inward and tune ourselves spiritually, and then we receive what we need to prepare and move forward through these times of rapid change.

If we are sincere when we ask in prayer to be guided through this transformation, we receive any help we need. Again it must be stressed: we must be selfless and sincere in our prayers and in our actions. The more we are prepared to help others during these times, the more guidance and help we receive ourselves. The increase in vibratory rate on the planet means more love and compassion for all.

∞ ∞ ∞

Every life form, including the earth, has a vibration. Humans, animals, birds, fish, plants, and even stones have vibratory rates. The change of vibration on the planet affects all of these. It affects everything.

One of the ways we can help to tune ourselves to the changing vibration of the planet is through contact with stones and crystals. Many are already using crystals and stones for a variety of reasons. The true power of the crystal is not yet known by the present civilization. Thousands of years ago, crystals were widely used as sources of power. Crystals can not only modify current, they can actually generate power when used correctly. Only a few of the technological possibilities of the crystal are used today. Stones and crystals can be beneficial to humans and animals by helping us all make the transition to a higher vibration. The crystal is especially useful because it holds, channels, and amplifies energy.

As mentioned before, it is important for us to tune to the changing rate of vibration of the planet for our health and well-being. There are several techniques that can help us tune ourselves more effectively. The most thorough and efficient of these uses crystals. We must proceed with the knowledge that crystals are powerful and must be used with respect and reverence. We must remember that crystals are entities unto themselves.

First, we each choose a crystal or a stone which we like, one with which we have an affinity. If we have been carrying the stone or have used it in any way, we had best clean it by covering it with salt water for a day. This procedure is important when using crystals because they do carry a charge, and this process clears the crystals. Once the stone is clear and holds no charge, we take it outside and bury it in the earth. It is best to bury it with the point of the crystal or stone pointing skyward and to leave the tip exposed. If the stone is small or buried deeply, let us put a marker by this buried stone so that we can retrieve it. Crystals do have a way of disappearing of their own accord.

The earth herself holds all the information we need to make this change in vibration. By burying the crystal, we are letting it absorb the information in the vibration of the earth. This exercise is most effective when carried out during a full moon because of the pull of energy between the sun and moon. This polarity stirs the vibrations of the earth and the buried crystal for a more thorough movement of energy from the earth into the stone. This movement of energy is very subtle but very real. Leave the stone buried for at least one day over the time period when the moon is full.

Once we each remove the stone from the earth, we hold it in our hands. We keep it near us as much as possible. We tune to it and it gives us information from the earth. We visualize the vibration in the stone moving into our bodies. We hold the crystal in meditation and it helps us adjust our vibration to that of the planet.

∞ ∞ ∞

Fifty years from the date of this writing, the earth is completely transformed. There is very little, if any, of today's culture left on earth. The children alive now at the time of this writing see and lead the new society which emerges on the other side of this great transformation.

Our eyes must focus not only on what we need to do to prepare for the transition itself, but also on what we want to pull out of these great changes. Few generations have the opportunity that we have now at the beginning of this new millennium.

The earth herself dictates much. As the earth shakes and realigns her energies, we can only pray and help others. Our visions, our ideals that come from the new level of energy on the planet are what inspire the children and lead them to build a new structure of society. The earth insists we take a different approach to our incarnation here. As the transformation progresses, it is up to us to tune to the information the earth is giving us, and to make it real for the young people in any way that seems appropriate.

∞ ∞ ∞

Most of us are familiar with the cycles of nature. The phases of the moon are monthly cycles; the changing of the seasons is a yearly cycle. There are cycles in existence that are much larger and much longer. We are at the turning point in a cycle that is thousands of years long. We are at a place that is similar to the time of a new moon, in that a new moon (when the sun and moon are aligned from the vantage point of earth) marks the end of one moon cycle and the beginning of another. We are at the end of one huge cycle and are about to begin another. Although this turning point coincides with the change in centuries and the change in millennium, it is a far greater cycle than either. The last time this turning point came here on earth, the last time the earth changed these great cycles, was so long ago that there are no historical records of the change. There is inevitably so much upheaval when the earth changes from one of these great cycles to the next that not much remains of the cycle that is ending and passing away.

Those of us who experience this change from one giant cycle to the next during our lifetimes are privileged to see a metamorphosis that we never dreamed possible. Certainly, nowhere in history is such a change documented. All that remains of the last great change are myths and legends. The movement from one of these great cycles to the next is so all encompassing and complete that the earth herself physically changes. Each of these great transitions is thorough. Each has its own special qualities. These qualities are based on what the earth needs at the time. We can look to what the earth needs now for clues as to what this great change of giant cycles might bring.

Again it must be emphasized that the major preparations for this great change need to be spiritual. There is no way we can know how to be properly prepared physically unless we are first spiritually attuned. Please heed these words, for others during the past times of great change did not, and there is nothing left of their cultures.

∞ ∞ ∞

When we humans are awake and active, we walk with our spines perpendicular to the surface of the earth. When we rest and sleep, we lie with our spines parallel to the surface of the earth. The energy in our spines is the energy that connects us to the universe. It begins in the skull and travels in waves up and down the spinal column. The energy flow in the skull and spine is beautiful, luminous life-giving energy. It is, in fact, our spirit; it is our life pulse. Both the time we spend perpendicular and the time we spend parallel to the earth's surface are important to this life-flow of energy and to our well-being.

The time we spend perpendicular or up and walking around, consciously acting and interacting, is creative time. The spirit energy in the skull and spine is literally pumped up and down. Our breathing, our movement, our thoughts and actions are all intertwined with the vigorous pump action of the spinal spirit energy.

When we lie down to rest or sleep and are parallel to the earth's surface, our orientation is different. This parallel time is receptive time, and the energy flow in the skull and spine is more gentle and evenly spread. During this resting time, balance is restored to the body. The spirit energy in the skull and spine becomes regular and even, much like the surface of a lake rippled with a light but steady summer breeze. When we are sleeping, resting, and meditating, we are in a receptive state. We are open to what our bodies need, to what we as human spirits need. This is why much is shown to us and much comes to us in meditation and in dreams. Time spent resting and meditating is essential for all of us as we prepare for the great transition. If we do not allow enough time for sleep, rest, and meditation, we may find that we are not aware of what we need and are not getting what we need to deal with these times.

The perpendicular time is, of course, very important also. When we are up and about, consciously acting and interacting with our environment, many insights can be gained if we have had sufficient rest. The perpendicular orientation can actively provide much of what we need if we have had adequate parallel time. Balance is the key.

It is important for us to understand the ebb and flow of our spirit energy, for we can use this energy in visualizations. The movement of this life-energy in the skull and spine is the key to the pulse of all life on earth. It is time for us all to be aware of it, to honor and respect it, to allow both the perpendicular and the parallel to find a proper balance in our lives.

∞ ∞ ∞

Let us take a person through the cycle of one day, from the parallel sleep state, through the perpendicular activity hours, and back to the parallel position for rest. The outline presented here is a guide to those individuals who wish to conscientiously prepare themselves daily for the upcoming transition. When we awake each day from sleep, we are rested, revived, and the energies in our bodies are relatively balanced. This is true, in part, even for those who are ill.

We join our example person as she takes her first waking breath. Still lying down, she breathes a deep breath of light and love, feeling the joy available to all on earth flood through her. Next, she says a prayer for the day, which includes a blessing for the earth, a request for guidance throughout the day, and thanks for what she has been given. It is also appropriate here for her to include a request for anyone who is ill or needs help. Next, she visualizes herself inside a huge golden egg of protective light. She sees life energy pulsing bright white in her skull and spine. In this way, she begins her day by feeling both protected and connected to the life-flow of the universe. This is done while lying down. All this takes only a few minutes.

On a day when she has more time, she might do some yoga, but today when she stands, she simply breathes deeply and stretches a little. This helps orient her to standing upright, to the perpendicular state of activity which she is entering for the greater part of the day. She washes, feeling the water as cleansing particles of light. Food is next, and she eats with reverence and thanks.

As she goes about her daily activities, she meets an obstacle which brings frustration. Later, she must deal with a difficult person. In both instances, she does not instantly respond, but takes half a moment to breathe deeply. This centers her energy and helps put the problem into perspective. Just that half moment provides detachment enough to foster a positive reaction rather than a paranoid one.

Partway through her day, whenever she can manage a half hour to an hour of solitude and quiet, she meditates. This process revives her and restores and balances her energy. She uses visualization and breathing techniques to relax and clear her. Sometimes she uses visualization in the meditation to help her deal with a particular problem.

As she proceeds through the day, she is always alert, always mindful of the changing flow of activity and energy. She knows she needs to be steady and operate from the base of light and love within her, but she must also be flexible enough to adapt to and learn from the changing patterns outside and all around her. She remembers that if she dwells on the past or projects into the future, she may miss the beauty that every moment has to show her. Anytime she feels off-center or unbalanced, she breathes deeply using the balanced breath (count on inhale, equal count on exhale) and visualizes her center radiating bright light. Each time she eats, she blesses the food and sees it helping her body become healthier and stronger. She observes what she takes into her body; she observes what words she speaks out. Always, in each day, she tries to do at least one thing for someone else, even if it is as simple as bringing a pillow or a cup of tea. She sees that serving others is important as a daily activity. She does not hesitate to say a prayer for someone, for a situation, or for the planet. This constant conscious tuning helps prepare her for the stress, confusion, and upheaval that come with great change.

At the end of her perpendicular day, she prepares herself for rest and revitalization. She washes. Her sleeping area is clean and ordered. She stretches again, perhaps now taking time to do some yoga and breathing. She knows the more balanced the body is when going to sleep, the more benefits she receives during sleep. Now she offers a prayer of thanks and asks that sleep may bring her body whatever it needs. She once again visualizes that bright golden egg of protective light around her as she lies down to rest. She feels the gentle pull of gravity evening out her energy as she stretches parallel to the earth's surface. She takes a deep breath, smiles, relaxes, and sleeps. All is well.

∞ ∞ ∞

The earth and the sky are full of many beautiful patterns, and we can learn much from them. The clouds form patterns across the sky which inform us of incoming weather. We watch the movement of the sun, moon, and planets before a glorious array of patterns provided by the stars. The patterns in sun and shadow, the patterns in the moving grasses, the patterns that seedlings make when they sprout out of the ground in the spring all contain information about the movement of energy on the earth. Many ancient civilizations knew that to observe and study nature's patterns were keys to understanding the Great Spirit, the Creator here on earth. Omens were often taken from patterns in nature simply as a way to read how the energies were flowing.

Many today who are close to the earth and observe nature have made the connection that these patterns are the God-force manifest on earth. Now, when the earth is changing quickly, it is essential to watch the patterns all around us, as they tell us much. They can tell us when the biggest changes come and where. These patterns can tell us where to be.

Reading patterns in nature and in society takes skills which are developed through patience and practice. Observation is only one of the skills. Even more important than watching the patterns is feeling them. An intuitive connection with the patterns must be developed so that they convey information through the feelings. Some may develop this skill to the point of actually hearing the patterns speak, another form of clairaudience. Others interpret the patterns with visual pictures, thus using clairvoyance.

The patterns speak to us and through us. Observing and interpreting patterns are ancient arts which are valid and useful. In fact, these arts can be taken to new heights of reverence and respect as we face a new millennium. Those that are drawn to these arts must be encouraged and supported, because it is through their insights into the patterns that surround us that we come to know when to be where and how to prepare. This book is meant to help many see with new eyes and hear with new ears in the face of this great change, this transformation of human consciousness.

∞ ∞ ∞

Every day is a new chance for us to prepare ourselves. Every day brings opportunities to refine our natures and to tune ourselves to the universal flow. The energy that flows through us is the very same energy that exists in everything on this planet and beyond. This is the "oneness" that is so often written about in spiritual and religious books. We are all "one" in that we all share this energy from a common source. If we take physical matter present on earth, we can study it and break it down to prove that all gross matter is made up of atoms. Perhaps not everyone can see or feel the life-energy present in all things, but everyone can grasp that, like the atom, the same energy is basic to everything.

If we approach each new day with the knowledge that we share this same life-energy with all things present in the universe, we have a proper perspective on our lives and on our relationships with all that surrounds us. We treat everything with a reverence that comes from the knowledge that we share with everything present the same basic makeup of matter and energy. This can be more than just conscious knowledge; we can *feel* this shared life force. We can feel the kindred energy in a pet, or a plant, or a fast-flowing stream. Of course, this universal life force manifests in millions of different forms on earth, but that is the illusion of earthly reality. Everything seems so separate, so different, when in actuality we are all constructed from the same basic matter, and are imbued with the same basic energy. It is the magic of creation, and it is all around us to be enjoyed.

If we begin each day with the knowledge of our connectedness to all things, we can better attune to the changes occurring all around us. The more we feel that life-energy present in ourselves, the more we feel it present in all things around us, the more we can sense what is happening, where we need to be, when to act, and what to do. The fact that we humans are all imbued with the same energy that fills all the universe helps us change with the times.

Instead of feeling fear and resistance when dealing with the major changes on this planet, we can feel that we are an integral part of it all. We can feel honored to be incarnated on earth in such an exciting time. We can feel the pull of the life-energy that is in all things drawing us into the spiral of great change. We can feel the thrill of flowing with this transition.

Our attitudes are extremely important as we enter this time of change. If we are prepared and welcome the change, we find our way through it. More than that, we see how we can improve the entire situation on the planet. This is a major cycle in which the life-energy is clearing and renewing itself, and moving all matter with it. We are a part of it. We can consciously help the transformation move toward a positive outcome. Human reaction can be pivotal during these times of change, for humans can offer resistance or we can flow.

Preparations now can help assure that this inevitable transformation brings positive changes for all matter, for all the life-energy present on earth.

∞ ∞ ∞

In any discussion of the upcoming transition, we must speak of the two emotions which are here to guide us clearly through it: love and compassion. It is up to us to make love and compassion a part of our daily lives, not only now in preparation, but as a living constant as the transition progresses. We can begin by simply praying that these two emotions come to the forefront in our lives. We can also do visualizations to actually transform other uncomfortable feelings into love and compassion.

All our lives, we have experienced a myriad of feelings, from depression to joy, from disgust to gratitude, from anger to love. Now the universe is calling upon us to channel our feelings, to uplift our emotions to those of the highest vibrational level on earth, love and compassion.

Emotions play a very important role in the great changes on earth. Emotions do indeed take form on another plane closely interconnected with the earth plane. With this knowledge, humans can proceed to generate love and compassion for the earth and for all life on earth in the face of this great transition. It is important that we do this both individually and collectively.

There are many ways amassing love and compassion can help. As the earth undergoes transformation, the love and compassion generated here and amassed on the inter-connected realm can guide the changes so that they are the most healing and joyful possible. We must begin now, feeling love and compassion for the earth and all life forms upon the earth. We have the opportunity to employ our emotions to help this great transition be a very positive change for the planet. We encourage daily attention to this by every individual. We encourage groups to generate love and compassion for the planet on a regular basis. Through channeling our emotions in this way, we are also refining our own vibrations, so that they are more in tune with the new vibrational rate coming to earth.

∞ ∞ ∞

The force of gravity is something with which all humans are familiar. There are other forces present on earth and in the universe that are not as apparent. One of these is the force that moves to balance, the force which many call karma. When a deed is done, there is a certain energy exerted. This exertion automatically sets into motion the forces that balance it. Of course, it is not as simple as this, but this is the basic principle. Sometimes it takes only a moment for the balancing force to make itself known; other times it may take centuries.

The force of karma moves to balance, but more than that, it moves to bring the energies on earth and in the universe into harmony. Sometimes the path to this harmony is difficult, painful, and filled with tribulations. It is time for humans to understand the significance of the force of karma. If humanity is to make a leap in consciousness, we must understand that we truly do "reap what we sow." If a person says or does something hurtful, something negative, to another person, a group of people, or to the earth, he or she triggers the karmic force. There is absolute certainty that this person sooner or later experiences the balancing force of karma. It may be an hour later, a year later, or even a lifetime later, depending on the circumstances.

These karmic forces are always present on earth just like the force of gravity. Just as gravity continually pulls us to ground, karma continually moves to balance. Time is not a factor, for the force of karma moves beyond earth lifetimes.

The following is far too simple an explanation, for the forces of karma work in very complex ways. Still, these are the basics, and they stand as true. A human does a helpful deed, emoting love and compassion. This is energy moving out from the person. Karma moves to bring love, compassion, and help back to this person at some time. This is energy in. Conversely, a human maliciously and hatefully does a hurtful deed. This is energy out. Karma moves to bring the same hateful energy back at the person, often when he or she least expects it. Energy back in.

The principles of karma are found in many religions and have been expounded upon by many spiritual leaders. Because the balancing force of karma works on a large scale throughout many lifetimes, humans do not often see instant returns for their actions. Many have therefore tended to disregard the existence of the karmic force.

It is time for humans to become much more farsighted. Reincarnation is becoming an accepted *fact*. We can move to see that our actions reap benefits or consequences far beyond our present lifetime. With the knowledge of reincarnation, humans can grasp the reality of the force of karma. We can see it as just as real as the force of gravity. Gravity anchors us to earth. We can feel it. We can see it working. We can also see and feel the great force of karma continually moving the energies of the universe toward balance and harmony.

Section Two

The Process

Everything on earth, in fact everything in the universe, is made up of vibrations. It does not matter if it is a rock, an animal, a human, or the earth herself, all is vibration. Scientists know this, although they describe the makeup of matter in terms of molecules and atoms. Electrons are constantly moving within each atom. This movement indicates the life force present. Atomic structure is vibration, energy, life force.

It follows that, when the rate of vibration changes for the planet, the vibration within each atom also changes. We are talking about fundamental change at the very root of our makeup. We are talking about change in every atom, every molecule, every cell on earth. There is a new energy pouring onto the earth plane. This energy is slowly but constantly raising the rate of vibration of the planet, and with it the vibration of every molecule. This means that we and our environment are changing. The changes are subtle at first, but are becoming more and more apparent each day. There are many who are tuning into and are beginning to work with this new vibrational rate. Conscious tuning to the changing vibration brings many benefits to each person and to the earth as a whole. Adapting to this new energy and to the new vibrational rate it fosters is essential for our well-being and that of the planet. This is an opportunity that the earth and her inhabitants have never had before. Many new teachings are surfacing now. There is much information available to help us grasp the incredible significance of this time.

It is up to each one of us to take the time to tune ourselves to the new energy present on earth. Each person can find a method of meditation and a number of visualization exercises to suit her or him. Our bodies and our environment are changing whether we wish them to or not. Trying to ignore the changes and hold onto the old ways of being brings disillusionment and often illness. The old ways are fading, passing away. Let longing for the past and clinging to memories of how things were pass away also. Let us, each day, tune ourselves to the energy that is present. We can each find our own ways of doing this. Again, there is much information about the many available methods. If we seek sincerely, we are led to what we need.

All great transitions bring with them a certain amount of turbulence and confusion. This book's purpose is to help minimize the chaos which usually accompanies great changes. With a certain amount of foresight and preparation, we can even feel gratitude and rejoice as the transformation occurs. Those who forcibly move against the tide of change increase the turbulence and violence. Those who flow lovingly with the transition find their way sooner and more peacefully to a new existence on this planet. Much has been said or written about taking the line of least resistance. In this writing, we are encouraging not only flowing with the changing world, but preparing for and helping with the transition. The more of us who ready ourselves and actively take part in moving the earth to a new state of being, the smoother and less chaotic the transition can be. In fact, the message of this book is that it is *essential* that we prepare and actively help. With our participation, distraction and disaster can be minimized.

Simply knowing about the upcoming transition is not enough. We must prepare ourselves in many ways. The first and most important form of preparation is establishing access to guided help. We all have this access and many are already utilizing it. Some connect to this guidance through intuition; some call this guidance their inner voice or their higher self. Others interact with spirit guides and gain assistance through them. It is necessary to connect with our own personal channel to this guided help now, before the major changes occur. Once events are in upheaval, we may not find the quiet and privacy needed to make the connection. If, however, we are used to turning inward for guidance, and have established a route to do this, we more easily continue to receive guided help through times of unrest. Also, much information is available to us now, through guided sources, to aid us in all phases of preparation for the transition. Obtaining guided help is a priority in the list of ways to prepare ourselves.

If any of us has difficulty hearing the inner voice, or trusting our intuition and understanding what it is telling us, the place to start is prayer. We simply pray for the type of guided help that is most comfortable and most useful to us to come to us. We must be patient and persist. Daily prayer is called for. Also, we must allow quiet time each day to go deep within and listen. The guidance is there. We need only quiet ourselves and tune to it. We feel it. We hear it. We see it.

All we need to know in this time of great change can come to us through guided help. Whatever our mode of access, we all connect to the same information. New doors, new channels for this assistance are now open for humans. We need only ask for this help with sincerity in our hearts and listen with open minds, and it is given to us.

There is a sense of peace and security and joy that comes once we establish our own channel to guided help and in-formation. Any question can be asked; any problem can be addressed. No longer do we feel alone when facing any change, any challenge in life. Daily prayer and daily quiet time or meditation time is recommended. The great trans-formation is upon us and we must take the time to tune in to the guided help and information that is widely available to us to assist us in all phases of preparation.

The great turn of events on planet earth brings great opportunities for healing. We can see peace and freedom many places where we never thought they would be only a few years ago. There is much light and love, much assistance being showered upon earth now. The very best that individual humans can do now is join in the healing process for the planet. Much has been destroyed and much has been lost, but the turn of the millennium is also a turning point for the planet and all life forms upon her. New reverence for the earth is being globally felt. New energy for conservation, new directives for restoration, new leadership in all arenas bring hope that the beauty and majesty of the planet can be maintained.

We all, as individuals, can help make the most of the opportunities present now. Keeping in mind that the earth is a sentient being, an entity unto herself, we can send love, compassion, and healing energy to her. The image of the earth as our great mother is appropriate, for she nurtures and sustains all life on this material plane. She interacts with and reacts to her children. She constantly changes, sometimes in subtle ways, sometimes in major ways which leave us awestruck.

The beauties of the mother earth are so numerous that it should be no problem for us, her children, to find something in nature that fills our hearts with joy, with thanks, and with love. If each of us could, each day, take a moment to experience that fullness of heart, that overpowering love for the earth and her beauty, and if each of us could then consciously send this love to the earth, much is accomplished. Feeling compassion for what the earth has endured at our hands is also appropriate. Visualize this love and compassion beaming right to the core of our mother planet and making brighter the light that dwells there. With each in-breath, we feel the love and compassion swell in our hearts; with each out-breath, we see the compassion and love flow to and brighten the earth at her very center. In this way, we can, as individuals, assist daily in the healing process now occurring on the planet. Whenever we see something, a sunset, a flock of birds, a lightning storm, something that moves us to appreciate the earth and her beauty, let us seize the opportunity to fill our hearts with love, and then consciously send that love to our great mother planet.

If we realize that our emotions actually take shape and form on a plane closely interconnected with the earth realm, then perhaps we can better grasp how much this simple visualization can help. If every individual, every day, consciously sends love energy to the earth, this love accumulates. It builds, amassing, taking form, until the time when it pours back into the material realm bringing transforming radiance and all-encompassing healing. Our mother needs us to help her in this way now. Our assistance is requested. We can help the transition on earth be one of true healing and love, and help the arrival of the new millennium be a time of rejoicing.

∞ ∞ ∞

We can look to nature for many clues as to how to refine ourselves, improve ourselves, and prepare ourselves for upcoming changes. Once the planet has stabilized and is operating at a higher vibrational rate, certain actions and ways of being are no longer appropriate and begin to fade out of existence. We are ushering in a gentler time, a time when yin or receptive female energy comes into its own as a major force, a balancing force, on this planet. This gentle nurturing energy permeates the planet bringing a time when violence, at last, is recognized as unnecessary and undesirable. This is a time when all creations of the Great Spirit or God-force are respected and revered. The Harmonic Convergence ushered in the first wave of this gentle, reverend energy. This occurrence has also been called the beginning of the age of flowers, and it is to flowers we can look for the essence of reverence and gentleness. Each blossom, as it opens, heralds the Holy Spirit present in all things. The delicacy, the color, the fragrance of each flower are earthly manifestations of the divine love which is always present. The flowers speak of the superior ways of gentleness.

We suggest sitting or lying with the flowers. It is best to meditate or commune with the flowers while they are still connected to the earth. We need only listen and the flowers tell us of the ways of gentleness and reverence. We need only open ourselves to the energy of the flowers to learn how we can refine our own natures to be more in tune with the upcoming time when respect and tender attention toward all living things is the norm.

The only way we can ever approach a flower is with gentleness or we injure it. The flowers are our great teachers for the new age. If we can learn not to harm a flower, we can learn the gentle ways of the upcoming cycle. If we can learn to communicate with the flora, we can learn much that helps us live in harmony on this planet. The flowers, the flora, bring light and love, gentleness and reverence to the earth plane. It is time for humans to do the same.

∞ ∞ ∞

Now is the time for many breakthroughs in our civilization. Many people all over the earth who are receptive to the new energy flooding the planet are seeing anew. Many connections are being made, many barriers lifted. One truth which is gaining wider acceptance is that all religions refer to the same Creator, the same Great Spirit, the same God-force. The various expressions of faith are part of the beauty and variety of life on earth. Religious disagreements and religious wars are nearing the end of their time on earth.

Another breakthrough involves the triangle or trinity used in Christianity and other religions. One point on the triangle is the great yin energy, receptive and nourishing, the spirit manifest in matter. All prophets and great teachers are spirit manifest in matter and are associated with this point on the triangle. The earth and all her beautiful life-forms sit on this corner of the triangle also. The point across from this is the great yang energy, creative and active. This point refers to the energies on this planet and others that move to balance and realign those forces which are the very cycles that we live and breathe. This point refers to movement, to the spirit as it flows through events and time. All social change, all political and religious movements, all events in history are associated with this point on the triangle. This point represents the action of the creative force, how it moves, how it flows in our lives. The third point on the triangle, the point above, refers to unity. It refers to the oneness we experience when we grasp that all we know, all we experience, is made of energy, of vibration. It is the spirit that lives in all things, in movement and matter. It is the basic energy, the basic vibration of all life. We are one with all creation because we are all made from the same basic energy. The feeling of oneness is associated with this point on the triangle. All three points as described can be found in every religion and spiritual teaching.

These universal truths are coming forward, promoting breakthroughs, illuminating us to the realization that our differences are illusions. Our differences are simply varying expressions of these same universal truths. We are one.

∞ ∞ ∞

It is easy for us to get wrapped up in the details and problems of everyday existence on earth. Much time and energy are spent on survival, whether it be in an affluent society where we move to continually accumulate material comforts or in a society immersed in poverty where we must continually struggle to find food, clothing, and shelter.

As new energy floods over the earth, more and more humans are seeing beyond the material plane. This new perspective adds a spiritual dimension to the lives of these people. Once we grasp how much more there is than just achievement or survival on the material plane, we are able to detach ourselves from the struggle for material goods. This is true freedom.

Seeing beyond the limits of the material plane is more than just possessing faith that there is more than existence on earth. It is knowing there is more. It is feeling and knowing that there are many realms besides the earth plane. It is feeling and knowing that we can also dwell on these other planes. It is feeling and knowing that death on earth is only the illusion of the end of life. Once we open our hearts and minds to the knowledge that there is so much more than just life on earth, our earthly struggles diminish. They do not seem so all-encompassing, so all-important. We have a new perspective on our lives. Of course, incarnation on the earth plane has much value. Spending our earth lives accumulating material goods, however, may not be the best use of our incarnation on this planet.

Information is available on what truly fulfills us as individuals during our earth incarnations. We can also learn how to make the most of our time here, but first we must be free of our attachment to accumulating material goods. We must detach ourselves from all the snares and illusions that surround us here on earth. We must eliminate greed. This is not always easy because we must still dwell here in a physical body which has physical needs that we certainly cannot ignore. Still, if we maintain a perspective that earth life is only one of many for us, then each daily problem takes on proper proportion and we are not so caught up in the struggle for achievement and material accumulation. In fact, in place of the struggle and strife comes an ease, an assurance that what we need comes to us when we need it. If this does not seem to be so, then it is time to look again at what we think we need, because perhaps what we think we need is not what we actually need at all.

There is too much struggle and hardship on this planet, and it does not have to be so. Greed has overrun the earth and it is time to change this. The opportunity for this new perspective which brings new ease into everyday life on earth is widely available now. Everyone can experience this new ease. To do so, we must be sincere in our hearts, and take time from our hectic existence to turn within. It cannot be emphasized enough: all the information and guidance we need can be obtained by going within. By taking quiet time each day to seek the truth within, by seeking with sincerity, we each can be blessed with new knowledge, new perspective, new ease with which to approach our lives on earth.

∞ ∞ ∞

The energies present on planet earth are changing, and there is no question that the quality and style of life here are changing as well. For one thing, the pace is intensifying. Also, structures that have been in place for many years are crumbling. The new energy present here is quickly making inroads, often into places we least expect. All that has been built on greed and the hardships of others is being undermined. The new energy is moving to bring harmony and balance to the earth. It is helping increase the speed and power of the karmic force.

The powerful energies now at work on this planet are beyond our earthly comprehension, but we are beginning to see their effects. Oppression of many groups, of many peoples, is being lifted. All over the globe, large groups are being formed to honor, to heal, to send love to, and to preserve our beautiful planet. Many leaders are changing their minds and their ways. The forces at work are very powerful.

It is not necessary for us to understand these powerful energies or for us to know all that is changing. It *is* necessary for us to be aware of the condition and events of our own lives. We can see the great changes reflected in our personal lives as well as on the larger world stage. How we conduct ourselves in our daily lives is all-important. We either align ourselves with the new energy of balance and harmony, or cling to the old structures based on material gain. The longer we hold on to the old ways and give our personal energy to them, the more likely it is that we are becoming a part of the cycle of disintegration. Our lives may very well crumble and be swept away with the old order.

We can daily tune to the new energy entering the earth plane and raise our personal vibration to align ourselves with it. This, of course, means major shifts in goals, in conduct, even in personality for many of us. If we keep in mind we are aligning with the new energies of balance and harmony for the planet, we can eventually bring balance and harmony into our own lives and easily let go of the old ways.

∞ ∞ ∞

Before the new ways come into wide practice, the old ways must pass away. It is rare for old structures to give way without some sort of demolition. This is especially true if the changes are major and are happening quickly. We must be prepared to face demolition and destruction in our lives and on this planet.

It is difficult for us to think of destruction as a joyful process, especially if we are particularly attached to material stability. Still, destruction and decay are a natural part of the cycles of the earth. Even the seasons tell us this. The late autumn, the Scorpio time of year, is when the vegetation dies. We can honor this time of death and dying as a time of clearing away the old growth in preparation for new growth in the spring. We can honor destruction of the old order in the same way, as a clearing away of old unneeded structures in order to make way for the new ways of the new millennium. It is a test of our courage, our faith, our knowledge of the workings of the universe to remain joyful when most of our familiar structures are being destroyed. Yet we can rejoice, because this time of change heralds fantastic advancements for the earth and for humans.

As we face the destruction and loss of our old lives, let us pray that we may be guided swiftly to the new ways of being available to us. An abundance of information and opportunities are flooding the planet as this great transition occurs. It remains only for us to seek them and make them a part of our lives. Let us not waste our energies on clinging to elements of the old order. Let us honor the old ways as we let them go, and then look forward to how we can build our lives anew. If we are prepared for the coming destruction and have a joyful attitude, always looking to the great steps forward we can make as a result of this transformation, then we can face these great changes without fear or sorrow.

∞ ∞ ∞

If we have a great deal of drive and direction, if we are sure of our goals, we must now take time to look within ourselves and reevaluate. Because we on earth are facing a huge transformation, we may need to rethink our goals and redirect our energies. Those of us who are highly motivated are often so caught up in daily activities or so bent on achieving certain rewards that we do not take the few moments each day to sit quietly and listen. If we take the time to listen to the world around us and most importantly to our inner voice, we can receive many insights and much information. We can see if our goals and our direction are suitable for the quickly changing times in which we live.

Those of us who are less sure of our direction in life are probably already seeking assistance. Looking into employment statistics and projections, job service counseling, and the like is a shortsighted approach. The greatest assistance comes from within. The truth of the past, the present, and the future lies within. Our inner voice can provide guidance and direction for each day and for a lifetime. Patience and discipline are necessary, but the rewards are great. Meditating or just sitting quietly and going within ourselves needs to be part of our daily regimen.

At first, we may be restless, our minds filled with thoughts, but once we learn to quiet ourselves, we find this time soothing, relaxing, refreshing. Once we find this calm and quiet place within us, then true guidance can come to us.

As the pace of events on earth increases and everything around us changes quickly, we may be confused as to how to proceed. Situations may not be what they seem, or they may change faster than we can imagine. In such times, it is necessary to have a stable base within ourselves that we can turn to for guidance, for information, or just for calm and quiet. It is very important that we cultivate this base of inner calm now, and do so daily. Our inner voice can then be there, ready to guide us through the upheaval of the great transition.

∞ ∞ ∞

Patience is necessary in all areas of life. With patience comes the sense of correct timing. Nothing is learned thoroughly or practiced skillfully unless patience is employed. So it is with the exercises and techniques described in these writings. Results may not always be immediate. If, however, we have patience with ourselves and with the rate at which we absorb and utilize the information, we definitely make progress.

Daily attention is necessary. This cannot be emphasized enough. Many of us already pray on a daily basis. We must somehow find the time and space for a quiet segment each day. Twenty minutes or a half hour is enough, although once we begin, we may find that we wish to extend this quiet time. We may find that two such daily segments are more suitable. Each of us can decide what feels right for us. No matter how we work this quiet time into our daily lives, it is essential that we do so. This time is sacred and there must be no distractions. The length of this quiet segment or the time of day we choose to take it does not matter. The important part is that we do take this quiet time each day.

It is appropriate to use this time in the following manner with personal variations acceptable. We begin with a brief prayer expressing gratitude and requesting guidance. Then we sit quietly and listen. We may use a mantra or another meditation technique to still our minds. Visualization and breathing are also appropriate. The important part is that we take the time to listen. In order to really hear our inner voice, we must learn to quiet our busy conscious minds, and this takes patience and practice. It is, however, not difficult, and most find this quieting of the conscious mind very relaxing and refreshing. Once we have stilled the busy sounds of our conscious minds and our conscious worlds, we have access to the truth which lies within each of us. Going within opens doors to the truth, guidance, and wisdom provided by the universe. Guidance on any situation, on any problem can be had. We need only quiet ourselves and listen. This is the essence of meditation, simple and pure. Each of us can tailor our daily meditations to our needs, as long as we always find the stillness and listen.

∞ ∞ ∞

All is well in our lives when we listen with an open heart and an open mind. If we approach each day with this openness, we hear what we truly need to hear. We can sort out what is true in the voices and sounds that move in and out of our daily lives. We can hear the truth of the inner voice. We can use both prayer and visualization to help us improve our abilities to listen and to truly hear.

The ability to listen with an open heart and mind is one of the greatest gifts we can give ourselves and others. It is amazing what we *do* hear when we approach each day in this manner. Listening in this way does not mean accepting all that is said to us as true. Listening with an open heart and mind helps us hear beyond the words and helps us understand the motivation or the emotions behind them. Listening with openness and compassion develops our intuition so that we can sense what is true and what is untrue in what is spoken to us. We can then go through the words and have insight into the reason they were spoken to us, be they true or untrue.

∞ ∞ ∞

Many of us experience the sensation of flying in our dreams. Flying is something humans have longed to do for centuries. The new energy and the new information pouring onto the earth plane includes instruction on conscious flying also known as levitation. Once humans learn how to focus their personal energy through meditation and visualization, levitation is an easy step. Once we begin consciously changing our cells and our tissue, we learn to align our physical mass differently. We can then learn to float or levitate our own bodies consciously, not just in our dreams.

Many gifts of knowledge and wisdom previously accessed only by sages and yogis are being made available to all humans. Some preparation is needed, but the time is right for humans to undergo a transformation of consciousness. In other words, we may all be yogis as we enter the new millennium. The opening in the veil between earth reality and the realms beyond is an opening within each of us. We are now more sensitive to subtle but powerful vibrations which before had passed us by. There are centers in our bodies which are newly opened. These centers can receive the new knowledge and wisdom flooding the earth plane and can help us adapt the rest of our reality to this new energy.

Those who are using meditation, breathing, visualization, and prayer on a regular basis are already seeing their lives transformed by this new ray of energy. These people are already receiving the new wisdom and are seeing their lives change and improve through the application of this knowledge. It is available to all humans. However, we must be in touch with our inner self, our inner voice in order to gain direct access to this information.

This new opening, this new ray of energy, knowledge, wisdom, and hope is meant for all the earth. It is up to us to center ourselves so that we can bring this new energy into our daily lives and onto the earth. It is a transforming energy which can elevate life on earth to a new level of peace, understanding, compassion, and love.

∞ ∞ ∞

Humans are complex beings. One of the most difficult things for humans to understand is the illusion surrounding self. Every human has a sense of being separate, and indeed we do each have our own bodies and psyches to care for. More than that, most of us have a sense of individual destiny which we move through life to fulfill. We have our own goals and our own ideas about what brings us happiness and satisfaction. It is very easy for us to get wrapped up in ourselves and our separate lives.

The self and all its trappings are an illusion. The self is the face we present to the material world. It really has little value beyond this! We have attached far more to the self than belongs there. We seek fame. We seek wealth. We seek power and control. Our sense of self-importance grows as we strive and accomplish on the material plane. Even those of us who accept a more humble lifestyle get far too caught up in the successes and failures of the illusion we call ourselves.

A new perspective on the self is needed for the new age. A new self-perspective can whittle away all the excess baggage we have attached to the self. If we view the self as merely the mask we present to the material plane, then many of our burdens are lifted. We no longer have to strive to make our name mean something. We no longer have the fear of failure riding us. We can look beyond the dictates of material success for true fulfillment.

If the self is just a mask, then what are we? We are the supreme energy of the God-force. We are one and the same energy as the Creator. We are emissaries of the Great Spirit. We are all connected. We are all one in that we are all made of this God-energy.

Once we see past the illusion of the separateness of the self, we can see that our fulfillment and our happiness are truly linked with the well-being of the earth as a whole and with all the people upon her.

∞ ∞ ∞

Much has been spoken and written about self-love and self-esteem. It is indeed essential for us to love ourselves, for only if we love ourselves can we truly channel love to others. Self-love, however, must not be confused with self-importance. There is danger in placing too much value on the self that is our face, our mask to the world. When we can detach ourselves from our mask, our ego, as it were, and see it, like the body, as simply a vehicle on this earth plane, then we can truly experience self-love. We can see ourselves as lighted beings, the essence of the Divine, an expression of the Creator. We can love ourselves as manifestations of the Great Spirit here on earth. Our flaws and our mistakes are challenges to help us grow into the light that is our birthright as expressions of the Great Spirit. Our mistakes, if properly heeded, turn us toward our inner light.

Self-hate and self-pity are every bit as dangerous as self-importance. Here again we are placing too much value on the self, the mask, the ego. When we get caught up in self-hate, we are exaggerating the importance of our ego. When we see ourselves as lighted beings, as made of the same energy as the God-force, then we cannot possibly hate ourselves, or pity ourselves for that matter. Self-hate and self-pity are dangerous in another way. Indulging in either can lead to a spiraling downward of our energy. The gulf between our lighted inner being and our outer ego-mask is widened. We see only the self which is our mask with which we are dissatisfied and unhappy. We lose touch with our center, the

God-energy in each of us. Our faults seem even more monumental and this generates more self-hate.

Prayer can break this spiral. Many of us can relate to reaching the point of such agony brought on by self-hate that we pray for relief. Prayer can bring guidance and a fresh perspective on our true being.

Each day we must love ourselves as vehicles for the divine energy of the Great Spirit on earth. If we take a moment every day to view ourselves in this light, to love ourselves and let the love present in the universe flow through us, then all temptations to self-hate, self-pity, and self-importance become less and less a part of our lives.

∞ ∞ ∞

There is excitement, but there is also sadness in these times. We see the earth being polluted and devastated by humans. We see much illness, poverty, and unrest. Yet there is a new energy afoot which many now feel. With this new energy comes an infusion of hope that perhaps the sad situation on this planet can indeed be reversed.

We inhabitants of earth need to consciously tune to this new energy, for it provides guidance for us in these times of great change. This energy is pouring onto earth from a newly opened door between the earth plane and realms beyond our knowing. We who dwell on earth need much assistance now, and we are receiving it from other planes.

The earth herself is playing an important role in the essential changes, for the earth is a sentient being unto herself. She is receiving this influx of new energy; she is absorbing it and is preparing to change in accordance with it. We inhabitants of this planet have choices of our own to make. We can tune to this new energy and increase our personal vibration in harmony with it, or we can choose to ignore it and continue on the way we have been going. Even if no human takes the time to consciously tune to and work with the new energy, the earth herself is doing so. The earth knows what is best and is moving to it.

Even though humans have made great strides in science and technology, even though humans have altered the forces of nature and the state of the planet, we cannot ignore for long this new energy and the changes it brings; nor can we stop it. It is beyond our control, and even beyond the comprehension of many. Yet the opportunity exists for us all to feel this new ray of energy and to consciously tune to it. This, in fact, is the best thing we can do at this time. There is help and guidance for all on earth, as well as much exciting new information coming in on this ray. It is up to us to make the best of the changes that this new energy brings.

A question that is often debated is the issue of how much control we really have in our lives? We do have choices. We can flow or we can resist. Resistance, however, is the cause of much unnecessary suffering on the earth plane. Flowing refers to tuning to the cycles at hand and working with them to learn and improve our lives on earth. Why would any of us resist? Flowing onward almost always means changing and sometimes these changes are radical. Often they are uncomfortable. Sometimes the changes bring loss, sorrow, and grief. Yet more often than not, resisting the changes brings more discomfort than if we had not resisted. More often than not, the changes occur whether we resist or flow, so our choice comes down to attitude.

So it is with the great changes coming to the planet. Our resistance to them only causes us more suffering. Even doing our very best to tune to this cycle of change and to flow with it, we experience much loss. The old ways are passing away, and with them some things that are dear to us. Loss is a part of the natural cycles of this planet. Death of a loved one appears to be a loss to those still incarnated. Yet this is an illusion, as are most losses. In times of great change, it is best to prepare ourselves to let go. Much that is old and outmoded is swept away. We must keep in mind that the energies of the universe always move to balance, so for all the old ways that are being swept away, there are new ways to be entered upon. If we face these times prepared to flow and release the old, then we can experience the great changes with joy. We can rejoice that the new energy and the new ways are here. We can embrace them. The earth is overjoyed that the time has come for this great transition, and so might we be. Let us relax, let go of the old, and tune to the new.

∞ ∞ ∞

We humans need a new attitude and a new approach to our incarnations on earth. There is far too much needless strife and suffering due to the way we humans now view our lives. There is so much joy available on earth. Humans miss much of it. We get so caught up in daily problems that the potential joy passes by unnoticed. We dwell far too much on the negative aspects of our existence, thereby increasing their importance in our lives. It is time for humans to see how much can be gained by reversing this perspective and emphasizing the joy. Strife melts away. Problems and challenges shrink to a more appropriate size in our lives. Instead of seeing our time on earth as bondage to worry, disappointment, and endless battles, we can see each moment, each day, as filled with wonder and joy.

When we begin to feel ourselves fill up with worry, fear, or despair, we need to sit quietly and breathe very deeply for a moment or two. If we breathe in through the mouth and out through the nose, we clear negative thoughts. Breathing in through the nose and out through the mouth clears negative emotions. Once we have calmed and cleared ourselves, we need to then take a moment to find some joy to bring into ourselves. Joy can come to us in the simplest forms. The beauty of the sunlight streaming in the room, the sound of a bird singing, the rustle of leaves in a spring breeze, the sight of the crescent moon at sunset all can bring joy to our hearts and minds. When we feel this joy, let us breathe it in and make it a part of our cells. If we do this every day, soon we have joy in all the cells and tissues of our bodies, and our outlook on earthly existence has dramatically changed.

Another approach to easing the stress and strife in our lives is as follows: When we are caught up in problems and overwrought with tension, we often go around and around about it in our minds until we are frustrated and depressed. Again, it is time to clear out the worry and frustration. If we are too overwrought to sit quietly and clear ourselves with breath, then walking out in the fresh air can help. Again, it is most helpful if we breathe deeply while walking. We need to visualize the worry and stress streaming out the out-breath. Then we can visualize breathing in clarity. Now we can begin thinking of all the things in our lives we have to be thankful for. Each time we think of something positive, we can breathe in gratitude and joy, again seeing the joy become a part of our being, our tissues, our cells, our very makeup.

Once we open our eyes to the beauty and joy that surround us, we are filled with a new appreciation for our lives on earth. Our problems then shrink to proper perspective and our lives include more ease and less stress. The more we look for the joy, the more we find it, the more we feel it, the more we make it a part of our lives and our very beings! We can become joy ourselves, and pass it on to others.

∞ ∞ ∞

In order to tune to the new vibration, the new ray of energy flooding the earth plane, we need to open our eyes to **see** in a new way. This new way of seeing is as easy as breathing. We need only look around us and appreciate every aspect of the natural beauty that is the earth. Some of us already have this special sight, and every day we are filled with joy and gratitude for the beauty of every detail of this earth plane. If we can view every snowflake, every leaf, every blade of grass as a marvel, then we are enjoying this new sight of gratitude.

This appreciation for everything that is natural to the planet gives us a reverence for the earth. This joyous way of seeing all the beauty that the earth presents changes our conduct. We can no longer do anything which might harm even the smallest part of the planet. Greed and selfish ambition fade away in the brilliance of the light that floods our beings when we view the earth in this way.

It doesn't matter where we live. We can always find some natural creation around us to evoke this appreciation and gratitude. The sky itself can inspire awe and wonder many times in a single day if we only take the time to look. It is a simple step to go from this feeling of wonder, appreciation, and gratitude to sending love to the planet. Each day we must make sure we have at least one moment when we appreciate the beauty and wonder of the creation that is our planet. When we do, we then need to send love to the earth and gratitude to the Creator.

This new way of seeing, which we shall call appreciation seeing, naturally opens us to feeling gratitude for the wonder that surrounds us. Once we can see and feel in this way on a daily basis, we are ready to raise our vibrational rates in accordance with the new ray of energy flooding the earth. If we have reverence and respect, appreciation and gratitude for all the details of creation on this planet, we can approach the great transition with hope, with joy, and in tune with the new energy present on earth.

∞ ∞ ∞

The veil between the earth plane and other realms has, in the past, closed off much for humans. This, however, is changing. With the new opening in the veil and the new information that is coming through it to earth, we can become aware of much that is newly available to us and much that has always been available to us but which we have not used. For example, it has always been possible to pass love between realms, but humans have not often realized this. When a loved one dies and the spirit of this person passes from the earth through the veil to the realms beyond, that person in spirit can both give and receive love. Love knows no boundaries, certainly not death. Far too often the friends and relatives of the departed human are filled with a sense of loss and are overcome with grief. If we humans begin seeing death as merely a transition, then we can surround these passings with light and love which is far more useful and helpful to both the departed person and those remaining on the earth plane.

It is indeed appropriate to send love to our ancestors. Many ancient civilizations included honoring the ancestors in their rituals. It is time to bring this practice to the forefront once again and surround it with love. We can use visualization and prayer to send love to those who have passed from the earth to other realms. When we do this, we hold in our hearts the knowledge that these departed persons receive our love and are aided by it.

It is time for us to be aware that love can and does pass from these other realms to us who now inhabit the earth plane. It is true that there are many who watch over us and send us love, although not many of us humans have been open to receiving it. Now, however, with the new opening in the veil, telepathic communications between spirit realms and the earth plane have increased. More and more humans are becoming aware of the guidance and love that are available from the spirit planes. Once we begin receiving this love and guidance, we can know security, peace, and bliss, perhaps for the first time in our human incarnation.

∞ ∞ ∞

The new ray of energy, the new opening in the veil between worlds, the change of great cycles all combine to make this a very unusual and exciting time on earth. Those of us who are fearful of change and of the unknown find this time particularly difficult. There are many opportunities for us to come to terms with our fears and to adapt to the new energies and the new time. We must be willing to try. We must be willing to open our hearts and minds and seek guidance.

Not only is love passing from other realms to earth, so is help. We need only ask with sincerity and patience, and we receive guidance. Guidance comes in many forms. Most often people receive guidance in the form that is most comfortable and most compatible with their natures. Some may receive help in their dreams; some may receive pictures or visions; still others may hear the guidance spoken. No matter how we receive the information, it is all conveyed to us telepathically. There are those in nearby realms whose joyful duty it is to help us on earth with this transition. These spirit guides are ready to send us all the information we need. We need only clear ourselves and open ourselves to receiving it.

Telepathy is a phenomenon that is now coming into its own. That part of our brain which deals with sending and receiving telepathic communications is being activated by this new ray of energy. Those of us who practice meditation and who are in touch with our inner selves are but one small step away from direct contact with spirit guides. Contact with spirit guides through whatever means can provide guidance, security, comfort, and love. It is important that we be clear, centered, and grounded when experiencing contact from spirit guides.

The new ray of energy flooding the planet is increasing the rate of vibration on earth, and with it our personal vibratory rate. New psychic centers in our bodies are being activated allowing us to pursue new avenues of learning. Telepathy is just one of these avenues, but it may be the most useful. Through telepathic contact, we can receive precise information about anything we need.

In times of intense and rapid change, we must reach out beyond our accumulated earthly knowledge for guidance from the realms beyond. Our spirit helpers are detached from our earthly problems, yet they still love us and wish to help us. We can turn to our spirit guides at any time for any reason.

Now, as humanity faces a giant transition on earth, guidance from the realms beyond is more important than ever. In fact, this telepathic guidance is the key to helping make this transformation joyful and successful as far as what is best for the earth. Our task is to open ourselves so that we are receptive to this guidance, and then adjust our lives in accordance with it. It is inevitable: our lives are changing. We might as well tune to the new energy and make the changes as joyful as possible.

∞ ∞ ∞

Love is the highest and most marvelous vibration available to us in this universe. It is the one energy that can pass through any barrier to any realm. Generating love energy for ourselves, for each other, and for the earth at this time makes all the difference as far as how we ride the changes.

Since love is an emotion, we can use visualization to increase the flow of love in our lives and the lives of those around us. Visualizations are very powerful when it comes to feelings. We can generate emotions and we can change the very content of those emotions through visualizations.

Let us try a simple visualization to increase the love in us and around us. This particular exercise cannot be done too much. It is best to begin by being relaxed and comfortable. If need be, we can use the balanced breath and/or the alternate breath to help us settle down. Now let's visualize a shimmering pulsing globe of pink light in the heart chakra area. This sphere is tremendously bright, luminescent, and sparkling. As we breathe in, we take the breath into this pink sphere and begin to expand it. We can visualize and feel the love energy filling our entire chest cavity. This energy pulses brilliant sparkling pink. We see it. We feel it. We watch it grow. Now that we have generated love energy in the heart chakra, we can do several things. We can send it up and down our spines, filling our head, our arms, our legs, every part of us with this shimmering pink light. We can see the pink love energy surrounding us and becoming part of our auras. This is helpful to those of us who need to love ourselves more. We can send this love energy we have generated out our feet and down into the center of the earth. This helps the planet. We can also send the energy to others whether they are presently incarnated or not, for love passes through all barriers. Simply envision the love energy streaming out of the heart and surrounding that person.

∞ ∞ ∞

When events occur that are beyond our comprehension, confusion often results. When events occur that seem to be beyond our control, we often feel helpless. Feelings of powerlessness, helplessness, and victimization exist all over the planet. This is a direct result of humanity's mode of operation at this time. We now operate for the most part out of our third chakras. This is the energy center in the body located about one inch above the navel. The third chakra relates to power issues. Power struggles cover the earth.

Now humanity has the opportunity to change this. We can raise our vibratory rates and lift ourselves up and out of the third chakra power struggles. It is time for humans to begin operating from the fourth chakra in our daily lives. The fourth chakra is an energy center in the body which resides in the area of the heart. This center relates to feeling and expressing love and compassion for others.

It is very difficult when we feel victimized to generate love and compassion for ourselves, for our oppressors, or for anyone! Quite a leap is necessary to move our energies from the third to the fourth chakra. Humankind has been trapped in third chakra power struggles for so long that an incredible force of will is needed to break out and to begin operating on a higher level.

Still, the energy to make this leap is becoming available. There are steps we can take to facilitate this change. First, we must detach ourselves from the throes of the power struggle, for if we are still caught up in it, we just keep going round and round. Visualization can help us detach. Picture the problem situation. Isolate it. Set it apart. Surround the picture with white light keeping it at a distance. Once we have detached ourselves, we can transmute the energy surrounding the problem, raising the level of vibration. We must always work to raise the vibratory rate. This is in accordance with the changing energy patterns on the planet. There are several ways we can raise the level of vibration. Breathing and visualization can both be helpful, but they are most effective when used together.

Once we have detached ourselves from the power struggle, the problem situation, and we have set it at a distance from us, we need to clean the third chakra area. Visualize a stream of soothing blue-green light flowing smoothly through the third chakra. This stream of light cleans and heals, for often there is hurtful, painful residue from power confrontations. As we visualize this stream, let us relax and use the balanced breath. Count breathing in; hold for the same count; breathe out for the same count; hold again for the same count.

Once we have cleared and healed our own power center, we can deal with that problem situation. Take the detached picture of the scene and spin it faster and faster until it is a whirling ball of white light. Then begin sending streams of sparkling pink light around the whirling ball. When the visualization is brilliant and beautiful, breathe it into the heart chakra. See it there generating love and compassion.

SEE ILLUSTRATION 3:

The Body with its Energy Centers or Chakras

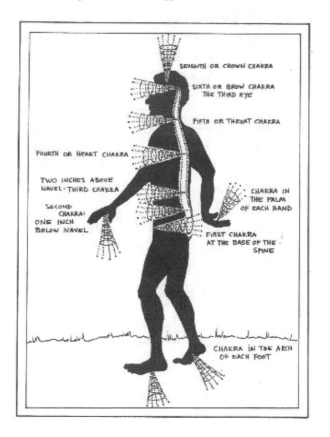

∞ ∞ ∞

The earth is blessed with large expanses of water. We humans are aware that we are made up mostly of water and that water is essential to all life on this planet. Now we can move to an even deeper understanding of the value of water. Water not only constitutes a large part of our physical bodies and nourishes those bodies, it also clears, tunes, and revitalizes our spirit selves.

The practice of baptism came out of the ancient understanding of the value of water as a spiritual cleanser.

Immersing ourselves in water, along with the use of visualization, can clean our bodies and clean our energy fields, our auras. If we find ourselves in an uncomfortable state, perhaps because of illness, anger, grief, or pain, we can visualize the problem within ourselves and see it extending out from us into our energy field. We can choose a color that we associate with the problem and see it within us and pouring out of us into our auras. Now we see the water, be it a bath or a lake or the sea, sparkling and shimmering. As we immerse ourselves, we visualize the undesirable color washing away. When water works on a spiritual level, it does more than just wash. It breaks up and disperses the problem energies. If we are creative with our visualizations, we find water helps to center, clear, and tune us in a more thorough way than we have ever before imagined.

The sound of water, for instance the sound of the ocean waves breaking on the shore or the sound of a swiftly running brook, is relaxing, soothing, comforting, even inspiring. Recordings of water sounds are now being used to facilitate relaxation and meditation. These water sounds clear our busy minds of their constant chatter so that we can relax and meditate successfully. For those who have keen hearing and are predisposed to clairaudience, the sounds of water can often bring inspired messages in the form of words and/or music.

Awareness of water as a psychic cleanser can help us view the gift of water in a new way. We can then use water on a daily basis to clear us, tune us, relax us, and generally improve our state of being.

∞ ∞ ∞

When we seek guidance with sincerity in our hearts, guidance comes to us in many forms and in many ways. For those who are especially visually attuned, clairvoyance is a psychic gift that can be developed. Guidance can then arrive visually.

The combination of light and water can aid in developing psychic gifts, especially clairvoyance. It is no surprise that many people have a fascination with sunlight on the water. The light of the sun reflected off of a lake, a stream, an ocean, or a puddle can move our consciousness into an open receptive state. Moonlight on the water opens subtle paths to our subconscious minds so that we are more open and receptive to guidance. The combination of light and water soothes and relaxes us, and clears that part of our minds which makes pictures for us. If we sit for a while gazing at moonlight or sunlight on the water, we may find ourselves in a rather fluid blissful state. It is but a short step from this state to one in which we connect with guided help through visions. We must be sincerely seeking this guidance and open to receiving it.

Another spiritually valuable phenomenon on earth is the reflection of sunlight and moonlight off the snow. Here water is crystallized in form, so the reflected light is especially powerful, nearly hypnotic. This light can cleanse our conscious and subconscious minds and open us to the possibilities psychic growth can bring.

When we find ourselves gazing at sunlight or moonlight reflected off the water or the snow, we can use breathing, especially the balanced breath, to ease ourselves into a clear receptive state. We let the reflected sunlight or moonlight filter in through our eyes to our minds and bodies relaxing us, clearing us, and opening us to the guidance that is available to all of us. Whatever guidance comes is tailored to our individual needs, but also to the needs of the planet at this time.

∞ ∞ ∞

Anger and aggression are present all over the planet. We see this on a global scale and we see this in our personal lives. To understand how to change this, we must first understand the psychophysics of anger and aggression. The emotion of anger and subsequent aggressive acts are generated in the lower three chakras, that is in the area below the waist and above the anus. For centuries humans have been operating primarily from these lower three chakras.

It is time now for humanity to change this. We have the opportunity through the increase in the vibratory rate of the planet to raise our level of operation up to the fourth or heart chakra and higher. This takes an incredible focus of will on our parts. We must consciously apply ourselves to this end. We have a great deal of guidance available to help us do this. The earth herself is helping, and the time is right. Still, we must be aware that the raising of our personal vibrations necessitates a conscious effort of will. If we apply ourselves, we find this raising of our energies flows quite easily.

Prayer, meditation, visualization, and breathing again are the keys. When we pray, let us pray not only for our own evolvement, but also for a healing for the earth. Let us picture a time when love and compassion (fourth chakra) step to the forefront of activities on this planet, and anger recedes. Let us picture a time when gentleness is the norm, and aggression and violence fade into the background. This is attainable. The time is right, but it is up to us to make these changes occur and then stabilize them. We can proceed with the assurance that we are working with the changing energy of the earth.

We must first effect these changes within ourselves. We must become comfortable with operating out of our heart area. Love and compassion must fill our lives and surround every activity. This is the natural progression of the energy on the planet now. If we align our personal wills with the will of the Great Spirit, we can make thorough and successful changes.

∞ ∞ ∞

Raising our energies up so that we operate from the energy centers located above the waist is an essential step for humanity. Here is a combination visualization/breathing exercise to help us move our energies up our spines. Let us remember that it is important that all seven chakras or energy centers be the same size, open, and clear, and that, in general, we wish to raise our energy from the base of the spine up and out the top of the head.

This exercise focuses on moving energy from the third chakra, located one inch above the navel, to the fourth chakra at the base of the sternum in the heart area. We are focusing on just these two because most people operate from the third chakra. This emphasis on the third chakra or power center has brought our planet to a place where greed and accumulation of money for power run rampant. It is time for a big change, and this change can occur once humans operate for the most part from their heart chakras.

This exercise is best done when we are quiet and centered as in meditation. Once we are familiar with the visualization, we can call it to mind when we are in a tense power struggle and it can help us react from our hearts. In a comfortable position, we begin the balanced breath. As we breathe in, we envision drawing energy up from the base of our spines to the third chakra right above the navel. Picture this energy as white light. As we breathe out, the third chakra brightens with golden orange light. Do this four times. Now using eight quick out-breaths or puff-breaths (the in-breaths occur automatically), we clear the pathway between the third and fourth chakras. Next, using the balanced breath again, we draw the sunny golden orange light from the third chakra up into our fourth chakra or heart area. As we do this, we see it change in color from pumpkin orange to brilliant pink. The in-breath sees the energy as colored light travel up the spine; the out-breath sees the heart chakra brighten with beautiful pink light. Repeat eight times or until the heart chakra glows with luminescent pink light.

There has always been some limited contact between the earth plane and other realms. There have always been those few who were gifted psychically and could receive telepathic communications through the veil between worlds. These gifted humans were seen either as religious prophets or insane deviants. At any rate, they were certainly not viewed as normal. This is another area where people's attitudes and understanding are changing. With the new opening in the veil and new energy flooding planet earth, telepathic communication with spirit guides and others who dwell on the related planes is becoming much more common.

There have always been some guided writings. Most have served as religious texts. A number of sections of the Bible, for instance, were dictated telepathically from beyond the veil. With the new opening in the veil, much information is being made available to those incarnated on the earth plane at this time. Most of this new information is being documented in guided writings such as this book.

We are entering a time when psychic gifts such as telepathy occur more often and are more readily accepted. Indeed, all of us have the potential to utilize that part of our beings which connects us to the realms beyond the earth plane. If we are open-minded and sincere, we can begin to find ways to expand our personal psychic potential. Exactly how we connect may be a bit different for every individual.

Those dwelling on earth now must become aware of the changing energy on the planet and the opening this brings to us. Each of us can know the wealth that lies within. Each of us can experience a special connectedness to the realms beyond earth and ultimately to the Creator. It is time for us to be more open and accepting of psychic gifts. It is time for us all to honor the connections each of us holds within ourselves to universal truth and to the Creator.

∞ ∞ ∞

Telepathy is receiving in our own minds the thought forms of another. That part of our brain that is the receiver has been dormant for the most part for centuries. Now, however, this area of the brain is being activated by the new ray of energy entering the earth plane.

To understand and use our telepathic powers, we must first be able to quiet our own restless minds. All forms of meditation teach us how to still our internal dialogue, or mind-chatter. Once we are proficient at quieting our own minds, we are ready to receive telepathic input.

We can receive thought forms from others whether the others are incarnate or discarnate. We can receive telepathic messages from someone sitting across the table from us, from someone across the continent, or from someone beyond the veil. This is because our thoughts take an actual form and exist on a nearby plane, and we can telepathically connect with these thought forms. We can achieve access to this plane through the veil surrounding earth's existence. The new ray of energy permeating the earth plane has provided an opening between our material plane and this nearby realm. That part of the human brain which can make the connection is now being activated. We can now use our own minds to tap into the thought forms that exist on this nearby plane. Of course, this is somewhat of a simplification, as are many things in this book. What is important here is that we grasp the basic concepts so that we can utilize the information by applying it to our own evolvement.

Telepathy is most useful in understanding others and in receiving guided help. It can also be used for communicating over long distances. Not only words can be sent and received. Emotions, especially love, can be telepathically communicated. Music and even scents can be telepathically conveyed. We are only at the beginning of discovering what can be done with the psychic gift of telepathy.

∞ ∞ ∞

There are certain truths now coming to light that are to be generally understood and accepted by humanity. These universal truths have always been present but have not been known or accepted by the majority of earth-dwellers.

The first of these is reincarnation. More and more people are beginning to accept the concept that our spirits not only live on after our earthly bodies die, but live many lives here on earth and on other planes of existence. The process of evolvement unfolds through many lifetimes, yet each incarnation is valuable. Some of the ancestors who were privy to the knowledge of reincarnation thought that humans would not value each individual lifetime if they knew they had many lives on earth. Now it is time for the greater picture of human evolvement to be known, understood, and accepted by all alive on earth.

This leads to the next universal truth: death is not the end of life, but is a transition from one state of being to another. Death, in fact, is much more joyful for the one who is passing than birth! The passing out of the physical body and out of earth incarnation is filled with comfort, light, and love. Once this truth is generally accepted, fear of death is eliminated from our cultures and from our lives. We fill our hearts with joy and love for the one who has passed rather than surround ourselves with grief and sorrow. We no longer see the passing of a loved one as a loss. Once we are in spirit form, we are much more versatile, and we can, indeed, communicate with those still incarnated. The separation is physical only. Many connections can remain between those who have passed and those on earth, especially if there exist strong bonds of love. This knowledge brings us a new perspective and attitude on life and death and a renewed respect for the vast workings of the universe.

∞ ∞ ∞

In times of great and rapid change there is always confusion. We all know the feeling of being completely befuddled. It is very easy for quick changes in events to unbalance us, and for the escalating rate of vibration to bring unbridled confusion. This is one of the reasons we must prepare. The more of us who do prepare, the less we suffer from chaotic confusion.

Clarity in times of confusion and chaos is not easy to come by. Even thorough preparation may not ready us for every wild occurrence. The first thing to remember is that it is better not to act when in the throes of confusion. Sometimes rapidly changing events surprise us and prompt an immediate reaction. There is almost always a way to step aside for a few moments to evaluate the situation. Only the most advanced sage can react instantly from a place of centeredness and clarity when faced with surprising and upsetting changes.

Overwhelming confusion can bring feelings of frustration and helplessness. This can escalate bringing more confusion and even despair. We must step outside the circle of confusion and ask for help. We must quiet ourselves using breathing and/or visualization and ask for guidance. Persistence is important, and so is asking with sincerity from the heart.

In order to go from confusion to clarity, we must reach a certain level of detachment. The more attached we are to the events, the people, the material goods, the more difficult it is for us to see our way clearly. Often the automatic reaction in confusion is to cling on. Instead, it is best to step back and ask for help in seeing the situation clearly. Once we are able to let go, very often the fog of confusion lifts, and we see and feel with clarity. In confusion, we must remember that if we pray for help, help comes. Meditation, visualization, and breathing are all tools to help us in times of confusion.

∞ ∞ ∞

We can operate daily from a position of clarity. We can do this without comprehending all the details of existence that surround us. Indeed, there is much about earth life as well as about the universe that is beyond the comprehension of humans at this time. Yet we can move through each day and through our lives in a clear and centered manner. We can step out of the fog of confusion into the light of clarity and knowing.

Knowing is very different from comprehending. Comprehension speaks of understanding with the mind, and we humans at this point use only a small part of our minds. Knowing is something we do with our entire body. Knowing uses all our senses, our intuition, our connectedness to the universe through our inner self. Through knowing, we achieve a position of clarity. Through knowing, we achieve an understanding that is beyond mere comprehension, an understanding that involves every cell in our bodies. At this point, most of us only catch glimpses of this knowing. The peaceful joy and absolute clarity that come with each glimpse motivate us to try to make this knowing, this connectedness, a greater part of our lives.

How do we achieve this state of knowing? We align ourselves, every cell in our bodies, with the holy energy of the universe. The actual vibration of each of our cells aligns with the universal energy of the Creator, the Great Spirit. The cells in our bodies change on a regular basis. Seven years from now, none of the cells in our bodies are those we have today. We can effect great changes in our bodies, our makeup, our beings, our energies by consciously aligning ourselves with the universal energy. We can make knowing a part of our very beings. Of course, this takes time, patience, and persistence. Our lives, however, improve as we proceed to change and realign our cells. We experience more and more glimpses of connectedness and clarity. We begin to know with our entire body/bodies on a more regular basis. Prayer, meditation, visualization, and breathing again are our tools to facilitate this process.

∞ ∞ ∞

The earth would be an entirely different place if the majority of humans spent each day operating from their hearts. Greed and power plays would fade away, and we would see hunger and much illness disappear. Yet this is a giant step for humanity, a step not many have made at this time.

Picture the spine as a flame. The flame burns at the base of the spine. It flames upward. If it is a small flame, it lights only the lower spine and the modes of activities associated with the energy centers of the lower spine: survival, sex, control, power, and accumulation of material goods. If the flame rises up the spine and lights the heart area, we operate in a more loving, giving, compassionate manner. It is time for humanity to fan the flame, to light the heart, to change life on earth as we know it now.

How can we fan the flame? How can we increase the size of our spinal flame so it reaches up and lights our hearts? We can use our breath along with visualization. We need to begin by finding a comfortable position, either lying or sitting, in which the spine is straight. Then we take a moment to quiet ourselves using the balanced breath. Next, we picture a golden flame at the base of our spines, right below the tailbone. Now, with each in-breath, picture the flame rising up the spine to the heart. With each out-breath, we fan the flame at the heart center, so that the entire heart area glows with golden light. See the beautiful, luminescent golden flame spiral up the spine on the in-breath, and increase the golden radiance of the heart area with the out-breath. We continue until we feel the heart area activated and energized. This breathing-visualization exercise only takes a few moments. If we take the time to do this early in the day each day, we can operate with and our lives can be filled with an abundance of love and compassion.

Section Three
Enlightenment Series

Enlightenment has meant many different things to many different people. In the new millennium the word enlightenment takes on another meaning entirely. Enlightenment is the word we can use to describe the state of those persons who have aligned themselves with the higher vibrational rate now beginning to infiltrate earth. There is no mistaking who these people are, and they are called enlightened. These are the humans who have consciously altered the makeup of the cells of their bodies so that they can vibrate and operate with the higher energy newly available on earth. This takes years of preparation, perseverance, and patience. Once, however, the cells of our bodies have been changed over so that they accept and utilize this higher vibration, we appear to have a glow or sheen about us. Also, once we are in this enlightened state, others can sense or feel the higher vibrational rate when they come near to us. That is why it is said there is no mistaking those who are enlightened.

Yogis have for many years practiced conscious changing the cells of their bodies. Never before on planet earth has this opportunity been available to so many nor has it been available in this particular way. Those who wish to take advantage of the opportunity that this new ray of energy brings us need only persist in daily breathing and visualization exercises, along with meditation and prayer. These exercises are geared to consciously changing the cellular makeup of the body so that we can accept and work with the higher vibrational rate.

Once we begin on this path, it is important that we persist. It is important that we regard these exercises as sacred and prepare ourselves for the fact that we may need to continue for years before we reach this enlightened state with our entire beings. The rewards are great: excellent health, unshakable balance, clarity and wisdom beyond our current knowledge, compassion and love for all.

SEE ILLUSTRATION 4:

The Layers of a Healthy Aura in an Enlightened Being

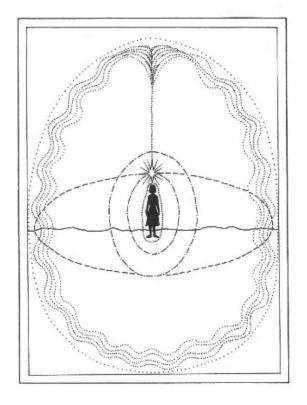

It is necessary for every human incarnated at the time of this great transition to come to terms with the new higher vibration flooding the earth plane. Those of us who take the time to prepare can invite this new vibration to become a part of our very beings. When this new higher energy lives in every one of our cells, we are said to be enlightened.

There are many ways we humans can incorporate this new ray of energy into our lives. The one thing we cannot do is ignore it, for ignoring this new vibration brings discomfort, illness, and probable death. This book provides many suggestions and exercises to help humans adjust and adapt in this time of great transition. We each need to find the suggestions that suit us and apply them to our lives.

We shall begin by outlining the process for those of us who wish to affect the actual changing of every cell of the body so that we resonate to this higher vibrational rate with every fiber of our beings. This is the most thorough preparation we, as humans, can do, but it requires a commitment of years and must be approached with reverence and sincerity of heart.

This exercise takes only a few moments, but must be done each day at the same time. The most appropriate time is right before sleep because our bodies do much rebuilding and regenerating while we sleep. Remember, it takes the human body seven years to rebuild or replace every cell, so we are talking about long-term preparation. In a relaxed position, we center ourselves using the alternate breath or the balanced breath. Then we visualize our entire bodies as lighted beings; see every cell alive with golden light. Simply breathe in golden light; see it going to every cell in the body. Breathe out and the light in every cell glows brighter. We hold this image of every cell glowing with golden light as we lie down to sleep. The golden light we visualize remains with us into the first hours of sleep and affects the transformation of some cells.

∞ ∞ ∞

It is important that we make this new higher rate of vibration our own. We must raise our energy levels to meet this new higher vibration. We must tune our entire beings to it. In this way, we are in synch, we are in tune with the flow of the great transformation. Each person is unique, so we must find the way best suited to each of us. Again, we emphasize that this new ray of energy cannot be ignored. It is affecting every molecule of the earth and all upon her.

Here is another way we can raise our personal vibrations to align ourselves with the new higher vibration. Again this uses our tools of breathing and visualization. Our bodies need to be straight, either lying on our backs or standing with feet spread slightly for balance. Visualizations are most effective if we first calm and center ourselves by using the balanced breath. Once we are practiced in using this breathing to clear and center ourselves, we need only take a moment or two to achieve a calm and centered state. Next, beginning at the feet, visualize a spiral of blue light moving up the legs, up the torso, up and out of the head. See it sparkle as it swirls and spirals around the body. As we breathe in, we draw the spiral of blue light up and around our bodies. As we breathe out, we see it flame out of the top of our heads. After visualizing the spiral of blue light four times, use bright emerald green for four times. Breathe in and see the soothing emerald light spiral around and through us. Breathe out and see it, feel it flame from the top of our heads. After four times using green, move to bright sparkling pink light. After four times with beautiful pink spirals, finish by visualizing brilliant gold spirals of light circling around and through us with the in-breath and flaming from the top of our heads with the out-breath.

∞ ∞ ∞

The adjustment of our bodies to this new higher rate of vibration can occur on many levels. There are those who actually change their cellular structure in order to tune completely to this new energy. Not every human can be expected or coerced to undergo the extensive preparation this requires. Yet some adaptation is necessary for those who continue incarnate on planet earth. We must raise our personal vibration to a certain level or we drop out of the energy flow of the planet and our present incarnation ceases.

Awareness of the transition this new ray brings is the first step. Quickly changing circumstances make all aware that the earth is experiencing some sort of major transition. Though many of us are confused, we are spurred on by this rapid change to adapt.

The second step is prayer. Confusion and rapid change bring the realization that we have little if any control over the whirling circumstances that surround us. We seek solace and guidance in prayer. If we pray with sincerity in our hearts, we receive the help we need to adapt to this new higher level of energy.

The third step is meditation, for in meditation we not only calm and center ourselves, we actually raise our personal vibration. Teaching and practicing meditation must become widespread as we enter this time of transformation.

For a more thorough tuning to this higher vibration, we can add the tools of visualization and breathing. The more steps we humans make on this path to a higher vibratory existence on earth, the more in tune we are with the changes, the better we adapt, and the healthier, more satisfying life we achieve for ourselves.

Almost all humans make the first step of awareness, and many go directly to prayer. The next step to meditation is a big one. Meditation must be encouraged in all cultures, in all walks of life, for it is a major key to adapting to this new time.

∞ ∞ ∞

The illumined path is the path we follow on our journey to enlightenment. Those of us who are on the illumined path change our lives day by day. Even the smallest details of our daily life on earth are addressed and appropriately altered. The key here is slow but steady change.

The process of changing every cell in the body is not as arduous a task as it may seem, although this process does necessitate daily attention. Focusing our conscious minds on this process for a few moments each day brings the steady change we seek. Those few moments we set aside for this each day are best taken in a calm, quiet space, such as the time following daily meditation. Each day as we devote a few quiet moments to the process of consciously changing our cells, we take a step on the illumined path. We find that we are refining and redefining our lives with each step.

As we continue slowly, steadily on the illumined path, we find that we are eliminating from our lives all that is associated with low vibrations. Such acts as lying, manipulating, cheating, stealing, and willfully injuring others we can no longer do without instant regret. As we change more of our cells to accept the higher vibrational rate, we completely clear the possibility of such actions from our natures, from our very beings. Instead, our actions and reactions include compassion, forgiveness, selfless service, understanding, and love. These then become part of our natures as we move further, step by step, on the illumined path.

It is important for us to remember that we can change only ourselves and our own cells. We can only inspire change in others by example, by simply living our lives on the higher vibrational level.

Much protection and guidance are available to those of us on the illumined path, for the earth, as she nears the transitional time, needs many enlightened leaders.

∞ ∞ ∞

The enlightenment of the human race can be accomplished only with cooperation and mutual support. The first humans to achieve this state of new enlightenment are the teachers who help others raise their personal vibratory rates. It is through cooperation and mutual support of these first teachers that healing and instruction groups are formed. The students in these first groups then go forth to organize other healing and instruction groups, and so on, until every human on the planet has access to enough information to make the transformation to an enlightened state. It is the duty of each of us who learns to then teach and help another.

The emotional climate on the planet is such that people are becoming more and more confused and disoriented as the rate of vibration increases. People are becoming ready to reach out for assistance. There is a point at which the vibration of the planet increases so much that no human can ignore it. It is then that these teachings spread quickly. It is then that the majority of humans incarnated at this time can adjust to the new vibratory level and find themselves enlightened.

It is very important that the basic teachings be solid, but that there is also some flexibility. Each human needs to understand the universal truths as well as grasp the fundamental techniques for adapting to this new energy. We then need to apply these to ourselves and our lives. A good example is meditation. There are many ways to meditate, many forms to use, but the end result is always to achieve the alpha state, a centered state of relaxation, awareness, and balance.

Now is the time for the first teachers to use this book and begin. It is important for us to support and help each other. Through exercising love and compassion, through these teachings, we can help in lifting the energy of the planet.

∞ ∞ ∞

Patience, perseverance, and prayer are all necessary as we begin to regularly and consciously change our cells. Each day we must pray with sincerity that we stay on the enlightened path. Each day we must consciously focus on changing the cells and tissues in our bodies. The exercises presented here must be used with regularity. Once we have selected an exercise that we find comfortable, we need to place it in our daily routine. It is best if we do these transformation exercises at the same time each day so they occur at regular intervals.

Blessed exercise for the transformation of the human body: Choose one toe. Focus on that toe. Use the mind to go inside that toe. Focus in until the very cells of a tiny part of that toe can be seen in the mind's eye. Choose one cell now, and begin to encircle and bathe this one cell in brilliant white light. Continue until the cell itself is clean, clear, and absolutely vibrating with pure white light. Once this cell is pulsing with bright white light, see this white light radiate out to the cells that surround this first cell. Envision this in three dimensions, so that the white light spreads slowly in the form of a sphere. Picture the cells that surround the first cell also within the sphere of white light. See them begin to vibrate with pure white light. Continue visualizing this until the surrounding cells seem clear, clean, and transformed by the purifying white light. Now enlarge the sphere to include the cells that surround these transformed cells and repeat the process, making certain that each cell is crystal clear and completely transformed into vibrating brilliant white light. To complete this exercise, begin breathing deeply. On the in-breath, see the bright white light generated in the toe spread up through the body. On the out-breath, see the white light brighten the head area and flame out of the top of the head. Each day choose a different cell in a different part of the body with which to begin this exercise.

∞ ∞ ∞

This series of exercises on enlightenment is meant for those of us who wish to seriously undertake the process of actually changing the makeup of our cells. Those of us who wish to do this must be dedicated and disciplined. The rewards are great. Once the majority of our cells have been transformed, we can operate in tune with the higher vibrational level of energy now entering the earth plane. Then telepathy and other psychic gifts are ours for daily use. Making this higher vibration a part of our very selves brings us a new and deeper understanding of the universe, stronger intuition, inner calm, and peace of mind beyond anything we now experience. We can actually be transformed into more evolved enlightened beings. The keys to these exercises are daily attention and strongly felt sincerity of heart.

Blessed exercise for the transformation of the human body: Sit quietly and comfortably. Focus on the breath. See the breath as golden light. Use the balanced breath to breathe in golden light and to breathe out golden light. Deepen the breath slightly. On the in-breath, see the golden light flooding the heart, the lungs, the chest area. On the out-breath, see the chest area glow even brighter. Deepen the breath a little once again, and visualize the golden light permeating the entire abdomen area as well. Again, using the balanced breath, breathe in deeply until the brilliant golden light reaches every part of the chest and abdomen. The out-breath increases the brightness in these areas. Now breathe slightly deeper again, drawing the golden breath down the legs and into the feet and toes. Once the legs and feet are glowing brightly along with the chest and abdomen areas, breathe deeply and include the shoulders, arms, and fingers. Use the same process. Repeat as many times as is necessary to visualize the areas aglow with brilliant golden light. Complete the exercise by including the head and by seeing the entire body as a glowing lighted being.

∞ ∞ ∞

Enlightenment, which has come to few on earth until this time, is now available to many. Enlightenment of the many is the key to the transformation of earth. It is a few at first who attain this state of enlightenment. Then, through focused teaching, many more follow the practices that lead to enlightenment. The rapid spread of these teachings and practices and the sincere desire of humans to change ourselves and our world bring positive changes to earth.

The exercises presented here are but one phase of the program which leads to enlightenment. The journey on the illumined path necessitates nothing less than complete transformation of our personal lives. Yet nothing less than this fulfills us as human beings. The further we travel on the illumined path, the more certain we are that this is proper, this is correct, this is the way we must proceed. When every breath that we draw, every act that we do, every moment that we are awake is filled with the knowledge that we are on this path to enlightenment, our lives are truly transformed.

All of us can begin by making this journey to an enlightened state our very first thought when we awake each day and our very last thought as we lie down to sleep. Beginning and ending each day with thoughts of this illumined journey bring joy into our first and last conscious moments. It is important that we connect in this way on a daily basis, that this becomes a part of our routine. One way to help ensure this conscious daily connection is to choose an object that reminds us of our journey on the illumined path, and then place that object where we are sure to see it upon awakening and upon lying down to sleep. Let us choose an object of beauty that harmonizes with our desire for personal transformation, an object that inspires joy and reverence in us. This object acts as a reminder to us and helps us make the conscious connection to the fact that our personal fulfillment lies in our steady progress as we proceed on the path to an enlightened state.

∞ ∞ ∞

We can say that we are enlightened when a majority of our cells has been transformed so that these cells align themselves with and in fact even contain the higher rate of vibration. This takes several years of patient, sincere work. This may seem like a long process to us, but the rate at which we can achieve this transformation is actually much faster than it has ever been before here on earth. We are all encouraged to take advantage of this time and begin the conscious transformation of our cells which leads to the transformation of all life on earth.

There are many exercises that can be used to affect this transformation of our cells. It is up to us to find the procedures we are comfortable with and we can enjoy. Then it is very important that we persevere, that we incorporate these chosen procedures into our daily routine, and do them!

Blessed exercise for the transformation of the human body: Sit or lie comfortably and relax using the balanced breath. We begin by visualizing ourselves inside a sphere of bright golden light. We see the luminescent gold light completely surround us. Next, the sphere begins to glow even brighter until the sphere itself, with us inside it, is entirely filled with brilliant golden light. Now we begin to absorb this light into our bodies and make it our own. We see the sparkling golden light pouring into our bodies right through the skin. We breathe it in, and, when we exhale, the golden light within us glows even brighter. We continue until we feel every part of our bodies, every cell, has absorbed this golden light. We see the light pouring in through the soles of our feet, in behind our knees, in through our abdomen, in behind the shoulder blades, into the heart area and the entire chest cavity, in through the fingers and the crook of the arm, in through the throat, the eyes, the ears, the nose, the top of the head. Now, we lie for a few moments, relaxed, seeing ourselves completely aglow with golden light, radiating this light from every cell in our bodies.

∞ ∞ ∞

If enlightenment is the transformation of our physical bodies and our earthly lives, then it is nothing less than revolutionary. This revolution, unlike most others on planet earth, is slow and gentle and filled with light and love. Like other revolutions, this revolution of light has leaders and followers. Unlike other revolutions, this one encourages the followers to become leaders and teachers, thus slowly and thoroughly spreading this revolution of light over the entire globe. This revolution makes all others seem insignificant because of its wide scope and great effects. This revolution of light has power and might above all other revolutions because it is being stimulated by an increase in the vibratory rate of the planet. The new ray of energy which is bringing this higher vibration to the earth is leading us to adapt our bodies and to revolutionize our lives. We are all touched; we are all affected. It is up to us to change and move with the times even if it means completely transforming our lives and life on earth as we know it. This is a true revolution.

Although the details in our individual lives may differ, the overall changes are similar. The old form of revolution, which generally included fighting and bloodshed, fades away as this new revolution of light comes into its own on earth. In fact, war and violence come to be seen as undesirable all over the entire planet. This revolution of light brings with it the first golden age of true peace for planet earth. Also, a new respect for the earth and for each other as lighted beings becomes widespread.

Not much in our lives is the same after this revolution of light. We develop new structures and new rituals in accordance with the higher vibration permeating the planet. We restructure our personal lives and our collective lives in accordance with the new ray of energy. With our cooperation, this revolution of light can bring great harmony into our lives and onto this entire planet.

∞ ∞ ∞

The lifting of the vibration of the earth and all who dwell upon her is a joyful process, and it brings much hope to the planet. The new ray of energy which brings the higher vibratory rate to earth is a gift from the Creator, and, like all gifts from the Creator, we must learn to use it and work with it. This takes awareness of the gift, a sincere desire to work with it, and the patience and perseverance to follow through. All the guidance that is necessary to do this is available to us now. So, we have the gift of the higher vibration permeating earth, and we have the guidance necessary to utilize it to change existence on earth for the better. This is hopeful and joyful.

We can experience this hope and joy every day as we consciously change our cells so that we can adapt to and utilize this higher vibration. The following exercise is for those of us who wish to experience joy while consciously working to change the cells of our bodies.

Blessed exercise for the transformation of the human body: We begin by finding a comfortable position. Then we relax, bringing peace to our inner selves by using the balanced breath. Next, we visualize a spiral or pinwheel of light about the size of a fist in the heart area. This spiraling light is mostly white, but also has ribbons of bright blue and pink light whirling around. As we breathe in, we see this beautiful pinwheel of light increase in size and brilliance. As we breathe out, we see it spin faster. We breathe in deeply and see the radiant spiraling light glow brighter and fill the entire chest area. We breathe out and feel it whirr faster. We continue and include the head and abdomen in the bright spiral of light. Then we feel it reach above our heads and down to our feet. By now, the pinwheel of light is rotating so fast that it is a brilliant pulsing blur. We breathe very deeply for a minute more, then we relax and feel every cell in our bodies vibrate with bright light, exuberance, and joy.

∞ ∞ ∞

Following the practices to become an enlightened being takes dedication. We must continuously renew our enthusiasm. This is not as difficult as it may seem because, even after a short while upon this illumined path, we can see change in ourselves. As we move step by step, day by day, we can see progress. It may seem, at the outset, that changing every cell in our bodies is an arduous task. In fact, it is just the opposite; it is joyous and invigorating. We are doing nothing less than changing ourselves into light! Again, it must be mentioned that we make progress only through daily attention. Although changing the makeup of our bodies takes years, we can only approach this change day by day. Dedication through daily practice and devotion to this illumined path through renewed enthusiasm and joy, these are the keys to successful progress.

Blessed exercise for the transformation of the human body: This exercise is best performed at dawn, for it calls upon the first light of the day to powerfully affect change in our bodies. To begin, stand facing the east with feet spread slightly for balance. Visualize a rod of golden light running down the spine and into the ground for further stability and balance. Call to the energy of the dawn light, either aloud or inside the mind, "Beautiful dawn energy of the east, please permeate every cell in my body with your golden light." Next, visualize brilliant sparkling golden light filtering down from several feet above the head. If this coincides with the first rays of the rising sun, it is a very powerful visualization. This sparkling golden light filters gently down both within and without the body. See it light the head area, the shoulders, the chest. See it light the arms, the abdomen, the legs, the feet. Breathe it in. Exhale and see the body glow even brighter gold. We continue until we see every molecule of our bodies glowing with brilliant golden light. If our intuitive timing is right, the rising sun bathes us head to foot in the first light rays of the day as we complete the visualization.

∞ ∞ ∞

Section 3: The Enlightenment Series

An enlightened person is one who has transformed enough cells of the body to accept and work with the higher vibration. There is no mistaking those who have reached this mark, for they themselves vibrate at a higher rate, and others can sense this. An enlightened person emits a glow of white light that radiates several feet from the body. Those of us who are psychically sensitive can see this light clearly.

It is indeed a slow, day-by-day process to achieve this transformed state, but the years of dedication bring many benefits. Health, exuberance, and seemingly endless energy come with this personal transformation, as well as a calm and a deep inner peace which radiates out to those around us. Psychic gifts such as telepathy, clairvoyance, and clairaudience are often in place and are being well utilized before the transformation to an enlightened state is complete. A person who holds and works with this higher vibration knows not violence, or selfishness, or greed, though others may perpetrate these undesirables. A person who has made the transformation to an enlightened state proceeds with integrity and undertakes all things with love, compassion, and a deep understanding of universal truth. This is because the majority of this person's cells hold this higher vibration which itself is universal truth and love.

The amazing fact is that all humans now on planet earth have the opportunity to make this transformation. We all must deal with the higher vibratory rate permeating the planet. This book provides detailed instructions on how to make the most of this increase in vibration. These instructions, if followed correctly and with sincerity and perseverance, can benefit ourselves and also the planet, along with everything that lives upon the planet. It must be emphasized that once we begin on the illumined path to enlightenment, we must make this our life's work, and we must attend to this work with daily attention and renewal.

∞ ∞ ∞

Enlightenment is a one-way street. Once we begin on the illumined path, we are compelled to continue. That is not to say that we never have times when we feel we are not making progress or times when we seem to be going back over territory we have covered before. The general movement is forward on the path, however slowly.

As we practice the exercises of our choice each day, we are affecting change in some of the cells of our bodies. Much change occurs on the subconscious level before we see it reflected in the conscious. It is important to remember that daily practice brings daily change, though this change may be subtle and minute.

Blessed exercise for the transformation of the human body: We begin by placing ourselves in a comfortable position with our spines relatively straight. Next, we use the balanced breath or another breathing technique to quiet and center ourselves. Once we have relaxed and centered ourselves, we begin by moving the fingers of each hand one by one. This movement needs to be very gentle. Simply lift each finger a little one by one. Now focus on the very tips of the fingers and visualize a strand of brilliant golden light running into the tip of each finger. We can visualize these bright golden strands running from deep in the center of the earth to each of our fingers, or we can see them running from the sky to the tips of our fingers, or we can even visualize a luminescent golden sphere suspended before us, and run the golden strands from that to our hands. The important part is that we see these brilliant golden strands run into the tips of our fingers, through our hands, up through our arms and shoulders, that we see them fill our neck and throat, illumine the entire head, and end in a bright flame coming from the top of the head. Breathe in and see the golden strands running; breathe out and see them and the flame grow brighter. Now repeat this process, but start by gently lifting each toe. See the golden strands running into the tip of each toe, through the foot, up the leg. See them fill the abdomen, the chest, the throat and head area, ending once again in a brilliant flame at the top of the head.

∞ ∞ ∞

Enlightenment is a state of the body, a state of the mind, and a state of the spirit. Enlightenment encompasses the entire being. The effects of enlightenment are great upon both the individual and the life of the individual. The step to an enlightened state is an important and necessary one for humanity. Enlightenment is the way of the new age, the new millennium, and we must begin to understand it now because the transformation has begun.

The increase in the vibratory rate of the planet is having a profound effect on people. Those who are particularly sensitive are feeling the need for adjustment and change. Those who are psychically active are receiving guidance and specific instructions on how to prepare themselves and help others. The planet is changing quickly, partly due to the activities of humans and partly due to the new ray of energy bringing the higher vibration to earth. The combination of these two forces is hurling the earth and humanity headlong into a major transformation.

Following the steps, the daily practices, that lead to an enlightened state is now extremely important for the survival of humans. The earth, by tuning itself to and adapting to this higher rate of vibration, is eliminating the lower vibrations. The earth is now moving to actually shake off the lower vibrations which have caused much distress. This is a necessary transformation in the evolution of both the planet and humanity. Those humans who do adjust and tune themselves to the higher vibration and eliminate from themselves the lower vibrations are the survivors on this planet. This is a crucial time. We must all pay attention to what is occurring and take the steps necessary for appropriate change in our lives. Fortunately there is an abundance of information available to assist humanity and to guide us all through this transformation. This book is one of many sources that exist for guidance in this time.

It is proper to note here that instruction specific to each individual is best received by going within. Guidance from within each of us coupled with instruction from without provides us with all we need to adapt and prepare.

∞ ∞ ∞

There is a joyful ease about the enlightened person. Because the bodies of enlightened persons are tuned to the higher rate of vibration, they automatically move to universal rhythms and act according to universal truths. Through daily meditation and prayer, breathing and visualization, the conscious and subconscious minds of enlightened ones are transformed as well.

Although daily meditation and constant refinement are necessary, we who strive for this enlightened state do eventually reach a plateau of ease. This place is reached when we have consciously changed the majority of the cells in our bodies and minds. It is at this point that struggle becomes ease. At this point, we begin to think, act, and react automatically with the universal flow. We are then vibrating at the higher rate, and we are, by the nature and makeup of our cells, tuned to the new ray of energy flooding the earth plane. Of course, it does take several years of conscientious application to reach this plateau of ease, but it is attainable for all of us humans who wish to try.

Once we have reached this turning point in our personal transformations, we notice how much more light we have in our lives. Situations which before would have caused us much distress and worry are seen in this new light and fade into unimportance. We actually do radiate much light from our transformed tissues, and most people can sense this. A few can even see this light.

The joy we feel once we have reached this plateau is immeasurable. We are then tapped into the higher energy of the creative force and this brings a new respect for everything on planet earth. Both our conscious and our subconscious minds are transformed, leaving useless thoughts and actions behind, and filling our minds and indeed our entire selves with this joy and light. Let us picture ourselves so, as we consciously move, day by day, toward this enlightened state.

∞ ∞ ∞

Following the illumined path step by step means incorporating selected practices into our daily lives. We choose the exercises which suit us, and we make them the cornerstone of each day. Our daily practice must be consistent yet adaptable, routine yet deeply felt. The few moments spent every day in prayer, meditation, breathing, and visualization are most important because it is during these times we are constructing our enlightened selves.

The following exercise is especially suited for those who feel very close to the earth and her cycles. It is essential that those of us who choose this practice approach it every day with heartfelt sincerity and a deep love for the earth. It is extremely effective if approached in this way.

Blessed exercise for the transformation of the human body: First we find a quiet beautiful location out-of-doors where we can place ourselves in a comfortable position. It is best if some part of our bodies can directly touch the earth. If this is not possible due to weather or location, then we must hold something of the earth in our hands as we proceed with this exercise. A quartz crystal which has been charged in the earth is ideal. Next, we use the balanced breath to calm and center ourselves. Then we focus on our deep love for the earth. We feel it swelling up in our hearts. We see it as glowing golden light in our chests. As we breathe in, this light expands. As we breathe out, it glows brighter. We continue until we feel our hearts literally bursting with sincere love for the earth. Now we take this golden light which is shimmering and pulsing with love, and we visualize it pouring from our hearts into the earth. We see it form an arc of sparkling light. We see it pour deep into the center of the earth. We see this now as half of a circle. Now we visualize energy from the earth making the other half of the circle, coming from the center of the earth up and into our bodies entering between the shoulder blades. Breathe out: we send golden light deep into the earth; breathe in: we pull golden energy from deep in the earth up into our own bodies. The circle is complete.

On earth, as the rate of vibration increases, all events escalate. This is one reason meditation is very important at this time. During meditation we slow our breathing and our heartbeat. It is not only a time of relaxation and rebalancing of our bodies' energies, it is also a time during which we detach ourselves from the quickening pace and the spinning events of the material world. We need this meditation time and this detached space in order to maintain a proper perspective on all events in our lives. We must remove ourselves from the whirl of physical plane activities on a daily basis. Meditation is one way to accomplish this.

Meditation brings many other benefits to us, too. The time we take for meditation is sacred time, and must be regarded so. We must respect each others' meditation time and space. We must encourage each other to take these sacred moments every day. We must do what we can to assist in the lives of others so that all of us have the opportunity to make meditation a part of our daily lives.

∞ ∞ ∞

Every moment we spend focusing on the illumined path is a moment well spent. Still, we cannot ignore the material plane, for we must make our way upon the earth as well. Every day we need to seek a balance between our inner work, our spiritual work, and our outer work, our duties here on the material plane. We have truly accomplished something when we not only balance the attention we give to the inner work and the outer work, but we also meld them together and view them as one.

The very best way to approach any work is by breathing deeply. If we have enough oxygen and circulation, we are much clearer. Then we must approach the work, be it inner or outer work, from a selfless standpoint. This is not easy. Most of us are accustomed to being motivated by personal gain. What we must grasp is the fact that we indeed gain the most for ourselves in the long run by adopting a selfless approach to all our work. Of course, the work we do on the material plane must support us, but if we approach this work, whatever it may be, from the viewpoint that we are here to serve others and to serve the planet, then we are on the right track. Of course, we undertake spiritual work to refine and improve ourselves, to help us be strong and clear in the face of adversity, but a selfless approach here is immensely beneficial. If we proceed with our spiritual work with the attitude that we wish to be strong, centered, and clear to better serve the planet, then we are truly on the illumined path.

We must allow time in each day to address both our spiritual and our material work. A daily balance is important. Of course, some days our material concerns take much of our time and energy. Other days we may have more time for our spiritual pursuits. As we approach each day, we need to make sure that our material responsibilities are tended to for that day, and we need to set aside an appropriate amount of time and energy for our spiritual work, such as meditation and prayer.

We must take each day and regard it as a jewel unto itself. We can admire all its facets, all its variations. We take each day and hold it as precious, and do the very best we can, no matter what our priorities, no matter what our tasks. The jewel holds within it both the material and the spiritual.

Along with balancing our inner work and our outer work, we need to integrate them. A selfless approach to both does much toward this end. If we are open and mindful of our spiritual work while we are proceeding with work on the physical plane, we can find many ways to apply our spiritual practices. Conversely, by operating with integrity and selflessness on the material level, we bring strength and verification to our spiritual work. We can turn inward to seek guidance with problems and challenges we face in the outer world. We can find signs and guideposts everywhere in the outer world that help us with our inner searches. The two are one. Our inner work and our outer work are one. Our journey upon the illumined path is one journey which includes our progress in our spiritual work and our progress in our material plane activities.

∞ ∞ ∞

It is a challenge for us, when confronted with a difficult situation, to face the problem with joy in our hearts. Often we dwell on the dark, the negative, the ominous possibilities, and do not see the entire picture. All problems bring us opportunities for learning and growth. The more difficult the situation, the more we can learn from it.

We need to examine the problem thoroughly. This may take some doing, as the toughest situations often evoke strong emotions. If this is the case, we must first deal with these feelings. We must name these emotions and ask ourselves why this problem stirs such strong feelings in us. We must be honest with ourselves. It is possible, through sincere self-inquiry and visualization, to detach ourselves from the emotional content of the situation. This makes it possible for us to see the problem from a new perspective, and we can perhaps see many more sides to the situation.

Once we have reached this detached perspective, we are ready to seek a clear path of action that may help to lead us not only to a constructive solution to the problem, but also to positive growth for ourselves. When seeking solutions, we must be free of desire for revenge. We must be free of selfish interests. If we act on selfish interests, more often than not, we find the problem worsens in the long run. This is why careful consideration must be given to any course of action. We need to meditate upon the situation. We need to ask, with sincerity in our hearts, that we be shown the correct way to proceed.

Once we are free of selfish motives, have asked for guidance in dealing with the problem, and have a little patience with ourselves, we find that we know the steps to take. We know clearly what to do, and, best of all, we feel deep inside us that this is the right course of action. We know that the way we address the problem benefits all who are involved. When we look back on the situation, we see that, although it may have taken us some time to reach a clear perspective and to decide on correct action, we have grown. We have benefited. We can now approach the next problem with more joy.

∞ ∞ ∞

The enlightened person has many responsibilities in the material world. Any of us who reach an enlightened state of being must become involved in helping and teaching others. This desire to serve others is natural and automatic to those who reach an enlightened state. It is best if we who are on the illumined path understand and prepare for this eventuality.

Once we set foot upon this path, we pledge to take a selfless approach to all we do each day. This is often not easy at the beginning, for we have been taught to protect our egos. There is a difference between acting from selfish interests which may seem to benefit us in the short term and acting selflessly which brings us long-term benefits. We are not advocating self-denial or martyrdom. We speak of simply serving others in a loving way that feels comfortable to us at the time. Serving selflessly means not expecting a return or reward. If we are operating from our heart chakras, this selfless approach to daily life is much easier. If we are stuck in the third or power chakra, we may fear losing control of our lives and resist undertaking purely selfless actions.

As we journey, step by step, on the illumined path to an enlightened state, we incorporate more and more selfless behavior into our lives. As we proceed in changing the cells and tissues of our bodies, we incorporate this selfless approach into our very beings. As our bodies accept and hold more and more of the higher vibration now flooding the earth plane, we naturally evolve toward selflessness.

We go slowly, one step at a time, moving at a pace which is comfortable to each of us. We must have patience with ourselves, for it is best if we move slowly and thoroughly. Changing the cells of our bodies is a slow process which takes years. We must press ahead with this daily work, yet be relaxed and joyful. As with all phases of our lives, we seek a balance here. Daily attention is essential to this process of transforming ourselves, yet we need to move ahead at a pace which feels natural and right. This is true also of incorporating a selfless approach into our daily lives. We do as much as we can each day with the knowledge that our ability and our desire to serve others increases naturally.

∞ ∞ ∞

Every day, as we proceed on the path to enlightenment, we may see what we want to change in ourselves. It is important not to become frustrated because characteristics and reactions cannot usually be changed overnight. The very first step, and it is an important one, is recognizing those parts of ourselves which we wish to transform. Often we must stand by and watch ourselves behave inappropriately, acting again and again in ways that we sincerely wish to change. We must not get angry or impatient with ourselves. Instead, we need to transmute the emotions of frustration, anger, and impatience into a heartfelt desire for a thorough transformation of our beings. The second step is to truly wish for change in ourselves. Sincerity is everything in all that we do to this end. Once we recognize what we wish to change, and we desire deeply to affect these changes, we must be comfortable with the fact that this type of intense inner change takes time.

Again, daily renewal of our purpose is essential. Each day we must align ourselves with the vision of what we wish to become. This can be done in several ways. We can pray on a daily basis for the changes we seek in ourselves. We can use visualizations, wherein we actually picture in our minds what it is we wish to change. We put a shape and a color to those parts of us which we wish to transform. For instance, if we tend to react in a hotheaded way and speak without forethought, we could picture this as flames shooting from our mouths. We then transform the visualization. Using the same example, we might see the flames turn into a spiral of pink light which increases in size and then folds back over us, enveloping us in pink light. Another technique is the affirmation. We write out very clearly what we wish to become. We must state this in positive terms. This means we do not list our faults. Instead we state what we wish to be, and then we read this every day. We can transform ourselves into beings of light and love.

∞ ∞ ∞

The enlightened state of being is available to everyone. This is a new development on earth. This opportunity is being made possible by the new ray of energy which brings with it the higher rate of vibration now permeating the earth plane. This opportunity for enlightenment for everyone is an essential step in the evolution of the human race. It is crucial that humanity as a whole acknowledges this opportunity and seizes upon it.

Many are aware that the human race may not survive on planet earth. We are fast approaching this major turning point. Pollution and desecration of the planet do not end as long as greed continues as the major motivation. A reversal of the situation on earth and true salvation for humanity can come (only) with the help of this new ray of energy. Every human being must develop a new respect for the planet and for each other. This new attitude must apply to everything we think and say and do. Each of us must be transformed from the inside out. This new ray of energy makes this unique transformation possible, in fact, probable!

This new ray of energy is a gift from beyond the veil. Its origin is beyond our knowing. Its presence and effects are undeniable. The instructions and knowledge contained in this book are coming in with the first major increase in vibration. All knowledge and guidance necessary for humans to make the most of the opportunity for enlightenment are being made available.

The combination of the crucial situation on planet earth and the introduction of this new ray of energy is propelling us toward a major transformation. This transformation occurs both within each individual and without in society and on the earth as a whole. This opportunity brings new hope for the planet and for the human race, but we must pay attention. We must apply ourselves and begin to make the necessary changes in our lives. The energy and the guidance now exist for us all to do this.

∞ ∞ ∞

There are numerous ways to achieve an enlightened state, but there are a few constants which everyone who wishes to tread the illumined path must undertake. The first is daily attention. Whatever procedures we choose, we must make them a part of our daily routine. The second is sincerity. We must approach all that we do to move toward enlightenment with the utmost sincerity. Sincerity is essential in all spiritual work. The third is selfless service. When we begin on the illumined path, we accept the fact that our lives, as well as our beings, are changing. Incorporating a selfless approach to all we do on the earth plane may mean major alterations in our jobs, our family situations, and our friendships. We must willingly accept the changes in ourselves and make the necessary changes in our lives on the material plane.

There are many forms of meditation as well as many different visualization exercises for us to choose from. There are several breathing techniques which work to quiet and center us, and, of course, what we say in prayer is very personal to each of us. We can tailor the specifics however each of us chooses. In this way, the program we undertake which moves us step by step on the illumined path is comfortable and joyful to us. We can enjoy and delight in the exercises and procedures because they suit us as individuals.

Since the journey to an enlightened state takes years, we may wish to incorporate a new visualization or try a different breathing technique as we proceed along. Changing and refining our daily program is not only acceptable, it is encouraged. We are changing, and so we may wish to change the techniques we are using. Some of us may find that our understanding and experience deepen as we continue with the original procedures we choose, and therefore find no need to change. Our sense of what is appropriate for ourselves increases as we move along the path. We can move along at our own speed in our own way. However, we must always attend to the constants: daily attention to the procedures we choose, sincerity in all our spiritual work, and selfless service on the material plane.

∞ ∞ ∞

We can greet each day with thanks in our hearts for the opportunity that has now been brought to the earth plane for all humanity. There has never been an opportunity such as this on earth. We are fortunate to be incarnated at this time, but we must take advantage of what we have been given. If we do not, we shall certainly see the demise of the human race.

This is a joyful time filled with new hope and the certainty that we can make a major transition. We must put all our fears and worries behind us and apply ourselves to the practices that bring about this transformation on earth. The time is right, and the desire for change on the planet is strong. Once the changes begin in earnest, they spread rapidly, like wildfire, because the climate is right for a major transition. Global communications facilitate the awareness of this uplifting opportunity. Many teachers, both incarnate and discarnate, are in place and are ready to help all who seek to make the most of this opportunity.

The transformation process is infectious. One person comes in contact with another who has made the transition to operating at the higher rate of vibration. The first person "catches" the desire to make this transition also. The second person can instruct the first or can lead the first person to a teacher who can then help.

This joyful transformation does not spread only from person to person on the surface of the earth, it also spreads from the earth herself deep into the inner fibers of each human. Those who are close to the earth already feel the increase in vibration directly from the planet. The earth is our mother, our host. We cannot long ignore the messages she sends to us as we dwell upon her.

There are also a few illumined beings who stand forth to help, to instruct, and to guide us. These enlightened ones coupled with increased guidance from beyond the veil give humanity all the instruction we need to make this great transition. The hope and joy available at this time are immense. It is time for us to immerse ourselves in the great transition.

∞ ∞ ∞

Comets are energy. Comets are beings. Some travel in a predictable orbit and some travel erratically. When a comet comes into view from the earth plane, it is a harbinger. Those that appear on a regular basis foretell changes on earth, just as those which appear to have no predictable path also do. Of course, there are always changes here on earth. Life on the material plane is a series of changes. The appearance of a comet says that a major global change is approaching.

The ancients saw comets as harbingers, but they did not have the global communications and the worldview we do today. They could watch the flow of life in their villages, but did not have access to viewing the entire planet. Now, with this global view, we can watch major transformations as they envelope the entire earth. The expected arrival of a comet is like a pulse which says, "Time for major change here again." The unexpected arrival of a comet into our earth view foretells a unique and surprising transition which is about to occur on the planet.

∞ ∞ ∞

For the first time, the illumined path is open to all humanity now incarnated. This offers great opportunities and great challenges. Since all humans now alive are at differing stages of evolvement, there needs to be a great neutralizing factor. This is arriving as a new ray of energy which is capable of lifting the vibrational rate of all humans. It does not matter where we are in our growth process. We can respond to this new ray of energy.

We humans must increase our awareness in several areas. Much has been said about the conscious and the subconscious minds; now we focus on our superconscious. The new ray of energy is providing a direct link for us between our conscious and our superconscious minds. Heretofore, the process was for communication from the superconscious to travel through our subconscious minds and then on to our conscious minds. Our evolvement was slower and often hampered by the maze of memories of prior experiences held deep within the subconscious mind. Now we are reaching a period of accelerated growth. The new ray of energy is providing for us the third side of the triangle which links the superconscious with the subconscious and now the conscious. Before now, connecting the superconscious directly with the conscious mind was possible only through years of yogic study. This great link is now available to all of us. Now we can tap directly into the higher mind, the universal force.

This connection from the superconscious to the conscious brings many psychic gifts to humanity. Telepathy, clairvoyance, clairaudience, guided healing, and more are available to those of us who wish to pursue them. This link is still new and still delicate, but we can strengthen it through meditation and prayer, visualization, and proper breathing.

It is time for all of us humans to be aware of this new connection occurring within ourselves. It is a gift, an opportunity to make a giant leap in our evolution both for individuals and for humanity as a whole.

∞ ∞ ∞

We follow the illumined path by conscious choice. Although this lighted path is newly available to all humans, not everyone chooses to follow it. Those of us who do choose to move toward an enlightened state consciously apply ourselves to this end. The link is made between the conscious mind and the superconscious, and we receive conscious guidance directly from the superconscious. This guidance comes in the form of psychic gifts such as telepathy, clairaudience, and clairvoyance. All of these psychic gifts bring messages to the conscious mind from beyond the veil.

Those of us who follow the illumined path receive much help and guidance. This guidance assists us in making the many changes in our lives on earth, changes that are essential if we are to continue on the path. Let us be mindful of the many gifts which are now coming to us on earth from the realms beyond. Let us be thankful and joyful, for all we need to make the great transformation is here for us now.

∞ ∞ ∞

Illumination is a gift, but it is also a responsibility. As with all talents and gifts, we must use them to serve others and, of course, the planet. There is extreme danger if, once we have reached an enlightened state, we choose to use it for self-gratification and other selfish purposes. If we do this, we are in more danger than if we had never begun on the illumined path at all. Selfish use of the power and magnetism that accompany the enlightened state multiplies our personal karma, and we become wedged in third chakra power struggles for incarnations to come. This is a mistake that must not be made on earth at this time. The very thrust of the new ray of energy entering the earth plane is to raise our vibrations and to lift us out of our seemingly endless struggles for power and wealth. Each of us who undertakes this journey on the illumined path must do so with knowledge of this danger and with dedicated resolve to move not only toward an enlightened state, but also toward a life of selfless service.

For generations upon this planet, we humans have scuffled and struggled for material gain. It is now time to lift our heads and look beyond our material struggles to a blend and a balance of the material and the spiritual. It can be seen that much joy and satisfaction can be gained from this balance. By honoring the spiritual and bringing it into balance with our material concerns on the earth plane, what we need comes to us of its own accord.

Even those of us who have been moving along the illumined path for years must continuously rededicate ourselves to a selfless approach to all we do. The use of increased knowledge, wisdom, power, and light gained from entering the enlightened state for anything other than selfless service is a dangerous mistake, one which we humans cannot afford to make on this planet at this time. There is a certain ease that accompanies selfless activities. We need to recognize this, enjoy it, and let it nurture our selflessness.

∞ ∞ ∞

Illumination is a responsibility for not only those who move on the path toward enlightenment, but also those who do not. This may seem strange to say, but those who choose not to undertake this study must support those who do. It cannot be expected that everyone incarnated on earth undertakes the daily regimen that leads to enlightenment, even though this path is available to everyone. Those who do choose to follow the illumined path are to be respected and supported by all.

It is the responsibility of every human alive on earth to tune to the higher vibratory rate now infiltrating the planet. We must raise our personal vibrations to align ourselves with the new ray of energy flooding the earth plane. There are many ways to accomplish this, the most thorough being undertaking the daily practices which lead to an enlightened state. The decision on how we deal with this new higher vibration on the planet is ours individually, but collectively we must acknowledge and we must support those who are dedicated to following the highest path.

It is those individuals who undertake the discipline and rigor demanded by the illumined path who lead and help us in the times of the great transition. It is for our benefit and the well-being of the earth that we protect and support these individuals. Without the guidance and help of those who follow the illumined path, the great transformation on earth may be extremely difficult, even disastrous.

Of course, the more humans who undertake the journey to enlightenment, the better for all humanity and for the planet. If we decide we want to follow the illumined path, we must set upon the journey with dedication, serious intent, and sincerity. Once we pledge ourselves and take that first step, forces are set in motion that align us with the new energy entering the earth plane. We receive much help and guidance to propel us along the path. Spirit guides and helpers intervene again and again to keep us moving toward an enlightened state. In fact, these helpers do not leave us alone, but continually and lovingly prod us along on our journey.

∞ ∞ ∞

Illumination is everyone's responsibility because we all must consciously choose whether or not to pursue it. The gift of the new ray of energy which is increasing the vibration of the planet demands that we consciously acknowledge the changes that are occurring on planet earth. We must then choose how we are going to deal with these changes, for they cannot be ignored.

Pursuing the path to enlightenment is, by far, the best use of this new ray of energy. There has never before been a similar time on earth. Never before has such a great gift been given to the human consciousness. It is the responsibility of humanity to gratefully receive and conscientiously utilize this gift.

Those of us who choose to follow the illumined path are given much assistance. This book provides specific information on how to begin the journey to enlightenment and how to reorganize our lives so that we steadily continue toward that goal. There are many benefits along the path, and, of course, many challenges, too. The pursuit of enlightenment is by no means easy because it requires dedication, sincerity, thoroughness, and perseverance on a daily basis. All of us who choose to follow the illumined path must reorganize our lives, although this is best done slowly. All of us who seek enlightenment must give ourselves in selfless service for the rest of our lives. This sounds like a tall order, but we find, as we journey further and further on the illumined path, that a selfless approach is natural to us. It is what the time requires. It is what the new ray of energy encourages. It is what the earth now needs.

Although this book provides specific information, most of us have problems and questions as we venture forward on this journey. Assistance is available from many sources. There are many psychic teachers, including the authors of this book, who are prepared to help. As this information is dispersed around the globe, the network of helpers increases. It must be mentioned here that the very greatest assistance comes from within. Once we learn to listen to the inner voice, once we make the lighted connection between our conscious and our superconscious minds, we have access to information and assistance specific to us individually. We all have assistance from beyond the veil. We all have guides who are there specifically to help us. Once we dedicate ourselves to following the path to an enlightened state, these guides become very active, and most make conscious contact with us, if they have not done so already. Through meditation and prayer, we can develop a rapport with our guides. We can ask for advice on any matter and they provide universal wisdom.

Once we have begun on this illumined journey, once we have proceeded on the path, we can feel the exhilaration of aligning our personal energy with that of the earth and the universe as a whole. We can feel the security of being looked after and assisted. We can feel the joy that is brought by this new ray of energy and hope.

∞ ∞ ∞

Love is necessary. Love must be incorporated into all phases of the journey to enlightenment. Letting love and compassion flow through us is one of the best ways to clear ourselves of blockages which hinder our progress on the path. Love is essential. Generating love and surrounding all we do with love help protect us, ground us, and tune us to the higher vibration, for love is the highest of all vibrations.

A reciprocal situation exists: as we generate more love within ourselves, we raise our personal vibration; as the vibrations of our beings become higher, love flows more easily through us and from us.

The new ray of energy now flooding the earth plane is bringing the highest vibration that the planet has known. This new ray brings with it universal truths that have, before now, been incomprehensible to humans. Now, however, we can not only comprehend these truths, but also make them a part of our existence on the planet. The first of these truths is how powerful love is and what love can actually do especially when generated on the earth plane from the human heart. Love has the power to cleanse and renew. Love has the power to heal and regenerate. Love has the power to transform us and all we do.

We can see love in a new way. We can see love as a high and powerful vibration which we can generate and send out from our physical bodies. As we proceed on the illumined path, we continually tune and retune our personal vibrations, raising them even higher. We can use visualization and prayer to help us literally vibrate with love. We can become power stations, generating love.

Love exists in the universe and on the earth plane whether we choose to tune to it or not. If we make the conscious choice to use our incarnated selves to generate more love, everyone benefits. The earth benefits as the vibration on the planet increases. We benefit as our vibration is heightened and our well-being is improved. All who come in contact with us benefit, as they bask in the radiant highest vibration of love.

∞ ∞ ∞

Love is the answer to many of the problems we face on earth today. When we humans learn to transmute our various emotions into love, the planet is indeed transformed. This again speaks of raising our personal vibrations to a higher level. If we can operate daily on a consistently higher vibrational rate, then it is much easier for us to respond to most situations with love and compassion. We can rise above the base emotions that are associated with the lower vibrations.

We humans are extremely valuable to the transformation occurring on earth because of our ability to generate emotions, especially love. One of the universal truths now brought to human consciousness by the new ray of energy is the value of human emotions. Once humans realize how much our emotions affect not only each other but also the vibrational climate of the planet, we begin to pay more attention to these feelings.

Once again it must be stated that all emotions are powerful and valuable, a truth that humans, until now, have failed to grasp. Now we are beginning to comprehend this truth. With the realization of the power of our emotions comes the responsibility for the feelings we do generate. We must remember that our emotions actually have an energy shape, form, and color. We generate these emotions and they retain their existence for some time, especially if they are reinforced.

Love is the most powerful and valuable of all human emotions. All emotions are valuable in that they are human expressions that take an energy form and affect the vibrations of the planet. Love and compassion are the emotions that not only align with the higher rate of vibration now infiltrating the earth plane, but also help us attune to this higher vibration. Love is so important at this time!

All emotions, no matter how base, can be transmitted into love. In fact, it is the responsibility of humans, especially those of us on the illumined path, to actively transform our emotions into love and to generate as much love as we can.

∞ ∞ ∞

It is essential for humans to understand the importance of this time. We are entering one of the great transitions on earth, one which sets the foundation for thousands of years. How we prepare and how we follow through on these preparations determine the very makeup of life on earth for the next great cycle. We have the opportunity to make great changes for the good of the planet and every life form which dwells upon her. We must, however, be informed, prepared, and so attuned to the changing flow of energy that our timing is perfect. These writings endeavor to help us accomplish this.

Even thorough preparation does not ready us for every twist and turn of circumstances during times of great change. We must maintain openness to guidance and flexibility of action. We must always be ready to adapt, always ready to learn from the changing environment.

There are no guarantees that we can turn this time of great change into a positive transformation for earth. There is the opportunity, but we must use our strength, our will, our determination, along with our patience, perseverance, and preparedness. Those of us who wish to turn this opportunity into positive changes for the planet find that every day there is something we can do. For one, we can employ visualization and create thought-forms and emotions which can help carry the planet toward specific positive changes. For another, we can in our daily interactions affect positive change through our words, actions, and selfless service.

The task is great. We must constantly pay attention. For many of us, this work is the most important and powerful work in many lifetimes. We are dealing with not just our personal karma, but also the karma of the planet and of humanity as a whole.

The decisions we make and the work we do now during this great transition affects the earth and all upon her for centuries to come. The incredible importance of this time must be grasped by all of us.

∞ ∞ ∞

The illumined path is very near each of us because it is within us. Those of us who are seekers may have already discovered this truth. It is essential that we apply what we learn on the illumined path to our material lives, but following the illumined path is an inward journey.

All of us upon this planet need quiet time to go within ourselves. Daily meditation is the best way to satisfy this need. Whether or not we decide to embark on the journey to enlightenment, we still need quiet meditation time, especially now as the vibrations of the planet are increasing. The faster events move, the more confusing situations seem, the more we need to remove ourselves for a short period each day. Using meditation to go within ourselves is the very best way to do this.

Learning and practicing meditation are the first steps on the illumined path to enlightenment, should we choose to undertake this journey. Daily practice is essential. The exact form of meditation we choose for ourselves does not matter as much as daily practice. In fact, we need to search until we find a form of meditation that suits us individually, one that we feel comfortable with and can grow to love.

Widespread practice of meditation is one of the absolute essentials in making the great transformation on earth a positive one. Meditation now applies to everyone's life. Daily practice of meditation opens many doors, both within ourselves and in the outer material world. The benefits are numerous.

Learning and practicing meditation are the first steps to more than the journey to enlightenment. They are also the first steps to a transformed planet. They are the first steps into a new millennium and into a new age. The more of us on earth who practice meditation, the more the vibration of the planet moves toward peace, compassion, and love.

∞ ∞ ∞

All the beauty that we see around us, great and small, can inspire us to send love to the earth. Everything from the simple song of a bird to a majestic sunset over a mountain range can connect us to the magic of this planet. We need to open our senses and use them to appreciate every detail of the wondrous creation called earth.

The earth now needs us to help her. The physical ways we can help are obvious: not polluting and cleaning up what we have polluted; not destroying and regenerating what we have destroyed. Beyond this, the earth needs emotional rejuvenation. For far too long we humans have approached the earth with disrespect and with callous disregard. It is past time for us to change our attitude and our approach to the planet. For one, we can begin to see and feel the earth as an entity, a being, an individual like each of us. We can begin to interact with this being on a one-to-one basis. Some of us already have very personal relationships with the earth. We can see and feel her as our mother, our host, our friend. If we approach her in the correct way–that is, with love and respect–she can teach us a great deal. If we all develop a deep caring personal relationship with the earth, then great healing and rejuvenation can occur, both for ourselves and for the planet.

Here is something we can do on a daily basis to promote strong ties between ourselves and the planet and to help with the healing process. Every time we notice something, even the smallest detail, of the wonder and the beauty that this planet gives us, we can send love to the earth. Simply visualize our hearts glowing with love for the planet. Visualize the light in our hearts as gold or pink, but see it and feel it strongly. Then send this love in a brilliant stream of light from our hearts right into the center of the earth. The more emotion we possess while doing this, the better. If we do this simple exercise with sincerity, we help ourselves and the planet in many ways.

∞ ∞ ∞

Once we have undertaken the journey toward enlightenment, we need to connect with others who are on the illumined path. This is necessary not only for mutual support, but also for strengthening the positive use of the higher vibration now entering the earth plane. For some of us, contact with others who are also on the illumined path inspires and motivates us. It is helpful, especially for those of us who are just beginning, to experience the higher vibration brought by the presence of those who have followed this lighted path for several years. It is absolutely essential that those of us who have undertaken this journey to enlightenment teach and help others who are interested in doing so. Once we embark on this journey, we automatically commit ourselves to selfless service, and one of the best ways we can serve is by helping others who are on the illumined path.

We all need much support and encouragement along the way, but the beginning is especially important. Always at the beginning we have much to deal with because we must reorganize our lives. Also, we must enter upon the path with the proper outlook and attitude. Contact with others on this journey can help ensure that the beginner understands that sincerity is essential in this undertaking. Also, the beginner can easily see, through interacting with others who have progressed on the illumined path, that this is a journey of many years, and it must be started with an eye toward self-discipline and perseverance.

There is something else besides mutual guidance and assistance which is accomplished by contact and communication between the travelers. When those who are on the path to enlightenment gather together, there is an increase in the vibratory rate of the group and also of the individual participants. Gatherings are very helpful to beginners, for they can personally experience the higher vibration brought to the group by those who have been on the path for years. In these gatherings, the best use of this higher vibration is always emphasized, and the group generates much good will and love.

∞ ∞ ∞

How we respond to the increased vibration on the planet is extremely important. The earth has raised her vibrational rate in a similar way before. The increase and decrease of the planet's vibration are cyclic, though difficult for humans to comprehend because these cycles are so huge. As is the case in the present day, in former times when the vibration of the earth increased to its highest rate, there occurred great transitions. As is the case in the present day, in former times there was always the opportunity to find the true meaning of these transitional times. There was the opportunity to understand and prepare, as there is today. It must be stated here that not one of the ancient civilizations which were faced with the intense transformational time on earth adequately understood or prepared for the transition. There were a few who were wise and understood the significance of the time, and they prepared as best they could, but the civilizations as a whole were lost.

There is one factor that is different this time as the earth moves toward her highest vibrational rate. This factor is the new ray of energy which is a gift to the earth from beyond the veil. It is actually a gift to humans to help us tune to the increased energy on our planet. This ray helps the earth as well because it encourages humans to generate love, compassion, and respect toward the earth, and this is exactly what the planet needs in her time of great transition.

We who are incarnated on earth at this time are blessed with an exciting opportunity never before available on this planet. We can, by thorough study, understanding, and preparation, make this transition an incredibly significant and uplifting transformation for the earth and humanity alike. It is up to us, however, to seize this opportunity, for if we do not, we need only look to former times to see the result. We have much help and guidance now. We can do this.

∞ ∞ ∞

It is not necessary to embark on the voyage to enlightenment to make positive use of the new ray of energy entering the earth plane. We must state again that following the illumined path to an enlightened state is the best use of this new ray, but this journey necessitates dedication, discipline, perseverance, the utmost sincerity, and a selfless approach to everything. For those of us who feel we cannot make such a commitment, there are other ways we can tune to this new ray of energy and make constructive use of the opportunity it brings.

We can raise our personal vibration in accordance with the increased vibratory rate of the earth and with the higher vibration brought by the new ray. We begin by consciously acknowledging that we wish to exist in harmony with the planet and the new energy now here. We then find a little time in each day to tune to this new energy. There are many ways to do this, so we all can find an avenue that suits us. Daily meditation and prayer are at the very top of the list, for there are no undertakings more beneficial than these. In prayer, we simply ask that our minds and bodies be open to the new higher vibration and that each day we move toward greater harmony with it. In meditation, we relax and open ourselves to this higher vibration, taking care to ground ourselves first.

Here is another way for us to tune to the new higher vibrational rate. This uses breathing and visualization, and should be practiced as often as can be managed. We must stand directly on the earth. The less between us and the actual ground, the better. Standing with bare feet on the ground is best but not always possible. Stand with feet slightly spread for balance, and visualize rods reaching deep into the earth from the arches in our feet. Send a third rod from the base of the spine for stability. Picture these rods going at least eighty feet down. They anchor and ground us securely. We need to make these rods out of a material we like, but it is best if we visualize them made of something that exists naturally on the planet, such as iron, wood, or gold. Next, we visualize ourselves standing in a ray of brilliant white light which streams down from above us. Our entire bodies are completely bathed in this ray of bright white light. Now we add the breathing. We inhale very slowly, very deeply, through the nose and the mouth. As we do so, we see ourselves pulling golden light up through the rods, up from the earth into our bodies. We also breathe in the white light streaming down from above us. We pull the white light in from above and the golden light up from below to a spot just above the navel, the solar plexus. As we breathe out, we visualize the gold and the white mixing in a sparkling spiral in the solar plexus. We inhale the white light from above and the golden light from deep in the earth. We exhale and see them glow even brighter as they mix, spiral, and whirl in our midsections. We continue this exercise, breathing slowly and deeply, until we feel the entire body tingling with the new welcome higher vibration.

∞ ∞ ∞

Following the illumined path, rigorous though it is, offers many rewards. Likewise, we find our conscious efforts to adapt our personal vibrations to those of the earth and the new ray of energy very beneficial. The secret to receiving benefits in both cases is perseverance. Whatever we choose to do, whether it be to undertake the journey to an enlightened state or to move to adapt ourselves to the higher vibration now on the earth plane, we must incorporate our efforts into our daily routine. We must keep at it. In both cases, we are altering our very beings, and this takes consistent action over time.

Every human on earth must deal with the increased vibration on earth. All must acknowledge its existence and move to adapt somehow. Whereas some adaptation occurs automatically through the subconscious mind, our conscious efforts to change and adapt are the key to a successful transition on earth. As we have mentioned before, the opportunity here is very great. We have only the smallest glimpse of the possibilities of this time. We must trust our instincts, trust the universe, and move ahead by applying our conscious efforts to whatever procedure we choose. This is the most important work on the planet at this time, for the future of the earth and of humanity depend on how those now incarnated handle this great transition.

Awareness of this transition and the opportunity it brings is essential. It is, of course, the first step, and it is the major reason for this book being written. Those of us who are aware must help others become consciously aware. Running about sermonizing is not the best approach, for we may be dismissed by others as fanatics. Instead, we suggest the following. First, we must remember that the increased rate of vibration on earth affects everyone, including those who are not consciously aware. Second, let us set an example by our own behavior. The more we tune ourselves to the increased vibration, the healthier, clearer, more centered, and more energized we are. Others, especially those who are ill or uncomfortable due to the higher vibration, then come to us and ask us. We can then help them become consciously aware.

∞ ∞ ∞

When undertaking the path to enlightenment, we must begin with the utmost sincerity and with an eye to the journey taking a number of years. It is very important for those of us on the illumined path to be able to sustain our practices for years. That is why the sooner we incorporate these procedures into our daily routine, the sooner we become comfortable with them, and they become an inseparable part of our daily lives. Of course, our lives change over the years, and so do our daily routines. It is essential that, no matter what changes, we continue the practices that further us on the illumined path. We must consider this work our priority.

Those of us who undertake the journey to enlightenment with sincerity and dedication are truly blessed. No matter what changes in our lives, we can be assured that the universe is caring for us and nurturing us in a way beyond our knowing. This is the most important work now being done on the planet, so those of us who are involved are guided and protected. We must hold in our hearts the knowledge of the importance of this work. We must hold in our minds the assurance that no matter what occurs in our lives, there is a way for us to continue this process to enlightenment.

We can look ahead to a time when we have consciously altered our cells and we can resonate to the higher vibration with our entire bodies at all times. It is then we can say we have reached an enlightened state. It is then we are called into service for the earth and for all humanity.

Once we have become lighted beings, we possess many powers and talents with which we can help others. It is absolutely essential that we employ these powers and talents in selfless service. There is much for us to do. We can teach. We can heal. We can bring joy, love, and compassion to a planet which sorely needs it. We can make a difference in the lives of many and help others tune to the higher vibration now flooding the earth plane. It is our work as enlightened beings which leads our planet through this time of transition.

∞ ∞ ∞

This series of writings on enlightenment is meant to instruct and to encourage all interested humans to undertake the illumined journey. The more of us who choose to set forth upon this path, the better for both the planet and the human race. Never before have the steps to an enlightened state been made so accessible to all humanity. The opportunity is great indeed, and it exists for all who wish to pursue it.

This unique opportunity has been brought to the earth plane at this time because we humans are at a crucial turning point in our evolvement. The development of our intellects and our scientific knowledge has reached an all-time peak. Now we need to balance these accomplishments with similar strides in the psychic and spiritual fields. The introduction of the new ray of energy onto the material plane here on earth brings with it all that is necessary for each of us to make significant psychic and spiritual breakthroughs.

The whirlwind of events surrounding the escalation in vibration on the planet makes it obvious to everyone that the earth is involved in a major transition. This great transformation is so complete that it affects every molecule in and on planet earth. Every human incarnated now must come to terms with these great changes. Many seek order in the chaos, but only those of us who turn within ourselves find peace and stability.

The key for all humans in this time of great transition is turning within for guidance. Everyone of us has the opportunity to realize this. All of us can turn inward for assistance. Meditation and prayer are essential tools in this process.

There is a new opening of the human consciousness at this time. We can expand the way in which we see, hear, and feel through seeking inner guidance. We can make connections through the veil that have not been possible on such a large scale before now. The potential of this time is very great.

Section Four
Order Within / Chaos Without

Every time the earth has undergone a major transformation, the civilization of the time has disappeared. It is as if the earth wished to clear herself and start over. We are approaching another such transitional time. If we look to the past for information, we might conclude that the civilization now present on the planet may disappear. This is indeed possible, even probable. There is really nothing we can do to stop this cyclical clearing of the earth.

We humans have, however, been given a tool to help us deal with this transformation. This tool was not available to ancient civilizations who had to face the earth's great clearing process. This tool is the new ray of energy which helps us increase our psychic awareness. This ray helps us tune to the changing vibration on the planet. It helps us understand, prepare for, and flow with the great transformation.

It is true that a few of the ancients were aware of the climactic nature of their times and were able to prepare, but the civilizations were lost. The few wise humans who prepared did survive, but had to begin over.

As we humans face another great clearing transformation on earth, we must feel joy and gratitude for the gift of this new ray of energy. This ray makes psychic awareness available on a large scale. Many more of us in this civilization have the opportunity to tune to the changes and prepare.

It must be stated here that the only way we can use this great gift of the new ray of energy is with a sincere spiritual approach. By using the psychic connections made available to us by the ray, we can learn how to change our vibrations and change our lives. Although some of us may resist changing our lives, we must remember that the earth is beginning a major transformation, so our lives may be greatly altered anyway. Hopefully, many of us welcome the guided advice brought by the new ray of energy and choose to change and prepare.

∞ ∞ ∞

A new day, a new time is approaching for the human race. This fact cannot be ignored. It is past time to begin preparations. Those who read these words are now aware. It is important to pass this book on to others so that they, too, may become aware and begin preparations.

Once we have taken the first step of awareness, the next step is going within ourselves for personal preparation and guidance. Meditation and prayer are essential tools in this process. The new ray of energy brings us the potential to consciously connect with guided help. We must, each of us, quiet ourselves, journey within, and make contact with our inner self, our higher self, and with our spirit guides and helpers. All of us can and, indeed, must do this. In this way, each of us can receive the precise information necessary for personal preparation. The information that comes to us through these inner journeys is specific to each of us, and it helps us each prepare in the most appropriate ways.

No less important is the third step of bonding with others as we prepare. We are all faced with a great transformation on this planet. No one is immune from the great changes which bring the new time to earth. We must help each other understand the significance of this time and prepare. We must encourage and support each other as we alter ourselves and our lives.

Change is very difficult for some, and these people need special love and support. Even with direct guided help, some of us find it difficult to make the changes that are asked of us. That is why we must bond and help one another. We are all in this together. We must help each other.

The further along we are in our preparations, the more we see the wisdom of taking the steps that we are asked to take in our guided meditations. It is important that those of us who are further along help and encourage those who are beginning. If we all love and help one another, we are already well on our way to making this transition a great leap for humankind.

∞ ∞ ∞

In the time of chaos and great transformation, there need to be those who are prepared. The more of us who are prepared, the more successful the transition can be. As the earth changes and civilization changes, let us move toward a new order of love and compassion, of respect for the earth and for each other. If we prepare properly, this can be achieved. This is not a utopian dream, but a real possibility for the earth and those who dwell upon her at this time.

We must approach this time of transition with a new outlook. We must see violence being minimized and eventually passing out of the realm of acceptability for the human race. We must see hatred and prejudice being replaced by compassion and understanding for others no matter what their race, their sex, or their background. This may sound fanciful and unrealistic, but times of great chaos very often force us to reevaluate our lives. If a number of us are prepared to move toward this new cycle in which we see love replacing greed and compassion replacing hatred, many follow us. During times of great transition, old structures disintegrate and everything is in flux. This is the time when those of us who are prepared step forward and establish new ways. We do so by setting an example and by helping others. If we are strong, calm, centered, and prepared, others turn to us for stability as the past falls away into dust. We need only be ourselves, for we have tuned to the higher vibration of the new ray of energy. Others are then drawn to us and wish to emulate us. When others ask for help, we give it gratefully and abundantly, for this is why we have prepared!

There are many challenges in times of great transition, but those of us who have properly prepared have all the resources necessary to meet any problem, even a life-threatening one. Remember, we are being guided and helped by many from beyond the veil. We are not alone in this great undertaking.

∞ ∞ ∞

The earth is truly blessed in this time of transformation. Many are watching from beyond the veil and are prepared to help in any way possible. The new ray of energy which is stimulating greater telepathic contact between the earth plane and other realms is making it possible for much direct guidance to flow to humanity now. We humans need only find the quiet space within and sincerely open our hearts and minds to receive this guided help. There is more communication to earth from beyond the veil than ever before. We all have the potential to make the necessary connections and receive information and guidance, but we must want this to occur and take the time to cultivate the quiet space within ourselves where this contact takes place. This takes consistency in daily application through prayer, as well as patience and perseverance. If we truly seek this telepathic connection and make the necessary changes in our daily lives to allow this to happen, there is no doubt we succeed.

We must be aware that making this connection opens our lives in a new way. We may now discuss any problems or ask any questions of the spirit guides who step forward to help us. Very often the guides provide direct answers and give specific advice. We must be open and ready to hear what the guides have to say, for it may not always be what we wish to hear. We must be willing to put our lives in order, for those who watch over us, protect us, and guide us are familiar with all we do. Once we make conscious contact through the veil, there is no room in our lives for behavior that is hurtful to others. The guides are there to help us as long as we are willing to abide by the great laws of the universe which we know in our hearts and our guides help us understand. Most often bringing guided help into our lives means great changes for us. If we are willing to flow with the universal energy, we reap many benefits in the long run.

∞ ∞ ∞

Although the illumined path is not for everyone, more humans can undertake this journey to enlightenment than ever before on the earth plane. We have explained that this is due to the gift of the new ray of energy which makes a connection for us which before was not widely available on the earth plane. The decision by the many to undertake the long journey on the illumined path is due to several factors. First, the information in this book and others is becoming widespread. Once humans have access to this information, many find it feels right to them. Something clicks, and they perceive the greater order of the universe. They suddenly grasp the reason for the escalation of events on earth. The sense of it all spurs them to undertake the journey to an enlightened state, for this is the best use of the energy of this time of great transition.

Some who have not before been seekers become disquieted, discontent, and perhaps even ill. The increase in vibration on planet earth stirs illness and discontent in those who hang on to the old order. These people seek relief from their maladies and in doing so find this information invaluable.

Many more begin the journey on the illumined path because they come in contact with those of us who have made several years of progress toward an enlightened state. Let it be known that there is no mistaking those who have journeyed for some time on this path. We can maintain strength and calm in the face of chaos. We have compassion for others and are always willing to help. We glow with a brighter light that some can see and most can feel. It is no wonder others are drawn to us, especially those who are ill and confused. We need not preach; we need only be, and others come to us and ask for help. Once these people are acquainted with the information now available through this book and others, once they see and feel the truth of it all as exemplified by those of us who have proceeded long on the path, the many feel much joy and hope, and they undertake the journey to enlightenment for themselves.

∞ ∞ ∞

The dawn of the age of enlightenment comes at a time when the earth is moving toward great change. Events upon the planet are unfolding at a rapid pace. Humanity certainly contributes to this. One after another, species of plants and animals are becoming extinct. The climate of the entire globe is changing. The earth cries out and moves toward a great transformation.

Now it is time for us humans who have facilitated so much of this change to take responsibility and take a stand. Many of us already feel in our hearts renewed respect and love for the earth. This passion must be contagious and spread across the globe to all people. There are many ways this can be accomplished. First, it is important to nourish this passion, this love for the earth, within our own hearts. If we think of it and feel it everyday and send love to the earth from our hearts, the love grows within us and within the earth as well. Second, we can learn to express this love and respect for the planet in a variety of ways. We can communicate in songs, in poems, in stories, in our everyday conversations. We can show our passion in drawings, paintings, sculptures, and prints. Best of all, we can show our love for the earth in our daily actions. Others then notice our reverence for the planet and take a new look at their own feelings and actions. Also, the simple act of pointing out something very beautiful in nature to a friend may have profound results. We can teach others to see the earth in a new way by sharing our vision, our joy, and our passion.

The opportunity exists for the earth and for humanity to rise together in love. The vibration of the planet is increasing and so must ours increase. The rapid pace of events may lead only to chaos and destruction, or it may lead to a transformation which brings the new higher vibration of love into our own beings and into the earth as a whole. It is up to us to live our passion and respect for the planet everyday, and to share what we feel with others.

∞ ∞ ∞

The opportunity for widespread enlightenment has come to earth at a time when humanity needs a major shift in direction. There is no question that we simply cannot go on the way we have been, plundering the globe and harming each other and ourselves by doing so. In a less benevolent universe, a civilization such as ours which has thrived on greed and profit would not have been given such an opportunity. Let us be filled with joy because the transformation is near and because we can take part. Let us be glad in our hearts that compassion and forgiveness are flooding the earth plane so that we may take advantage of this opportunity for change, let go of the past, and build a new civilization based on the higher vibration of love. It is a great task, but we have much assistance, including help from the earth herself. In fact, the earth plays a major role as the vibrations of the planet increase and more earthquakes occur, more volcanoes are activated, more turbulent weather circles the globe. Change is afoot. We must prepare. Let us not approach this preparation with fear, paranoia, or anxiety, for it is our joyous duty to pay attention and prepare.

The timing is such that many who are now incarnated on the earth can reach personal fulfillment only through dedicated service to the earth and to the process which can lead many to enlightenment. This book is written specifically to encourage all who are interested to undertake preparations for the great transformation and begin the journey to an enlightened state. Those of us who feel dissatisfied with the current situations on the planet, those of us who are restless and desire change, we are the ones who must step forward and begin. Once we decide that this must be our path, let us pray for strength and guidance. Let us realize that we are truly blessed as we set forth to prepare.

∞ ∞ ∞

Centuries ago, the last time the earth came to a time of great transformation, there were only a few humans who understood the meaning of the time and made preparations. This time, there exists the opportunity for many to be enlightened and prepared. There are many differences between the earlier time and now which make this possible. For one, today information is spread around the globe at lightning speed. We are no longer isolated in our separate villages. For another, the human mind has evolved to the point where it can realistically make the next evolutionary step. Also, we have been given the gift of a new ray of energy which helps to facilitate this evolutionary step. This step involves the use of a part of our minds which before now has been activated in very few humans. Now, however, the increase in vibration brought by this new ray of energy coupled with the increase in the vibratory rate of the planet are working to stimulate that part of our human brain which handles all psychic concerns. This means that many of us have the opportunity to increase our psychic awareness and psychic abilities. Our increased psychic abilities allow us access to guided assistance from beyond the veil which helps us make precise preparations for the transformation of earth.

This book is being written to help all of us take advantage of this opportunity.

In order to tune to this new ray of energy and increase our psychic awareness, we begin with prayer and meditation. We offer up a prayer of thanks for the opportunity brought to us at this time, and we ask with sincerity that we be allowed to make the best use of it. Daily meditation is the other place to begin, for we must make a quiet space for ourselves in each day in order to tune to this higher energy. It is no secret that our links to the universal mind lie within us. We must all be able to quiet ourselves and go within on a daily basis.

Once we are comfortable with daily meditation and prayer, we can begin to add breathing and visualization exercises which are geared to helping us increase our psychic abilities. Here is a simple visualization with which to begin. Breathe slowly and deeply using the balanced breath. Focus on the sixth chakra or the third eye, which is located on the forehead above the bridge of the nose. Now move the focus just behind the third eye. Picture a brilliant golden sphere in the area behind the third eye. Be sure to see this sphere as luminescent gold. As we breathe in, we see the sphere expand slowly. As we breathe out, we see it glow even brighter. Once the luminescent sphere of gold has expanded enough to fill the area behind the third eye and below the top of the head, we move our focus to the center of this brilliant sphere and hold it there. We are now in the space where we can make use of our psychic abilities and receive guided assistance.

∞ ∞ ∞

In centuries past, the tumult of the time of great transformation on earth destroyed the civilizations. As we face another great transition on this planet, we need to examine what there is of value in our present civilization that we may wish to save and carry over to the new cycle. Great strides have been made in many technological areas, yet not all of these advances may apply as we enter the new time. In many ways, we are shaping the new cycle. We are laying the foundation which affects many generations to come. Our decisions, our actions have far-reaching effects. This is one reason for taking the time and making the effort to receive guided help.

The new ray of energy now flooding the earth plane is bringing with it a new opening in the veil which surrounds earthly reality. It brings new connections between our conscious minds and the great superconscious or universal mind. It brings access to information which helps us understand the great cycle of which we are a part and helps us take appropriate action. We must take advantage of this opportunity. We must cultivate the gifts brought to us by this new ray of energy. If we do not, we are no different from those civilizations centuries ago which were destroyed in times of great change on earth.

We can begin by giving thanks for the opportunity afforded to us by the advent of this new ray. We can ask with sincerity that we be open to learning all that this new ray has to teach us. We can continue by following procedures which raise our personal vibration so that we may tune more easily to this new ray. We have spoken of the four practices, the cornerstones which help us raise our vibratory rates: prayer, meditation, breathing, and visualization. By making these practices a part of our daily lives, we invite the new ray of energy into ourselves and our lives. We must undertake this work with the utmost sincerity and respect and with the knowledge that our lives as we know them are changing forever.

The earth is changing, and so our lives must change. Do we not wish to face these changes with understanding and guidance? The alterations we must make in ourselves and our lives in order to raise our personal vibrations and tune to the new ray are small in comparison with the huge changes that come with the great transformation on earth. We may make these changes now in peace and privacy, whereas the changes must be more difficult to make when faced with disorder and chaos. Preparation is the key to facing the great transition with strength and with calm and centered beings.

All the information we need to prepare as individuals and as a global civilization is available through guided assistance. We need only follow the steps necessary to connect with this guided help. All of us who take the time to make a quiet space in our daily lives, who approach this opportunity with sincerity and thanks, who persevere in the aforementioned practices, can consciously connect with all the help and guidance we need in this time.

∞ ∞ ∞

We all have duties in the material world, even if they are simply to keep ourselves clean and healthy. We have responsibilities also on the spiritual plane as they are reflected in earth life. We have the responsibility to treat everything and everyone on the planet, and the earth herself, with the utmost respect. Carelessness in our actions and disrespect for the living spirit in all things have been great human failings on this planet. Our greed for material gain has blinded us to that which is truly valuable. It is time to see with new eyes. Once we realize that the Great Spirit lives in all things, everything from a pebble to an elephant, we can no longer thoughtlessly destroy that which has been given to us on earth to nurture and protect.

Nothing should be taken and used without acknowledging the God-force within it and respectfully asking for the privilege of using it. Giving thanks for everything we take from the planet is also an important spiritual responsibility. Once we take these spiritual duties to heart, we must necessarily change our approach to daily living. We must proceed through the day feeling true gratitude for everything we have and use. We treat everyone and everything with respect, for all has been put into our path for a reason.

We are given what we need on the earth plane to learn what we need to learn and to grow. When we see with new eyes, we recognize even the most stubborn obstacles as gifts from which we can learn a great deal. If we approach all that we encounter with reverence and with the knowledge that whatever comes to us we need right now, we have taken a giant step on the path of our personal evolution. This is not always so easy to do, for sometimes we encounter distressing situations filled with hurt and pain. Sometimes we are given something we are sure we do not want, such as a toothache or a broken bone, yet even these challenges have a place and a purpose in our personal growth. This is often a difficult concept to grasp, yet it is an important one for us to see with our new eyes.

∞ ∞ ∞

Anytime we are faced with problems and challenges in our earth lives, we are being given gifts that help us learn and grow. We are not used to perceiving our troubles as gifts, yet once we learn to see with new eyes, that is to see through the illusions of earthly reality, we comprehend that that is exactly what they are.

Once we achieve this new vision, we obtain an ease not known to us before on earth. We welcome challenges with the knowledge that they are important stepping-stones to our growth. We see our problems moving us in the proper direction for our evolution. The ability to pierce the illusions of earthly reality with this new vision is one of the greatest tools we have at this time. To see with new eyes is to recognize what is truly valuable on the earth plane. Our old value systems based on accumulation of material goods dissolve away in the bright light of this new vision. This new way of seeing brings with it a feeling of security and trust in the universe.

Throughout the centuries, sages who have spent their lifetimes in deep inner contemplation have been able to achieve this new vision. Yet today it is widely available to us. This is partly due to the connection between our conscious and superconscious minds being facilitated by the new ray of energy. Our ability to achieve this new way of seeing is also being aided by our inner journeys through meditation and visualization. Once our conscious and subconscious minds accept this new vision as presented by our superconscious mind, we have taken a great step forward, for we are no longer subject to the illusions which engulf all earth life. When we see with new eyes, we see what is truly valuable on earth, and we are able to change our lives accordingly. Everyday old mysteries unfold before us in the light of this new vision. Even death itself takes on a new face once we see with new eyes. We accept this gift of a new way of seeing with much gratitude.

∞ ∞ ∞

Many hundreds of years ago, the last time the earth underwent a great transition, there was much chaos, much destruction. As we on earth come full cycle to another time of transformation, we are again facing upheaval and all that comes with it. This is the time that our new way of seeing becomes very important. We can use our new vision to see that the chaos, destruction, and upheaval are gifts to help us usher in a new era on the planet. We must be able to see with new eyes that the falling away of the old order is indeed a blessing. We must be able to use our new vision to see through the loss to the benefits that come with a thorough clearing away of the past.

It is very easy to become shaken and unsteady in times of great and rapid change. We must, therefore, prepare ourselves by building our inner strength and stability. With the assistance of guided help coupled with daily meditation and prayer, we can be strong and calm under any circumstances. The duty of those of us who prepare is to aid those who have not done so. We need not seek out people to help, for they flock to us. Our calm strength acts as a magnet to those who are shocked and disoriented. So we must be ready not only to deal with this great transition within ourselves, but also to help others handle the changes.

This may seem like an overwhelming task, but remember that we have much assistance from beyond the earth plane at this time. We can continually turn to our guides and helpers as we all work together to bring about a new cycle of light and love on this planet. Although the potential is there for this to occur, it is up to us to make this opportunity a reality on earth. We are faced with perhaps the greatest evolutionary step that can be potentially made by humans on the earth plane, for we can transform our very way of being and with it the nature of our civilization. It cannot be emphasized enough that all efforts and all work toward this end are extremely valuable and in fact necessary for our survival.

∞ ∞ ∞

In times of great change, those of us who survive and prosper are those who have inner stability. While everything on the material plane is in tumult and transition, we can maintain an inner calm through preparation and guidance from beyond the earth realm. The time to begin such preparations is now, for events on earth are already changing more rapidly than before.

The very best way to begin all preparations is with meditation and prayer. Our prayers include thanks for the opportunity we have been given to make such preparations, and also include a request that we receive guidance in doing so. In our daily meditation, we establish a zone of quiet inner calm to which we can journey when events around us in the material world are chaotic and upsetting. Through practice of daily meditation, we can increase our inner calm and inner stability. We may often need to call upon this zone of strength and quiet within ourselves. We must have this inner space so well established that it is easy and comfortable for us to journey there no matter what is occurring in the outer material world. This inner space of calm, quiet, stability, and strength is very sacred. It is while we are in this sacred space that we receive guided assistance in all matters in our lives. It is especially important that we cultivate this sacred space in order to receive guided help in making preparations. All that we need to know can be shown to us or told to us if we establish this meditative space and spend adequate time in it each day.

We are at the turning point of a great cycle where we have much guidance and assistance in order to help us deal with the changes and begin the new cycle in the most positive way possible. We need only take the time to seek this help through prayer and meditation. As always, it is very important that we be sincere in our pursuit of knowledge and assistance. If we hold in our hearts the desire for what is best for the earth and the human race, then all is well.

∞ ∞ ∞

In times of great change, we must operate from a place of inner peace and stability. We must be prepared to serve others in any way we can. We therefore have much to do. As chaos and confusion increase on earth, we must not neglect the time we take each day to center and balance ourselves through meditation and prayer. No matter how demanding our situation might be, we must continue with this daily devotion, for it is through these practices that we renew our strength, regain our balance, and maintain our inner stability and peace. It is not selfish to take this time for ourselves each day, for we are able to function better and serve others in a more complete way if we are operating from a place of inner calm. It is very important not to let the rapidly changing events on the material plane jostle us and keep us from this time of daily renewal. No matter how selfless we are in using our time and energy to help and serve others, we proceed in a much clearer way and we are ultimately much more effective if we take the time we need each day to go within ourselves to center.

There is much danger in being swept away by the whirlwind of change on earth. We must be able to make a peaceful space for ourselves no matter what the situation. We cannot wait for the outer world to be quiet so that we can meditate. We must be able to create our own quiet inside ourselves no matter what goes on around us. We must be able to go within for renewal and guidance no matter where we are, no matter what is happening. If we can meditate only in a certain room at a certain time, how do we proceed if this room is no longer available to us?

Our strength lies within. Once we truly grasp this fact, we have the confidence we need to go within and make a quiet meditative space for ourselves no matter what is going on around us. We can enlist the help of friends, both incarnate and discarnate, to aid us in finding the time and space in each day for prayer and meditation.

∞ ∞ ∞

In times of great change, we must use all we know and all we have practiced to bring love and compassion into every aspect of our lives. Love and compassion are energies of the highest vibration. The earth needs as much love and compassion as we humans can generate. The times are intense, and there is danger of much needless destruction and pain unless we consciously surround ourselves, our families, our lives, our earth with love and compassion. We must lift ourselves up and away from the old order of greed and the ruthless actions that accompany it. We must change our values and see that violence is unnecessary and undesirable in any form. Unless we do these things, the earth can fall into a whirlwind of violence and destruction so intense that absolutely nothing survives, not even the planet herself.

In times of such incredible and rapid change, we must absolutely be prepared and be strong and calm within ourselves. Only then can we surround ourselves and all around us with the love and compassion which is so very needed now.

Here is a simple visualization that we can do anytime, several times a day if we wish to. We begin by taking a deep breath. As we breathe in, we feel the heart swell with pink and golden light. As we breathe out, we see this light flow out of the top of our heads like a huge brilliant fountain. The pink and golden light showers everything around us with love and compassion. We can make the fountain larger with each breath until we have covered the earth with this light. We must be sure while doing this exercise that we feel the love and compassion in our hearts, that we feel it deeply as well as see it as pink and golden light. This is a simple but very powerful exercise. It can be done anywhere, anytime, as often as we wish. It helps to raise the vibration of all around us, including the earth.

∞ ∞ ∞

In times of great changes, we must be so thoroughly prepared that nothing upsets us from our center. We must have so thoroughly established our inner calm and stability that all disturbing outer events do not unsettle us. Such thorough preparation takes time and dedication. This book is available to help us make thorough preparations.

Nine days of singing and celebrating bring many people together in order to further preparations. These gatherings are filled with joy and a heartfelt welcome of the new cycle. During these days of celebration, those who have been preparing individually come together to continue preparations as a group. These group celebrations cover the globe as awareness of the arrival of the great transition moves many humans to change their lives.

Although much of the preparation must be done on an individual basis, we cannot face the chaos and destruction on our own. We must have a network of individuals who are able to communicate telepathically and are proceeding with these thorough preparations. Mutual support is very important in these times. No matter how thoroughly we prepare as individuals, we need the support of others to remain centered and joyful when facing the great transformation on the earth plane.

This celebration of nine days is the way to solidify this mutual support and to accomplish even more. For one, we can raise our personal vibration, the vibrational level of the group, and the vibrational rate of the planet through group singing, prayer, chanting, and meditation. For another, we can form joyous bonds which help us in times of extreme challenge, for let there be no doubt, the great transformation brings the most challenging times the earth has ever known. The nine days of celebration help us focus on the opportunity we have to make this great transition a truly positive change for the planet and for the human race. The nine days of celebration inspire us to move forward with determination. This celebration solidifies our inner strength and assures us that we can accomplish what we are setting out to do, which is nothing less than establishing the foundation for a new way of being on earth. We need the confidence generated in a group setting, for we surely could never bring about such a complete change on the planet on our own.

We can look to the nine days of celebration to generate much love for each other and, of course, for the earth. The love we generate around the planet during these nine days can make a tremendous difference in the outcome of the great transformation, for we must remember that although we have the opportunity to bring this new way of being to earth, our success is not at this time assured. We must proceed with heartfelt sincerity, dedication, and perseverance, and with a joyful outlook, for we can, through our efforts, bring the greatest most positive change the earth has yet known.

∞ ∞ ∞

In times of great change when we need to encircle all we do with love and compassion, we need also to be ready to guide and serve others. All that we do in these times is extremely important, for we are manifesting the great transformation of ages. Every thought, every emotion, every breath must be geared toward helping all the energy of this transition move toward positive change for the planet. We must hold in our hearts and in our minds the new structure of values based on love and respect for the earth and for each other. We must seize this opportunity, for we do not have another for thousands of years. The basic principles upon which we need to focus are outlined in this book. The basic preparations and procedures to carry them through are also addressed in these writings and others. All this information is brought to the earth plane now in simple straightforward terms. Everyone is encouraged to read, to learn, and to take all this to heart. We have here a guide to changing our lives that we may change all life on earth for the better.

∞ ∞ ∞

This time, of all the ages of the earth, is very significant. It cannot be stressed enough what a rare and important opportunity we have before us. The joyful news of this opportunity must be spread far and wide. We can solidify our own hope for the planet by informing others about this time of transition and all it may bring to the earth plane. The more of us who are aware of this time of change and its great significance, the more of us can prepare and the greater our chances for affecting a positive transition.

The psychic energy on the planet is increasing, thanks to the gift of the new ray of energy. Our ability to tune to this psychic energy is also increasing. Much information is now entering the earth plane through psychic channels. When we converse with others and inform them about this time of transition, we can suggest that verification can be had through their own psychic connections.

Even skeptics cannot deny that changes are occurring very rapidly now on this planet. Even the most unbelieving humans can sense the increase in the vibration on earth. All of us who are now incarnated need only open our hearts and minds to the possibilities of the time. All of us need only ask for this new psychic connection and we have access to it.

Everything that is found in these writings can be verified by using the new psychic energy now available. We can all receive personal instruction through telepathic means. In fact, personal guidance is essential in all preparations we make.

In order to access this new psychic energy, we need to do a bit more than be open to it and ask for it. We must be sincere and patient. We must allow quiet space in every day so that we can connect psychically with our superconscious and with our spirit guides. This increased psychic awareness is available to all on earth who pursue it properly.

∞ ∞ ∞

Regardless of how things seem on earth, all is well in the universe. Our vision must go beyond the material realm. We must recognize that our earth lives are but one tiny part of all that exists in the universe. This wide vision helps us and steadies us when everything is in great flux on earth. We can go within ourselves to the many worlds inside us for solace, peace, stability, and love. The road that lies deep within us is the one that offers us access to the many realms beyond our earth life. Through meditation and selfless dedication, we can learn to make many inner journeys to the realms beyond our earth lives. These inner journeys can become a part of our earthly existence, but we must also be acutely aware of events on this planet, as this is where we are incarnated and have our lessons now. The inner journeys we may take to other realms are useful in that they help us deal with life on earth. Our priority must always be our actions, reactions, and interactions on the earth plane.

The opportunities for us to make great strides in our personal growth exist all around us on the material plane. We may travel within for information, for stability, for calm, for peace, but while we are incarnated as humans on this planet, our growth comes through our actions on earth. We may withdraw and go deep within ourselves for centering, for strength, for guidance, but we must apply what we experience during these inner journeys to our lives on earth. We are incarnated on earth for a purpose: to learn, to grow, to evolve. Therefore, we must pay attention to all we do while acting, reacting, and interacting in the material realm.

Now, during the time of great change upon this planet, we can be actively and consciously a part of more than just our personal evolution. We can, through our efforts and actions, affect the evolution of planet earth and the human race as a whole. It is an important time to pay attention to all events on earth.

∞ ∞ ∞

All is well in the universe, although this may not always seem to be reflected in events on earth. The earth now faces monumental change. This is in keeping with the natural order of the universe. Also, we must realize that it is time for the earth and for humanity to evolve. We have reached new heights in scientific knowledge and technology. This has set the stage for even greater evolution. Now it is time for our spirits and our bodies to make similar great strides.

Such a tremendous leap for humanity must be prepared for. There must be those who step forward to lead. This book is written to help all those who prepare to guide humanity to a new way of being on this planet. It is time for this to happen, but success is not assured. Only through thorough preparation, sincere dedication, perseverance, and love by those who choose to lead can we hope to achieve a successful transition to a new order on earth. These leaders must selflessly and tirelessly serve the earth and all humanity in these times of great change. The task is great, but success is attainable.

Those who choose to lead in this time are blessed and have much help and guidance. It is these leaders who make the difference between a successful transition and disaster. These leaders have strength and help from beyond the veil, for the earth plane is now showered with light and love as we face the great transformation. These leaders are the link between all humans now incarnated on the planet and all the divine help and guidance that is now available through the veil. The challenge is very great, but the rewards for the earth and all who dwell upon her are even greater.

Although undertaking the task of leadership at this time is very serious, it is also filled with joy. In fact, joy is the number-one emotion that all leaders must indeed feel as we near the time of great transformation.

∞ ∞ ∞

In times of great change, there is much to prepare for. Of course, our material needs must be met. Yet our values must necessarily shift so significantly in a time of great transition as to make our material needs much different than we see them now. We find new wealth in all the earth has to offer. We abandon the trappings of the civilization which is passing away. Therefore, when we prepare, we must look to the new values as guideposts.

Some of these new values were held by our ancestors. For instance, love and respect for the earth were a way of life to some of the ancients, as well as a belief that the earth herself offers up all we need in life. These are important values which must be renewed in our time.

Another value that must be regained from ancient times is a love for the world within ourselves. Deep inner journeys shed much light on life on the material plane. We must value the time we spend going within and view this time as very sacred. This is where we hold our calm, our strength, and our peace in times of great change. This inner world must be honored and respected and must become as comfortable to us as the outer earthly realm. This can be achieved through daily meditation and prayer.

There are new values on the horizon for the new cycle which is now arriving. Peace must be held in the highest regard. Peace must permeate every aspect of our earthly lives, and this necessarily eliminates violence. Compassion must be held in every heart and permeate every action. We must learn to value compassionate acts most highly. We must also learn to value our emotions, especially love, which is an emotion of the very highest vibration. The time we spend transmuting our various lower emotions into love must be seen as valuable sacred time. We must begin now to orient ourselves and our lives to these new values as an important way to prepare.

∞ ∞ ∞

Never before upon the earth plane has there been such a challenge or such an opportunity for the human race. We have come to the point where we either fall or soar. There is no middle ground. We must realize and take to heart the incredible significance of the time. All we have to do is look within ourselves and we find the truth of this matter. We have within ourselves the connection to universal truth. We need not rely on others, for we can turn within ourselves to verify.

One of the first things we must do as we face this time of great challenge and great opportunity is learn to go within ourselves for the truth. Life on the earth plane is full of illusions and half-truths. It is time for us to see past the illusions to the truth of human existence on earth. We need not be frightened. It is a joyful picture, for we humans have much potential. We have merely been stuck for hundreds and hundreds of years in the whirling illusion of profit and material gain. It is time for us to realize with every cell in our bodies that single-minded pursuit of material wealth is entirely useless. We need only see our evolution in a larger sense. We need only grasp that our time on earth is but a small fraction of the life of our souls, and our time here on the earth plane can be much better spent.

This dawning of a new consciousness for humanity is a great turning point for the human race. At last we can set about realizing our potential on the material plane. This challenge, this great opportunity, has been a long time coming. We are ready now to face it, to grasp it, to change life on earth for the betterment of all. This great change excludes no one. This wonderful opportunity is available to all incarnated on the earth plane. We need only see the truth of it for ourselves, for the truth is within us and all around us. Then we are ready to undertake this great change.

∞ ∞ ∞

At all times, as we make preparations, we must remember that events on earth are not what they seem to be. The illusion of earthly reality is very strong in times of chaos and unrest. It is an automatic reaction of humans to grasp onto the material when our lives are unstable and unsettled. Yet those of us who are wise to the illusion surrounding the earth plane know that it is time to let go of the material and trust our spiritual insight.

When we are embroiled in intense changes in our lives on earth, we can get so caught up that we believe the illusion. It is very important that we keep a spiritual perspective throughout all our preparations and throughout all that occurs. Only by seeing through the illusion surrounding the earth plane can we proceed correctly. Only by utilizing a universal viewpoint can we make correct decisions for these times of change on earth.

We must not let rapidly changing events unsettle us. We must not lose our center in times of great flux. We must be prepared to meet the overwhelming changes with an inner calm and strength that is unshakable.

If we see this great transition on earth as our entrance into a new cycle and into a new way of being on this planet, then we can let go of the old structures, the old ways, and we can truly rejoice. If we open our hearts and minds to this new cycle and all it brings, then we have no need to regret all that passes away.

Events on earth may seem destructive when they are actually purifying. All that has been built for hundreds and hundreds of years may seem to be uselessly crumbling away, when actually this clearing process is necessary for us to establish this new way of being on earth. The ties to the old ways must be severed, and this may seem painful. The pain is not necessary. We must pierce the illusion and welcome the new cycle with love and light and joy.

∞ ∞ ∞

Whenever we need to, we can find strength and guidance. This has been true throughout the centuries, and it is especially true now as we face the time of great transition. The knowledge of the availability of this strength and guidance brings us comfort and security not readily found on the earth plane. Once we experience the wellspring of strength we can tap within ourselves, once we connect with the truth of the guidance that comes from within, we lose all fear in the face of great change.

It is very important for us to be strong and calm in times of great chaos. This is the first step in being of service to the earth and to other humans. The next step is to utilize the inner connections we have made in order to receive specific guidance. We can go within and seek help with any situation that arises. When we are involved in constant service upon the earth plane, we need to seek this guidance on a daily basis. The third step is to consciously radiate love and compassion not only to each person we encounter, but also to the earth as a whole. This also needs to be a daily practice. If we begin each day, before we interact with anyone, with the prayer and the visualization that we radiate love and compassion to all we meet, we then manifest this throughout the day. If we begin each day by feeling love and compassion in our hearts, and then we visualize this love and compassion as brilliant light radiating from us to all around us, we radiate to all throughout the day.

Each day is different and presents new challenges and tests. Yet if we approach each day with strength and calm, with the truth of our inner guidance, and with the light of love and compassion, we can face whatever each day brings our way. We need all of these resources in order to proceed in selfless service on the earth plane. Selfless service is essential. It is the key to laying the groundwork for the new cycle. It is up to us to build a strong foundation so that the new cycle flourishes in light and love.

∞ ∞ ∞

All is well when people gather together in love. When people gather with peace in their hearts, much can be accomplished. Although we may not agree on every detail of how to proceed, when our goals are the same, we can move forward in harmony.

Gatherings are an important part of preparing for the great transformation. We gather for many reasons. We join to share experiences and to offer mutual support and encouragement. We gather to rejoice and celebrate. We come together to raise our vibrations and our spirits. We join together so that we can accomplish much.

A group of like-minded people can affect events on the earth plane in a more significant way than can a single individual. This is a major reason why those of us who are involved in preparations for the great transformation must periodically come together to join our energies. There is much to do.

Rejoicing and raising the vibration of the group by singing, chanting, and dancing are excellent ways to initiate any such gathering. Once we feel a harmonious vibration permeating the entire gathering, we are ready to discuss specific actions we wish to undertake as a group.

All who are gathered are dedicated to selfless service, for this is accepted as a way of life by those who are on the illumined path in preparation for the new cycle. Therefore, there is never a shortage of projects that can be undertaken by such a group, or by us as individuals for that matter. In times of great change, many basic material needs must be met, and many spiritual needs must be addressed and nourished. As we decide how to direct our group energy, we must permeate all we say and do with love and compassion. We must work together to peacefully bring to the earth plane the new values for the new cycle.

∞ ∞ ∞

Every time we move to action, we affect the vibration of the planet. It may seem that our individual actions are insignificant. We must realize that every action we take on the earth plane may be repercussive and may affect our own futures as well as the future of the earth. If we grasp the fact that our actions on the material plane are what make our mark in this earth life, then we are more thoughtful about what we do, how we act and interact.

Many ponder the reason for our existence in this earthly reality. Many spiritual sources offer the same answer: earth is a learning place. Here on earth, we face the tests offered by the material realm. We are all ultimately familiar with the challenges of life on earth and of life in a physical body. If we also held the knowledge that our actions during our incarnation on earth mark our development, our progress or lack of it, then we might approach our life here with a different outlook and attitude.

It is really quite straightforward and simple. The material challenges we encounter on the earth plane help us refine ourselves, help us grow, and help us evolve. We do not take our earthly bodies when we leave this plane, but we do take the results of our actions and experiences here. Our spirits travel on to other levels of existence taking with them what we have learned during this earth incarnation. Our spirits always enter the earth plane with specific challenges to face. We come to earth to refine and develop ourselves in certain ways. Our actions are our marks. Our actions show how well we have faced and learned from the challenges the earth plane presents to us.

Although the earth is a resilient being, our actions do affect her. Our actions set up vibrations that not only mark our spiritual growth but also mark the evolution of the planet. Once we are entirely aware of the ramifications of our actions, we proceed on the earth plane with integrity and love.

∞ ∞ ∞

Dearly beloved, those of us who inhabit the earth, to all of us this charge is made: we must make great changes within ourselves so that we may survive the great transformation on earth. Humanity has brought itself to the brink of such a fate, for if we humans do not acknowledge the great transition and adapt ourselves to the time, we may perish. This sounds severe, but the effect of humans upon the planet has been and continues to be severe. We are faced with nothing less than transforming ourselves in the face of extinction on this planet. We must change our values. We must change our outlook. We must change our very way of being upon the earth, for if we do not, we bring about the end of human existence. All as we know it must change as the great transition progresses, and so we must change right down to the makeup of each cell in our bodies. This is very true and very serious business.

We need only look around us on the earth plane or turn within for verification. It is a time of crisis, as the time of any great transition must be. Yet these words are written, not to cause panic or distress, but to move each of us to address the changes which must necessarily be made. There can be no escape or avoidance. Only leaving the earth plane through death gives temporary pause from the responsibilities now facing all of us incarnated on earth. It is best if we take a deep breath and face the situation exactly as it is: we evolve or we perish. Our evolution can only be achieved at this time through our conscious and concerted efforts.

Let us be comforted by the knowledge that forgiveness, compassion, and love now flood onto the earth plane. Although we are charged with a very difficult task, we are given much assistance. We, in fact, have all the help we need to make the changes within ourselves and within the human race as a whole. We need only ask with sincerity for strength and guidance, and it is ours.

∞ ∞ ∞

All inhabitants of earth must be prepared to flow with the changes that come to the planet. Those who cannot adapt to the new ways must necessarily perish. This is the simple fact of evolution.

The evolution that comes to humanity and to earth is called the great transformation because much is altered in a comparatively short period of time. We are talking about changes that range from those that occur deep within the cellular structure of the human body to those that affect the face of the planet.

All is well because it is time for these changes. All is well because the earth is on the threshold of a great evolutionary leap. We are incarnated at one of the most exciting times on this planet, but we must be ready. Our outlook concerning this transition is very important. If we welcome the changes and are prepared to change also, we can experience much joy and exhilaration. If we resist and cling to the old structures and the old ways, we can suffer much loss, grief, and pain.

To all of us who inhabit the earth, now is the time to open our hearts and minds to guidance from beyond the veil and from the earth herself. All that we need to learn and know to adapt in the time of great change is available to us, but we must take the time. We must make space in our daily lives to receive the guided information that helps us. We need not rely on others, for a wealth of information and truth lies within each of us. We need only seek it with sincerity.

The pulse of the planet tells us much. We need only listen and the earth tells us a great deal. She speaks to us in many ways. If we take the time to say a simple prayer that our ears may be open to hear what the earth has to tell us, we begin to receive much helpful information from the planet. We are ushering in a new era of communication with both heaven and earth.

∞ ∞ ∞

Each time a human soul enters or departs from the earth plane, there is a change in the vibration of the planet. Thus there is always a slow evolution on earth, as those humans whose work is completed pass on from earth life, and those whose work is beginning are born. In this time of great change, many are being born who are here to undertake the work of establishing new ways on earth. These souls who come now to the planet have been schooled on other levels and are thoroughly prepared for such a great task. Each time one of these evolved souls is born onto the earth plane, the vibratory rate of the planet increases and so does the probability that the great transition may be successful.

When we speak of the success of the great transformation, we speak of the positive evolution of humanity. We speak of a time of love and compassion upon this planet, as illness, greed, and violence fall away. Some have spoken of this time as the Golden Age of earth, a time when humanity first realizes its divine potential. Of course, earth remains a place for us to learn, but the lessons must necessarily be of a very different nature from the ones we face now upon this planet.

As we look to the time of great transition, we must welcome and honor the souls entering the earth plane, for they are the leaders of the new cycle. It is to these children we look for establishment of a new way of being upon this planet. We must love and nurture them well, for they can be of great service to the earth and to all of humanity. These souls bring to earth with them a higher vibration gained from many levels of previous experience. We need only look into their eyes, and we can see the light and love of the universe.

Part of the preparation for the time of great change is the care and protection of the children. Much light surrounds this generation. Much guidance comes to us regarding their health and well-being.

∞ ∞ ∞

Every day we are one step closer to the great transformation on earth. Every day that passes is precious in that it is time for us to prepare. We must not lose a single day of preparation. We must begin now to alter ourselves and our lives on earth. This is not idle chatter, and it need not be seen as a warning or threat. Instead, let us view these changes as natural, as necessary, and as very positive for ourselves and the planet.

It is time for those who have not done so to take the first step. It is essential for those of us who have begun to renew ourselves daily and continue each day, each step.

This book outlines many ways to begin. The most straightforward and familiar is prayer. We need only pray with sincerity that we wish to begin, and we ask for guidance in doing so. If we take a moment now and say such a prayer, we have taken the first step. We have begun.

Once this first step is taken, all is set in motion in our lives. Within us and without us the changes enter our lives. Let us turn to these writings and others for daily assistance, for not one day must be missed, not one step forgotten. Once we begin, we must continue, giving our attention every day. As we proceed and we change, our lives change. We find that we have incorporated much that is helpful to us into our daily lives.

For many a daily routine is necessary, especially at first. Taking quiet time for meditation and prayer at the same time each day, whether it be dawn or bedtime, assures that we incorporate these practices into our lives. Soon we find our outlook and our actions also change, and as we proceed day by day, we find all our waking moments are filled with the necessary changes. These alterations are best done gently and gradually. This is the most positive preparation. Then we are ready for the more jolting changes that come with events on earth as the great transition proceeds.

∞ ∞ ∞

Now is the time to take these writings to heart. Now is the time to search deep within ourselves for the wellspring of guidance. The truth of this time is known to all of us. We need only turn within to know it for ourselves.

There are those few who have been preparing for many years. Now is the time for the masses to recognize the significance of the time and begin preparations. We cannot undertake such preparations half-heartedly. We must proceed with thoroughness and sincerity. This may not have been the way some have taken action in the past, but we are embarking on a new path here. Every day we begin anew and can do better than the day before if we wish it. There is no reason to be discouraged by what we have done in the past. This is a new time, a time for change, a time for the past to fall away.

Everyone can and indeed must participate in these changes on earth, for they affect everyone and everything. Since the great transformation cannot be ignored, our best course of action is to learn about it, make personal preparations, make group preparations, and accept all the changes with joyful hearts. It is truly an exciting and challenging time to be incarnated, for we have the opportunity to make great strides in our spiritual growth, which is, after all, one of the reasons we undertake life on earth.

Now is the time to put aside the distractions of the past and focus on the transition to the new cycle. We must accept flux and rapid change, for it may be some time before we settle into the calm, the peace of this new cycle of being on earth. All on the planet continues to change until the past is entirely lost to us, and we have only the new ways. Therefore, the sooner we embrace the new cycle, the sooner we find peace in our lives. For some, letting go of the material trappings of the past may be difficult, but they disappear no matter what we do. It is best to go deep within ourselves to seek what is truly of value now.

∞ ∞ ∞

Every day our attention must focus in part on the changes we need to make in our lives in preparation for the great transition. These changes must necessarily begin deep within us. They then manifest in our earth lives. All preparations also begin by going deep within ourselves. The wealth of information and guidance we can access by turning within is immeasurable. All of us can touch the core of truth within our very beings. Once we realize this, our daily meditation time becomes extremely valuable to us. All of us must take the time each day to quiet ourselves and listen. It is the only way we receive information specific to each of us. We receive daily help. We receive long erm guidance. We receive what we need in order to make the necessary changes and preparations. None of our individual preparations are exactly the same, for we are all facing different challenges on earth and we are all at different levels in the evolution of our spirits.

We all have those who help us and guide us from beyond the earth realm. It is time for these helpers to step forward and take a more conscious role in our lives. These guides bring us exactly what we need to know in order to make the appropriate changes and preparations. Our guides are tuned to our specific needs and help us in any way they can. In order to receive this help, we must open our hearts and minds and sincerely seek it. We must take the time each day to find the quiet place within, for it is here our guides can connect with us and consciously communicate.

It is comforting to know that, as we face monumental changes on planet earth, we have much help and support from friends beyond the veil. It is to their advantage to help us now, but we must give them the opportunity. We must realize that we cannot make the proper changes and preparations without first making the deep connection within ourselves which links us to universal truth and love.

Section Five

Leaders for the Time

Everything in the universe is in spin. Cycles and more often spirals are the natural movement of the universal flow. Once we grasp this truth, we can more easily understand the times of great transition on earth. Periodically there is a quickening of events on the planet followed by shifts in the outer layers, which include the atmosphere and nearly always the earth's crust. These cyclical events from the human perspective occur at very wide intervals of thousands of years. Many hundreds of generations arrive and depart between these great turning points on earth. By the time the earth is ready for another great transition, the last one happened so long ago that only sketchy legends remain to remind humanity of its occurrence.

The time of another great transition is approaching. It is once again heralded by an increase in the vibration of the planet and by rapidly changing events. Humanity and the planet herself are both at a new spot in our spiraling spin. We face tremendous challenges and incredible opportunities not before available to us in this realm. It is a sink-or-swim situation.

We humans have advanced our technology to the point where we can extend life and can also annihilate all life-forms on the planet. This time of great transformation can mean an incredible leap for human consciousness or, at worst, it could bring an end to life on the planet. It is up to us. Those of us who are now incarnated upon the earth plane are faced with great responsibility, for we are the ones who can carry humanity through this great transformation into a new golden age of light and love on earth. This can be done. We have much guidance and help. We can do this!

Much information, such as the writings contained in this book, is now arriving on the earth plane to help us at this crucial time. We have every reason to take a positive joyful approach to this exciting time of transition.

∞ ∞ ∞

As events come to pass, we each see with clearer vision that the time of the great transformation has arrived. We have been slowly approaching this change for many years, but now the pace quickens and we are very near the great transition of cycles. Those of us who think that there is nothing we can do to alter the course of events on earth are mistaken. It is true that we cannot prevent the great transformation from occurring. We can, however, use this time of great change to improve conditions on the planet for the benefit of the earth herself and also for humanity. There is much we can do, but we must be prepared and dedicated to our course of action.

This text provides the basic information we need to begin preparations and to visualize a new way of being on earth. We must begin and take all preparations seriously because the time of the great transition is upon us. We cannot ask the changes to wait for us to be ready.

All preparations, be they group or individual, must begin with a clear vision of the possibilities of the new cycle which we would like to see become reality. The new cycle can be a golden age on earth for both the planet and humans alike. We must provide a strong foundation for the new ways so that they may be firmly established.

We can set a tone of harmony upon the planet. We can establish a new value system here on earth which encourages love and respect for the planet and for each other. With the new opening in the veil surrounding earthly reality, we are given much information about our existence in this realm.

We now have a new perspective on earth life, and this helps us let go of our old beliefs and establish a new way of being here on earth. We have help every step of the way from those who guide us from beyond the earth realm, but it is up to us, those of us who are now incarnated here on earth, to make this new way of being a reality on this planet.

∞ ∞ ∞

At least once in every lifetime, we have the opportunity to reach through the veil and pierce the illusion surrounding earthly reality. If we recognize and seize this opportunity, we then possess realizations that affect the remainder of that incarnation. Our lives can never be the same once we see through the illusion. We must necessarily conduct ourselves differently because we have been touched by truth.

The new opening in the veil is making this opportunity available more often to more people. Universal truth is now flooding the earth plane. Those of us whose hearts and minds are open have already realized the significance of this time, as we awaken to the truths of earthly reality and the illusions fall away.

This piercing of the illusion surrounding the material realm is a necessary step toward the evolution of humanity. This new sight coupled with the great change of cycles sets the stage for a great leap for humankind, for life on earth, and for the planet herself. We humans must take advantage of the gifts of this time. It is up to us to bring about this evolution by working with the energy that is present. It is important that we fine-tune our personal vibrations so that we are aligned with the vibration of universal truth now widely available. We must prepare ourselves to be steady and strong within, as the earth plane undergoes momentous change. We can use this time of change to shape the future of all life on earth. Armed with realizations about the illusions and truths of earthly reality, we can move to establish a new value system, new codes, new standards, and even new rituals here on earth.

Times of great change call for great actions. Let us not fall short of our potential as we face this time of great transition on earth. Let us open ourselves to the truth of this material reality and let this truth guide us as we change our lives and all life on earth.

∞ ∞ ∞

Every time we take action on the earth plane, we are taking a step in the spiral of life. With forethought and guidance, we can make sure that each step is beneficial to our development and to the evolution of the earth. We are approaching a time when every individual action is important to the success of the great transition on this planet. If we truly want the great transformation to bring a new way of being to earth, we must consciously direct our actions to this end. Any actions that lead away from this purpose only weaken our chances of success, and in this case, success means not only the evolution but also the survival of humanity.

As we take each day, one at a time, we must refine our natures and our actions. We must eliminate those acts which necessitate a step down on the spiral, a step away from our purpose. This is important, for every individual human action adds or detracts from the energy available on this planet for a positive and successful transition.

In order to be completely in tune with what actions are positive and helpful to this purpose, we need to examine ourselves, our personalities, our modes of action. This is not an overnight task, but a study that most often takes years. Many of us are seekers and are already moving to improve our lives by refining our natures. Now more specifics are available through guided assistance. We can learn to use every event in our daily lives to help us see ourselves more clearly and to continually improve our way of acting and interacting.

We must act with integrity and with hearts filled with compassion. We must surround all we do with light and love. Never before on this planet has there been a time when individual actions were so important as they are now. Each of us contributes to the actual form and the result of the great transition. The transformation occurs no matter what we do, but the shape that it takes, the events that occur within it, all rest on our actions, so now is the time to examine and refine our modes of action.

∞ ∞ ∞

As the sun rises each day, we can make a new beginning and refine ourselves and our lives even further. The dedication of daily attention is essential to all preparations. We must impress upon all humans the importance of focusing on preparing for the great transition. We must pay attention to the very details of our daily lives, as well as to our values, our beliefs, our outlook, and our goals. Every part of ourselves and our lives on earth must be scrutinized in the light of the new information now flooding onto the material plane.

This information is coming through many channels and can be verified by turning within ourselves, for we hold the core of universal truth within each of us. The many veils, the many illusions surrounding life on earth are being lifted, and a clear picture of the material realm is now available to those who seek to see it.

For starters, we on earth are a part, a very small part, of a gigantic network of realms. We can exist on many levels, each with its own set of experiences. Now we are incarnated in human bodies and are here on earth to undertake the learning process available on the material plane. There is much to learn here. Just grasping how to maintain a healthy human body can prove to take many earth lifetimes. All social interactions and social structures are grounds for our development. In fact, if we are open to it, we can learn and grow from just about everything we encounter on this plane of existence. Unfortunately, the illusions surrounding material reality have clouded many a mind. For instance, many use their earthly incarnations to pursue material wealth at the expense of others and of the planet. Some use violence as a means of obtaining what they want. Some manipulate and use others for their own gain or pleasure. All of these are futile acts, for they harm those who do them far more than we humans have ever before realized. It is now time for humanity to see the big picture, that is the workings of the universe beyond this one tiny realm we call earth. Once we do, we can change our lives on earth with enthusiasm and determination.

∞ ∞ ∞

Every time we go forth and act on this material plane, we affect the vibrations of the planet. It does not matter how insignificant the action may be; the effect, though subtle, still exists. Humanity must realize that the actions we take are the imprints we make during our lifetimes. Our actions are the measure of how we have evolved throughout our various incarnations. Careless acts, thoughtless acts, reckless acts may make very undesirable marks not only on the fabric of our own lives but also on the earth. The repercussions of selfish acts go far beyond the brief moment in which they are done.

Our thoughts, our words, our actions are ours here on the earth plane. We have free will to think, to speak, to do what we choose. This is the challenge of this realm of existence. We must learn that our thoughts, words, and especially actions have far-reaching effects. We must learn the value of compassionate thoughts, loving words, and selfless acts. If we do not grasp the significance of this, we have little hope of utilizing the opportunity now available to us through the great change of cycles.

The new opening in the veil is helping us see many truths. The truth concerning our actions on the earth plane is a very important one, for it is through our actions that we not only survive the great transition, but also vastly improve our way of being on this planet.

The time of preparation leads us to the threshold of the great transformation. We must prepare so thoroughly that we are free of careless actions and inappropriate responses. Many of us now incarnated are working on clearing ourselves of past patterns. It is time for us to make new patterns not only in our personal lives but on the planet, too. These patterns must include the automatic response of love and compassion toward ourselves, toward others, and toward the earth. We must be able to respond in a selfless manner, for it is through acts of selfless service that we can establish a new way of being on earth.

∞ ∞ ∞

Every human incarnated upon the earth is experiencing the rapidly increasing vibration of the planet. We can all feel this within ourselves and see it reflected in events all around us. The reality of the great transformation is upon us. We must prepare ourselves to let go of the past and all that is associated with the past. Those who insist on clinging to old, outmoded structures may suffer a great deal. It is best if we prepare for a time of incredible flux during which the old ways crumble away. The most suitable approach is joy and excitement. We are establishing a new way of being on earth! We are laying the foundation for a huge new cycle thousands of years in length! How we proceed must necessarily affect humanity for hundreds of generations to come. Our responsibility is great indeed.

Since it is useless to cling to the past, we must turn our faces toward the new cycle. We must open our hearts and minds to the possibilities of the time. A combination of forces and events offer us humans powerful tools for entering this huge new cycle and laying the groundwork. The natural cycle of the earth has brought us to this great transition, allowing great changes to occur all over the globe. Those that watch over us and guide us from beyond the veil are sending us much assistance now. New information and energy are flooding the earth plane. We have all the help we need to realize the incredible potential of this time of change. We need to first access this information, and, second, we need to put it to use, for if we do not act upon the guidance that is given to us, the great potential of this transition does not manifest.

Our actions are what carry us through the intense changes and establish the new way of being on earth. Our actions can lead us to a great golden age on this planet. We can move into a time when we see through the illusions which have hindered and blocked us in the past. We can, through our actions, initiate a time of harmony between the earth and humanity which lasts for centuries.

∞ ∞ ∞

Every day we are one step closer to the great transformation. Once we realize this, we also know that not one single day must be lost as we begin preparations. Each day we must take some time to focus on the great transition and what we can do to prepare. Soon we begin to incorporate changes into our daily lives. Soon we find we are evolving toward a new way of being as we ready ourselves and our lives for the great changes on this material plane.

All personal preparations must be made with guided help from within. We cannot pretend to know the details of appropriate preparation. We must rely on the new information flooding the earth plane which we can verify by turning within. Also, our guides and helpers can give us specifics which apply only to ourselves as we move to make changes in our personal lives. The inner connection to the core of universal truth within each of us and to our spirit helpers on adjoining planes is of the utmost importance. Once we have established this connection, we have all the help and all the detailed information we need to make appropriate personal preparations.

This connection can be made more easily by some people than by others, but it is available to everyone. We must not be discouraged if we do not achieve telepathic communication immediately. Our brains are learning to operate in new ways, and this often takes a little time and effort. If we sincerely seek guided help, if we pray consistently for it, this assistance comes to us. If we allow ourselves some time each day for quiet and meditation, we are well on our way.

Guided help comes to each of us in different ways, but the information, whether it comes in the form of words, pictures, or strong feelings, is meant to assist us in our personal preparations. The stronger our telepathic connections, the clearer and more exact the information can be. Each day we can use this valuable assistance to understand the changes and refine our lives.

∞ ∞ ∞

Every time we turn our thoughts and actions toward the great changes, we change ourselves. We humans change and evolve as a natural process. Now it is time to take conscious action as to exactly how we change. It is a simple process, really, for whatever we hold in our hearts and minds, we become. We need only be consistent in what we think and feel, and we see our beings evolve accordingly.

Now we have important reasons to undertake conscious change. The well-being of the planet and the human race depends on our concerted efforts to affect conscious change. The time is now to begin filling ourselves with thoughts and feelings that help to prepare us for the great transformation.

Once we realize that we have this control, that we can change our energy and our very cells, we must not hesitate. We must undertake a daily program that addresses the changes we wish to make in ourselves. We must be very clear about where we are headed before we begin. We must be prepared to be very thorough and to persevere, for daily attention is essential.

If we wish to change our cells so that they may vibrate at a higher rate as the planet is doing, if we wish to adequately prepare ourselves for the great transition, then we must fill ourselves with appropriate thoughts and emotions. The emotions of love and compassion carry the highest vibration and are most valued. We can learn to transmute other lower emotions into love and compassion. Our minds must hold a trust of the universe, an openness to guidance, and a willingness to serve. We can achieve a deep understanding of ourselves, of others, and of the time by being open to the guided help that is available. We can solidify all thoughts and emotions through our actions of selfless service.

Conscious change does take time, which is why we who write this book urge all humans to begin now. With daily application, we can all see and feel the changes, and the joy accompanying these changes.

∞ ∞ ∞

All is well when we pause and open ourselves to that which is around us. We can only live each moment one at a time. True harmony can be had by experiencing whatever each moment brings to us. If we are open, we find the present brings us exactly what we need. This may sound too simple, but it is one of the truths of earthly reality. With all the talk of preparation for the great transition, we must not lose our ability to experience each moment. The present is important, for it is in the present that we exercise our free will. Each moment we live, we think, we feel, we act, and in doing so we possibly change our vibration and perhaps our direction, too. This is all part of the wonder and the illusion of life on earth. We are given a sense of time as a tool. We can remember the past, and we can project our thoughts to the future, but we can only think, feel, and act in the present. It is how we deal with each moment that makes our mark in earth life.

If we accept the value of the present moment, we can more easily let go of the past, and we are, perhaps, less anxious about the future. It is true that whatever we need for the present moment is available to us. All we need to do is open ourselves. We must first realize that what we desire and what we think we need may not always be what we actually do need at that moment. Once we accept this, we can be open to the truth within ourselves and to whatever outer earthly reality brings to us. Once we open our eyes to this way of seeing, we may be amazed at the wealth of information that surrounds us. We are speaking here of tuning to the subtleties of life, for there are layers of them to observe. Sometimes an occurrence in the outer world triggers an inner experience, for our outer and inner worlds are really one. We may begin to notice that our inner struggles are surprisingly addressed by what comes to us on the outer earth plane. If we relax and open ourselves, we find that all we need to address any issue is available to us in each moment, in each breath.

∞ ∞ ∞

Every moment, every breath, we determine how we act or react. Sometimes our actions stem from conscious thought, sometimes from subconscious patterns. Whichever may be the case, it is our will, our self-determination that spurs the action. It is important for us humans to understand that we do indeed decide, whether consciously or subconsciously, what we think, what we feel, and what we do.

Sometimes subconscious patterns trigger certain reactions in us. It may seem as though we have little if any control over these reactions. We can change these subconscious patterns if we wish to do so. We must first clearly recognize the patterns that we wish to change. We observe all the details and intricacies of this pattern. We pray with sincerity for help in altering this pattern. Next we choose either words or pictures as our vehicle for change. We describe in words the positive result of the change we wish to make, or we picture the positive change in our patterns.

It is essential that we describe or picture the positive end result of our efforts to alter our subconscious patterns. We must write or visualize the way we wish ourselves to be. We must be thoughtful and careful in doing this. Once we have the words or the picture, we simply connect with them on a daily basis. We just spend a few moments each day repeating the words or clearly visualizing the picture. In approximately one month, we notice that our subconscious patterns are altered in the way we wish them to be.

We are approaching a crucial time period during which we must be able to rely on both our conscious and subconscious reactions. Every breath, every moment, we must be striving for positive change upon the planet. In order to do this, we must be free of unnecessary, harmful, detrimental actions and reactions. Our wills must be focused on positive change for all humans and for the earth, and all actions, conscious or subconscious, that interfere with this must be weeded out. We have self-determination, it is true. Now we must use it constructively, for it is up to us to effect a positive transformation on this planet.

∞ ∞ ∞

Every day we face challenges in our earth lives. These tests and problems take on a much different perspective once we see them in relation to the changes that are occurring on the earth as a whole. Some of our troubles may then seem insignificant, but others come forward as important life challenges that we must face before we can move forward. It is essential that we deal with these life challenges as we prepare for the great transformation.

As we prepare, we open ourselves to a new way of being on earth. In every case, our personal challenges must be met and dealt with before we can undertake this new way of being. We must not let any problem slide by. We must examine every challenge and take appropriate action. It is not that we must solve or eliminate every problem. We must simply be aware of our challenges and be prepared to change with this awareness in mind.

We are constantly moving to refine our natures. We must be cognizant of our areas of challenge as we do this. This is not to say we dwell on them. We recognize our personal challenges, we accept that they exist, but we hold in our hearts and minds that which we wish to become. In this way, we are moving toward a new way of being without becoming bogged down by our problems and without ignoring them either.

It is important that we possess both recognition of our challenges and a sincere desire to change and move on. We must not be discouraged, for it takes many years to evolve into a new way of being. We are moving. We do change.

Our personal transformation goes hand in hand with the transition occurring on earth. We are, after all, a part of the entire great picture. As we tune to the events, the changes, the vibration of the times, we can sense what needs to be addressed in our own lives. We can see how we need to change in order to move toward a new way of being.

∞ ∞ ∞

Every day as we move closer to the great transformation, we refine our natures so that we may be ready. There is more to do than prepare ourselves individually, although this is the important first step. We must make circles of preparation around us. In other words, our families, our neighbors, our friends must also become aware of the needs of the time. We can make these circles of preparation in many ways. We begin by setting an example, by changing and refining our own lives. During this process, we shower love and compassion on those within these circles. We serve them with joy in our hearts. In many cases, these friends, neighbors, and family members ask us about the changes they see in us. This is an opening for us to pass along information such as that which is contained in this book. For those who do not approach us and ask, they may be gently encouraged to turn within for solace and stability as the events on earth move quickly, and all seems to be in flux. Some may feel devastated as the old order crumbles and begins to pass away. We can offer comfort and hope. We must always be ready to serve whomever crosses our path. Those within our circles merit special attention, for we interact with them more often or they live close by. By serving our family, friends, and neighbors with light and love, we construct important circles which protect them as well as ourselves in these times of upset and chaos. If we extend the vibration of love to all around us so that it exists in all our lives, our neighborhood is protected.

As we continually examine and refine our individual natures, we must begin to manifest these changes in our everyday lives on earth. Now that we are aware of the need for these circles of preparation, we can begin slowly to make them. Our actions must be consistent and filled with love. We must remember, no matter how much we meditate and prepare ourselves individually, our actions out on the earth plane are what make the difference.

∞ ∞ ∞

Although this truth may be uncomfortable, we always get exactly what we need each moment of earth life. We must begin to view our earth lives in terms of the underlying universal truths. Once we do this, we recognize that what we desire and what we think we need are not always what we truly need for the growth of our spirits. For numerous centuries, those who have inhabited the earth have been caught up in the pursuit of material gain. This quest for material wealth still drives many humans. It is time to shatter the illusion that wealth on earth comes from material possessions. The truth is that accumulation of material objects increases our challenges on earth. Conversely, giving material possessions away to others brings us ease on our path. It must be mentioned here that this is true only when we give sincerely and without expectations of return.

Of course, there must be a balance in our lives. We must have certain basics in order to live in the material realm. We speak here of those who are driven to accumulate material wealth and who place much value on physical possessions. If we are tuned to the truth, we know that lasting wealth on the earth plane comes from the refinement of our natures, the growth of our spirits, the evolution of our souls.

Achieving the balance between the material and the spiritual during our lives on earth is one of the greatest challenges we face as humans. There are several ways we can meet this challenge day by day. We can keep in our hearts and minds that which is true and lasting wealth, wealth that goes beyond the material realm. We can practice generosity and selfless service. If we are willing to give some of what we possess to others, we begin to experience the wealth of spirit. Finally, each time we desire something material, let us picture ourselves giving it away to someone else.

∞ ∞ ∞

Every day as we move closer to the great transition, we have opportunities to prepare for the changes. These opportunities come in many forms, some deep within us, some in the outer world of earth life. We have the opportunity every day to go within ourselves to affect lasting changes. These changes range from refining our natures to actually altering the cells of our bodies. These deep inner changes cannot happen all at once, but must occur slowly and steadily over time. That is why we often speak of daily attention, for it is through conscious application every day that we make such deep and thorough changes in ourselves. The same holds true for the changes we wish to make in our interactions with others on the earth plane. Daily attention is needed to make sure of thorough and proper change. We must make sure we clear ourselves of resentment, jealousy, revenge, selfishness, and other reactions which hold us in low vibratory patterns.

The overall goal for all changes and preparations is to raise our personal vibration. We do this by filling ourselves and surrounding ourselves every day with the highest possible vibrations, those of love, compassion, understanding, and forgiveness. We change our very cells so that they may more easily vibrate at this higher rate. We refine our natures so that we may spontaneously act and react with love and compassion in our daily lives. Each day we must take a little time in prayer and meditation to consciously move toward these changes. Each day we must try to apply these changes and refinements to our actions on the earth plane. We must not be discouraged. Such changes take time, but they do come through daily application. Let every instance when we fall short be a motivating force. We analyze, we refine, we pray for help and guidance, and then we do much better next time. We pay attention every day to these changes and preparations.

∞ ∞ ∞

Every day, every breath, as we move closer to the great transformation, we have opportunities to improve our natures through serving others. Our dedication to selfless service makes the difference as chaos increases on the earth plane. Many prophecies have spoken of this great transition and its ramifications for the human race. This book has been transcribed so that all humans are aware of the possibilities of this time of great change. We must be totally aware not only of the opportunities for a positive transformation to a new way of being on earth, but also of the disastrous consequences that may occur if we do not pay attention to what needs to be done. We can surely imagine the violence that could occur and the harm that could come to every human alive if these great changes are not taken seriously and proper preparations made. The greater the number of people who are made aware of this approaching transition, the greater are our chances for positive change during this important time. As we spread the knowledge of this great transformation, we must emphasize the opportunity for an incredible positive step for humanity. Hope and joy must be in our hearts and on our lips as we speak of the great changes. Yet we must not neglect to talk of the seriousness of the time and the importance of proper preparation. It does not take much to imagine what could happen in a time of global chaos if we humans do nothing to improve our ways. On the other hand, if many people upon this planet understand the demands of the time and are willing to prepare and to change, then we open the door to a new era on earth.

As we prepare, the most basic change we must make is to incorporate selfless service into our daily lives. We must make this a part of our very natures to the point of automatically responding to all situations by thinking of the needs of others. We put our own needs and desires aside and actively help all those around us. If many people proceed with this selfless approach, we assure that the changes are positive.

∞ ∞ ∞

In times of great change, chaos and confusion are natural and are not harmful in and of themselves. We humans must prepare ourselves so that our automatic reactions are filled with love and compassion. This means deep inner change for many of us. So often we react from guilt or fear or anxiety or insecurities that lie buried deep within us. We must begin to change this now, so that when we are called into action, we automatically move to serve others with love and compassion in our hearts.

It is up to each of us to prepare ourselves in this way. This deep inner change takes time, which is why we must begin now to alter our old patterns. The very survival of the human race on earth depends upon many of us understanding these changes!

When the material realm is in great flux and there is much chaos and confusion, we may not often have time to think and analyze what we should do. We must be ready to react automatically from our hearts. We must be so full of love, compassion, understanding, and forgiveness that we have not a moment of hesitation. We move directly to serve whoever needs our help.

If many of us are prepared to act selflessly, we can use the opportunity brought by the great transition to establish a marvelous new way of being on earth. The vibrational field of the human race can be raised to new heights by our selfless actions. Those who have not prepared cannot help but be influenced by the love and compassion that pours from those of us who are ready to serve in this way.

As the old structures and old ways crumble, we all can be swept up in the rapid changes. Those of us who are prepared can use the fluctuating situations to help raise the vibration and the awareness of those who are lost and confused. If we know basically what to expect, and we have prepared ourselves thoroughly, we can be calm and strong, and we can be a solace to many in times of great change.

∞ ∞ ∞

We must be very thorough in all our preparations. We must do nothing less than revolutionize our lives on earth in the face of the great transition. If we have thoroughly changed ourselves and our lives, we can flow easily in times of great change. We can be strong and centered while others who have clung to the old ways are seized with confusion and panic.

There are many reasons why we must work daily toward a complete inner transformation. The challenges come quickly and forcefully as events on earth continue to speed up. We must be so thoroughly prepared that no occurrence, no matter how devastating, shocks us and throws us off balance. This is no easy feat, for we are facing a time when the entire structure of life on earth which has been built up for thousands of years is completely dismantled. We must build a new structure within ourselves based on universal truth, love, compassion, and forgiveness.

This new inner structure offers many benefits to those of us who build it and to those around us whom we serve. The very vibration of our beings increases so that we are in tune with the changes occurring on earth. We can radiate harmony even in times of great chaos. Our presence is calming and reassuring to others, and therefore they flock to us for comfort and help. While others may view the destruction of the old order with horror, we approach each day with hope and joy. Our attitude is infectious, and soon others also see that the changes are ushering in a great new cycle for earth.

Those of us who persevere with sincerity and dedication upon this path of thorough preparation have access to guided help through firmly established channels. This guided help is indispensable. Our spirit guides can help us know exactly when to be where and what words and actions are appropriate. We must have the patience and discipline to take the time and to pay attention every day to the changes we must make within ourselves. Our own transformation must first be complete.

∞ ∞ ∞

As the new millennium progresses, most humans realize that great change is facing the planet. Many feel that all is out of control. Events roll along so quickly that there is no time for planning and analyzing. This is why we must pay attention to that which we can control: our individual selves. We can control our thoughts, our feelings, our actions, even the makeup of the cells of our bodies. This control of self can be learned, but this learning takes time and patience. We must be gentle and loving with ourselves as we clear our beings of unwanted, unnecessary, detrimental thoughts, feelings, actions, and reactions. We must proceed one step at a time so that all our inner changes are thorough and proper. Because this deep inner change takes time, we must begin this process now. Many have begun, and many more must start if we are to be prepared for the times that are out of control. We must always keep in mind that this is a joyful process. We are honing our natures. We are increasing the very vibration of our beings. We slowly, thoroughly, systematically clear ourselves of all thoughts, feelings, and actions that hold lower vibrations, such as greed, jealousy, and violence. We consciously move to rebuild every cell in our bodies with the higher vibration of light and love. In this way, we have control. We no longer react in ways that are hurtful to ourselves or others. This slow, controlled changing of our individual selves is one of the most important steps in preparation for the great transition. The more of us who take the steps to be prepared in this way, the better are our chances for a positive transformation.

The human race has the opportunity now to take an incredible evolutionary step. It is, however, up to each of us to exercise the control we have here on earth over our individual selves. We may not be able to control events on the planet, but we can change ourselves, and this ability makes the difference in times of great transition.

∞ ∞ ∞

In these times of great change, we must not only prepare ourselves thoroughly, we must also be open to guidance every moment of every day. In this way, we know how to proceed even in the most confusing and chaotic situations. As we prepare and change ourselves, we also develop our abilities to connect with guided help. This is an important and necessary step in our preparation. As we refine ourselves and raise our personal vibrations, we increase the possibility of directly receiving guidance. Each of us receives this guided help in the way that suits us best. If we are visually oriented, pictures and images flash in our minds providing direct guidance. If we are drawn to words and music, then we hear our guides speaking to us in our minds. We need to develop whichever connection is best for us so that we can turn inward for guided assistance whenever we need it.

In times of great transition, we cannot rely on the old structures of society to give us support, for they are crumbling away. We must turn within and then we can receive all the strength, support, and direct guidance we need. If we have developed and firmly established our inner channels for guided help, we can call on our guides at any time for assistance. We need only have prepared the way and proceed to seek all guidance with sincerity in our hearts. There are much comfort and joy in our inner connections to guided help. Taking the time to cultivate these direct communications is one of the most rewarding practices we undertake in our entire lifetimes. The love that we share through the veil with our guided helpers is beyond anything we can imagine.

We must open ourselves to the possibilities that exist. We must work to raise our personal vibrations, and we must pray each day that direct connections be made. With patience and trust, with sincerity, we move with certainty toward a direct, working, loving relationship with our guides. They are eager and ready to help us. We need only open and reach out to them. They are there.

∞ ∞ ∞

All is well when we trust the universe, for there is an eternal order beyond our knowing. Even when we are confused and upset by events on earth, we can reach deep inside ourselves to find the strength and stability inherent in the universal order.

We can learn much by viewing and analyzing the events in our lives. If we look carefully and analyze with an open mind, then we can see that certain issues and challenges have been brought to us again and again so that we might learn and grow from them. We are given free will on this earth plane. We can choose how we handle these issues and challenges within a larger universal framework. We choose our attitude, our approach, our actions. We have a certain potential to evolve. If we ignore the issues and challenges that life on earth brings to us, or if we mishandle them, then we meet them again and again until we learn, grow, and evolve.

The universe can and does embrace both the structure of fate on a larger scale and the random element of free will on a smaller scale. This universal truth is reflected in many areas of life on earth. We can see this truth in the unfolding of our personal growth on the earth plane. We can see this truth in the makeup of an atom where there is a certain set structure but there also exists the random behavior of the electron.

We can be assured that the universal truths we speak of in these writings permeate all aspects of our sphere and others. Once we learn and understand the certain universal truths that apply directly to our incarnations on the earth plane, we can construct a set of values for ourselves that is solid and stable. Once we base our lives on these values, we achieve an inner stability and strength that can carry us through even the most upsetting times. This larger understanding makes the difference as we change and refine ourselves and our lives. We need to constantly seek the truths inherent in the universal order and apply these truths to all aspects of our lives.

∞ ∞ ∞

Every day, as we move closer to the great transformation, we find more and more we can do to prepare. As we examine each aspect of ourselves and our lives on earth, we see what is appropriate and what must go. Each day we realize with clearer vision the direction we must take in order to extricate ourselves from the bonds of the old structures of society. We need not focus on eliminating the old ways as much as we must concentrate on filling ourselves with new values, new priorities, and new practices. The old values naturally fall away in the light of the new ways we embrace.

We can use breathing to clear ourselves. Breath is one of the most useful tools we have to clear away all that is unnecessary and unwanted. We can use the balanced breath and the alternative breath on a daily basis to slowly, thoroughly clear our beings of the old ways, the old values, the old structures. At the same time, we draw into our beings the higher vibration of light and love. Just a few moments each day of simple breathing exercises can keep us moving toward a new way of being. If we establish a daily pattern or routine in which we take the time to sit quietly and clear ourselves with the breath, we automatically build new structures to replace the old.

Over time, we notice the differences. We see what is falling away and is no longer of any importance in our lives. We see what is coming into focus as most important to us.

The new value system based on love, compassion, forgiveness, and respect for the spirit in all things is coming to the forefront on the earth plane. This value system is the basis for our new way of being on this planet. It is time for us to fill ourselves with these new values and let the dictates of the old society pass away. If we wish to prepare, if we wish to be attuned to the great changes, we must begin by changing our personal inner structures. In this way, we flow joyfully into the new time.

∞ ∞ ∞

Although it may not seem so on earth, all is well in the universe. The universe is vast and beyond our knowing. However, it is time for humans to catch a glimpse of what lies beyond our earthly reality. We have for too long been cloaked in the illusion that what we experience on earth is all there is. Now the way is open for those who are incarnated on earth to see beyond the illusion. We need only be open to the knowledge that is now pouring onto the material plane from beyond the veil surrounding earthly reality. Our openness is very important, for if we are closed to the possibilities that exist in the universe, we have little chance of receiving this knowledge. It is best to take a deep breath and admit that there is much beyond the small sphere with which we are familiar. Once we have done this, we have opened the way to expand our knowledge of the universe.

The knowledge that is now flooding onto the earth plane is appropriate for the time. It is a valuable gift. At last we humans can grasp the significance of earth life as seen against the greater backdrop of universal truth. This knowledge alone can change our approach to our earthly incarnations, for once we see our human existence in relation to the universal order, we know what is important and what is not.

We humans who are incarnated now must take this new perspective to heart and let it change our lives. The knowledge is here now for a reason. Our expanded view of the universe is essential if we are to proceed in the appropriate way. Once we obtain this knowledge, this greater view, we can no longer cling to our old ideas and ways. We let them pass away, just as the decade, the century, and the millennium pass away. It is time to fill ourselves with the light, the love, the joy, the understanding that this knowledge brings. Now we can eliminate fear of death. Now we can trust the universal flow while understanding and exercising our free will here on earth. All is well. The time is here for us to know this, to feel this, and to rejoice in a new way of being on earth.

∞ ∞ ∞

People incarnated on earth at this time face a tremendous challenge, but it is a challenge we can rise to meet. Every day more of us humans realize our psychic potential, more begin to use the telepathic connections available to us, more become aware of the significance of the time. It is an exceptional time on earth, for the evolution of humanity is at hand. One way or another, the great transformation does occur on earth. The results of this great transition are dependent on the actions of those of us now on this planet.

A sparkling new ray of light, of hope, of knowledge has pierced the veil surrounding earthly reality. This ray shines equally upon all humans. Each of us must be open and receptive to this new ray in order to gain the benefits it brings. Those of us who are sincere, who seek to improve the ways on earth, those of us who take quiet meditation time each day are probably already aware of this new ray of energy. This new ray is available to all. We need only go within ourselves to seek our connection to it.

The gifts brought to the earth plane by this new ray are greater than anything humanity has known before now. We at last have the ability to see our earth lives in the perspective of the vast workings of the universe. We at last have direct access to all the universal truths that apply to our earthly existence. We at last have the opportunity to consciously communicate through the veil in order to receive guided assistance. These are great steps indeed for humanity.

The most beautiful part of all this is that these gifts are available to everyone. We need not be a priest or a guru to obtain the knowledge this new ray brings to earth. We need only be sincere in our hearts and take the time to go within ourselves to make the necessary connection. Of course, patience and perseverance are necessary. The rewards are great. We must be ready to set our feet upon a new path, for the knowledge brought by this ray shatters the illusions of the past and clears the way for a bright new future for earth.

∞ ∞ ∞

Ever since we humans first inhabited the earth, we have had a purpose in being here. This purpose is simply this: to evolve spiritually while dealing with the challenges of the material realm. Throughout the centuries, there has been guidance available to us in order to help us tune to this greater purpose. This guidance has come in many forms. Many religions all over the world are based on these various forms of guidance.

Now is the time for a great evolutionary step for humanity. The guidance that comes now to earth can potentially light each human being from the inside. This means that we can move beyond belief. We can know within ourselves the truths inherent in the universe. We can move beyond faith and trust in our priests, gurus, and other spiritual leaders. We can trust the knowledge and the light within ourselves. We have access to divine knowledge. We need only go deep within ourselves.

We need, however, to learn to trust ourselves and the connections we make to universal truth and knowledge. This may sometimes be quite difficult to do. We humans have many obstacles that may prevent our access to the core of universal truth within each of us. It is up to each of us individually to search ourselves, to delve deep into the darker sides of our natures, and to bring to light any facet of our personalities which may hinder our progress. The process takes perseverance and a willingness to look at, examine, and accept our shadowy sides. We must proceed in this way in order to establish clear connections to the universal truths and the guidance that is available to each of us. If we do not deal with our personal shadows, if we shun them, avoid them, or push them away, they most certainly hinder our evolution. We must be willing to bring the darker aspects of our natures into the light. Once these shadows are identified and embraced, they no longer interfere.

∞ ∞ ∞

People incarnated now upon the earth have a great opportunity and a great responsibility. We who dwell now upon the earth plane must usher humanity into a new cycle and a new way of being. This is a great task with great rewards. We need not feel overwhelmed or alone when faced with such responsibility. We have been blessed with new gifts which can help us and guide us through this great transformation.

This book explains these new gifts and how we can and must use them. It is time for all humans to have direct conscious contact through the veil surrounding material reality. This gift of direct communication has never before been available on such a wide scale. Along with this gift of direct contact comes the gift of blessed assistance from those who dwell in associated realms. These spirit guides and, in some cases, angel helpers are ready to help us face the incredible challenges that come with the great transition. We are blessed with all the guidance and assistance we need in these times of great change.

Through our direct contact with spirit helpers, we can obtain the gift of a new perspective on earth life. We can at last ascertain the purpose of earthly existence. We can at last grasp the universal truths that form the framework for our experiences on earth. These are indeed very great gifts.

Great also is our task, for we must do nothing less than transform our beings and in doing so transform all life on earth. The great transition occurs regardless of our desires or actions. However, we can work with the changes happening on the planet to bring about this new way of being on earth. We must open ourselves to the incredible potential of the time. We must adapt and prepare ourselves, making use of our new gifts.

These writings are here now to help make all aware of our new opportunities and challenges. The verification for all that is written here can be had by going within and making that direct connection through the veil to the universal truth and guidance which is now available to all on earth. No longer need we rely on what others tell us. We can experience this truth and guidance directly. We can know for ourselves. This is a very exciting prospect for humans today.

When we speak of direct contact, we mean exactly that. We each can make direct and conscious contact through the veil to those who are ready, willing, and eager to help us. We are on the threshold of an entirely new phase of earthly existence. It is up to us to take the time and to have the patience and perseverance to establish these conscious connections. We can do this, for the time is right.

The prospect of contacting those in other realms may arouse fear in some of us. There is no need to fear. Those who wait to assist us are filled with light and love. We must, however, clear ourselves of old prejudices, fears, and mistrust, and surround ourselves with love, compassion, forgiveness, and trust in the universe.

∞ ∞ ∞

Blessed are those of us who take these writings to heart and begin to make changes in our lives. Everyone who undertakes the thorough preparations that are called for is guided and helped in every way necessary. The key to achieving a complete personal transformation is steady progress. We need not berate ourselves when we think we are not moving quickly enough. As long as we give daily attention to these inner changes, we move ahead. Sincerity and thoroughness are more important than speed.

Daily focus is essential, for each day we can add another building block to the foundation of our new way of being. Thoroughness is important, for we must examine every detail of our lives. Our natures must be completely scrutinized. Again, we proceed just one step at a time. We do not wish to become overwhelmed and perhaps stymied by the tasks before us. We must realize and accept that this process takes years. If each day we take a deep breath and a small step, we are doing well.

The essentials of our daily focus are outlined in these writings. It is up to each of us to choose our daily program. We need to be comfortable with this program. It must fit into our current life on the material plane. Most probably this program evolves over time as we change and evolve. The basics, however, must remain constant. We need to pray every day with sincerity. We need to find a quiet time and space every day in which to meditate. Daily breathing exercises and visualizations are also important and extremely helpful.

We can tailor these basics to our current needs and situations, but we simply must attend to these practices every day. It is up to us to fit them into our earthly schedule. Soon we may find that our earthly schedule is based on and around our daily devotional practices!

As our personal transformation proceeds, we watch our values, our habits, our very thoughts and feelings change. As a result, the earth life around us also changes. We can rejoice in that our evolution is part of the great transformation on earth.

∞ ∞ ∞

Every time we offer up a prayer with sincerity, we are heard. Every time we pray for help with our personal transformations, our way is made a bit clearer. Every day as we rededicate ourselves and refine ourselves a little more, we move closer to the time when our personal transformations are complete. We must not be discouraged by events in the material realm nor by our own shortcomings. We must have a new outlook. We must view any hindrances as tools to help us.

Each time we encounter a challenge which throws us off balance, we must not let this problem deter us from our path. Instead, we face and examine the challenge and ask how we may learn from it. Often the very situation we need to spur our spiritual growth and move us toward our personal transformation comes to us in the form of a problem or hindrance. This is why we must learn to value these challenges, for without them we would not make sufficient progress.

When facing an upsetting problem, one that stirs our emotions, we must first work through and transform the feelings surrounding the problem. Only then can we gain a perspective on this challenge and see it in terms of our spiritual unfolding. As long as we are immersed in the emotions of the situation, we go around and around over the same ground. If we follow the procedure outlined here, we can turn any problem situation into an opportunity for spiritual growth and an occasion for rejoicing.

When the challenge arises and we are engulfed in the emotions it brings, we begin by experiencing the feelings as deeply and as totally as we can. We must not avoid the emotions involved, for they are a valuable aid to us. Often we can use visualizations to help us identify the feelings. We must go deep to the root of the feelings.

Once we know we have contacted our emotions concerning the issue, we move to transform them. Again, visualizations along with breathing exercises are valuable tools. We picture the emotion with form, color, movement. We see the feeling vividly in our mind. We consciously move to place all our emotions into this visualization. Once we have done this, we are ready to transform this picture by surrounding it with whirling gold and white light. We can feel the heaviness of the emotion lift off of us as we breathe deeply and spin the visualization ever faster until it is a whirling globe of brilliant light. Once we have cleared the emotion from around the problem, we can see much more clearly what the situation is and what needs to be done.

As we progress in our personal transformations, we find we face deeper and more profound challenges, some which date back to former incarnations. This deep cleansing work is essential. We must face every personal challenge we hold within us before our transformations near completion. This work may at times seem endless, but we need not despair. We have much help and guidance as we undertake this sacred work. We need only ask for help. Our sincere prayers are powerful. They activate the forces of the universe to help lift us out of the shadows and into the light.

∞ ∞ ∞

Sacred be these times on earth, for there is more communication between earth and other realms than ever before. A great challenge has been placed squarely in the lap of the human race, but we are not alone in facing this challenge. We have many evolved spirit helpers on our side whose pleasure and duty it is to guide us in these times of change. We humans must realize the significance of these times, for through our spirit helpers we have access to much information that has not before now been widely available. When so much of heaven floods onto the earth plane, the times are sacred indeed.

The knowledge and wisdom that are now permeating the earth plane are so pervasive that even those who try to ignore or block out these gifts cannot help but be affected by them. The vibration of the earth plane is changing and all who dwell in this sphere mu : be affected. We humans cannot deny that we are of the earth; we are bonded; we are linked; we must change as the earth changes. Fortunately for us, these great changes have the potential to be incredibly positive, but it is up to us to make them so. It does not matter how much knowledge, information, and guidance we receive. We must apply this wisdom to our lives on the earth plane or all is for nothing. We humans are the vehicles. We are the ones who can make this great transformation on earth usher in a golden age for humanity, a new way of being on the planet. It is up to us. We must accept this challenge seriously and joyfully.

Our spirit helpers smile and rejoice whenever we apply their guidance to our daily lives. We are then actualizing our potential in these times of great change. We now have available, through our guides, all the information, all the help we need to deal with every facet of our changing lives on earth. We must learn to go deep within ourselves and trust the connections we make. We must trust that the universe is providing all that we need to meet this challenge and realize this opportunity.

∞ ∞ ∞

People who are alive during these times of great change must take heed. We must be aware of what is going on around us and within us. We must watch and listen with vigilant eyes and ears. By fine-tuning our awareness, we can learn a great deal. The knowledge that comes through such attentive observation is profound.

This focused awareness goes hand in hand with increased intuition. As we develop our skills of observation, we also increase our intuitive abilities. We strive to reach a point where we can not only see clearly what is happening, but also respond appropriately.

We can increase our intuitive abilities by carefully watching what goes on within us. We note our feelings and responses. When we find a response that is inappropriate, we have found a key that may unlock much information about ourselves. We can, if we choose to, delve deep into our psyches in this way. We can root out lifetimes of karma through this simple method of observation.

Once we have identified an important life issue, we have taken a giant step. From this point on, we are conscious that our inappropriate actions and reactions are rooted in this issue. We can no longer experience an uncomfortable feeling or react in an out-of-sync manner without the knowledge that this issue is the basis of it all.

Change begins from the moment we identify the karmic issue. Our skills of observation coupled with a desire to change move us forward. Once again it must be stated that prayer is an important, if not essential, tool for helping us process these life issues. If we pray sincerely that we wish to be released from these karmic challenges, we open the way. We move forward, however slowly.

All is well when we search within ourselves for the truth of any situation. Events that occur all around us may show us much, but the truth lies within. We need only be aware of this fact, and then observe how universal truth manifests in our lives.

∞ ∞ ∞

Upon the earth plane, we must always deal with physical reality and the challenges this brings. We must, however, refrain from getting so caught up in these challenges that we lose our greater perspective. When earthly worries and troubles press down upon us, we must pray to be released from their blinding grip. Once we regain a more universal perspective, our challenges do not seem as overwhelming and we more often see a way to begin to meet them. This sounds simple, and so it is. Sincere prayer can lift the cloud of troubles which fogs our path. We then see clearly how to proceed. Through our sincere prayers, we invite holy assistance. We can take comfort in the fact that we do not have to face our earthly challenges alone. We have help. Sometimes this help arrives whether or not we ask for it, but it most certainly arrives if we do.

Of course, it is up to us to initiate a course of action which moves us to work through our earth challenges. We can receive guidance as to how to proceed, but it is up to us to act, to put this guidance to use. We can receive vibrations which strengthen us and help us see our path clearly, but it is up to us to take the necessary steps to move forward on this path.

Earthly troubles can indeed overwhelm us, and when they do, we feel helpless and lost. Inviting guidance through prayer and centering ourselves through meditation are the two most useful and effective ways to meet our problems. Often our challenges run deep and there are no simple straightforward solutions. We can only move forward one step at a time, one moment at a time. We need, however, to be certain that each step is well placed on the road to resolving our earth challenges.

Also, we need to take a deep breath and to not be impatient with ourselves. Our earthly challenges are complex and not easily unraveled. Through sincere prayer and daily meditation, we cannot help but proceed in the correct way.

∞ ∞ ∞

One millennium ends; another begins. It is the turning point of the ages. Those of us who are fortunate enough to be incarnated at this time witness much. We can now witness with more than just our physical senses, for we now have the ability to reach through the veil surrounding material reality. We can now consciously have experiences which reach beyond the earth plane. This is part of our new way of being on earth.

These experiences can take us to the other realms which surround the earth plane and even farther. Such travel takes preparation. We must know beforehand in general what to expect. Otherwise such experiences may be unsettling, even frightening.

The first step is the realization that our physical bodies stay planted on the earth plane. This is where we are incarnated now, so it is to earth and to our physical bodies that we return. The second step is becoming acquainted with our etheric and our astral bodies. It is the higher etheric body which can travel to other planes of existence. It is the astral body which can travel on the astral plane here on earth. We can be conscious or unconscious while traveling in our spirit bodies. As our psychic abilities increase, we are able to have more fully conscious experiences while out of our physical bodies and in our spirit forms. The higher etheric body and the astral body are both very real and very luminous. Once we have experienced conscious awareness while out and about in our spirit forms, we get used to the friendly glow of the spirit body.

Movement while out in the astral body is much the same as when we are conscious and moving in our physical bodies. We can, however, do more because we do not have the gravitational pull of earth acting upon the astral form. We can leap and even fly when in our astral bodies, which can be very exhilarating experiences!

Once we humans can consciously travel in our higher etheric bodies on a regular basis to other realms, we develop an entirely new perspective on earth life. Our limited scope is expanded. We know for certain that there is much that exists beyond the earth plane. We have access to knowledge and experiences which cannot be had while bound by our physical bodies on the material plane.

∞ ∞ ∞

Only once in many centuries do this great transformation and this great opportunity come to earth. We are very fortunate to be incarnated on earth at this time, for we can witness the change of ages. We must open our eyes, our ears, our hearts, and our minds to the possibilities of the time. If we do not, we lose the one chance for humanity to make a great evolutionary step.

Already many are aware of the unique new energy permeating the earth plane. Already many are tuning to this new energy and increasing their psychic abilities. This new ray of energy does not discriminate. This new energy is available to everyone on earth at this time. We do, however, need to acknowledge its existence and open ourselves to the knowledge that it brings.

It must be emphasized that increased psychic abilities and increased knowledge of the universe do not often occur for us instantaneously. Most often we open ourselves slowly over an extended period of time. Our physical bodies and our spirit bodies must increase in vibration in order to tune to the gifts of this new ray. Although once in a while an event sparks a dramatic rise in our personal vibrations, more often we slowly raise our vibrational rate through daily breathing exercises, meditation, visualization, and prayer. This slow method is preferred because it is kinder to our bodies. We must often process out much which holds us in the low vibrations, as we move to increase our vibratory rate. This takes time, patience, and persistence, but the results are incredibly rewarding. Often we must choose to eliminate certain practices from our lives, certain characteristics from our natures, the ones which hold us in the low vibrational patterns. This obviously cannot be done overnight, but is often the work of many years.

Still, we can begin today. We can start now by taking the first step. This step is simply acknowledging this new ray of energy and wishing that we might be open to receiving all the gifts it brings.

∞ ∞ ∞

As the change of ages on earth reaches its peak, there is much chaos. Former societies and structures have, at this point, completely disintegrated. Whereas many humans may think that this is a giant setback, in actuality this breakdown is necessary, for the way must be cleared for the new cycle on earth. In order to begin to build again, we must be ready to turn our backs on all that has gone before which no longer applies to the new way of being on earth. We must be clear. Our values must be strong, for we are building the foundation for a new society which may last for many centuries. We must be strong within and dedicated to the new ways.

Very often on earth, we humans become very attached to what we know, to what is familiar. In the time of great change, much that is familiar passes away. We must be prepared to let go. If we attempt to cling to any of the old ways for comfort and security, if we grasp onto objects from the past for comfort, we are only prolonging the agony, for we must eventually let go. We must bless the past and let it be. We need to fill our hearts with love and light and rejoice at the prospect of a great new cycle for the earth.

This is not to say that absolutely nothing carries over to the new cycle. We must be very careful and very clear about what we bring over from the past to make part of the new ways. The opportunity to begin again on such a grand scale does not happen often on earth. That is why the information contained in this book is now being brought onto the material plane. Preparation for this great change is essential. We need compassionate leaders who not only have guided help, but also have a clear vision for this new golden age for earth. These leaders are comforters who have strong inner connections to universal truth and who know what elements of the past are appropriate for the new cycle. This information is here for them and for all who wish to prepare. The more of us who have a clear vision of the new cycle, the more complete and joyous the transition can be.

∞ ∞ ∞

Only once in many thousands of years do we have the opportunity that has come to us now in this time. This time and this opportunity are valuable to the earth and to humanity in many ways. We must increase our awareness so that we can take advantage of every facet of this opportunity. It is best if we waste nothing that is brought to us in this time of change.

Again, we can begin simply by praying that our eyes be opened to the possibilities of the time. During periods of great change, all in the outer world is in flux. If we have inner stability and strength, and a vision of what needs to be done, we can move ahead with confidence. Our inner connections must be strong, and we must listen to the guidance that comes through to us. In this way, we can clearly see how best to proceed so that we can help manifest the most joyous possibilities of the time.

When years of both inner and outer preparation bring us to the point of action, we must not hesitate! We must be ready to step forward. Our appropriate actions are essential for the transformation on earth to be positive and complete. Years of inner and outer preparation hone our skills to the point where we know, either through intuition or through guided help, when to act and what to do. Our inner strength and stability coupled with our outer flexibility help prepare us for whatever situations we encounter. We must be ready and able to adapt, while never losing our center, our inner connection to universal truth.

The most important quality we must exhibit as we step forward into action is compassion. All the leaders of the new cycle must be known as compassionate humans. As the times become more and more chaotic, we begin every day by filling ourselves with compassion so that we may express this to all whom we encounter during the day. We can alleviate much suffering and bring much joy if we proceed in this way. We can radiate light and love to all around us, and help to usher in the great new cycle on earth.

∞　∞　∞

Every day, as we draw closer to the great transformation on earth, we must give thanks for what is being brought to us. As we watch the old order slipping away, we must turn our attention to the new way of being on earth. Our values must shift, just as the earth herself shifts, if the transformation is to be successful and complete. These values are based on universal truths, truths that we can each discover for ourselves through introspection and meditation.

Once we consciously connect with these universal truths, we can give heartfelt thanks that it is time for new ways to be established on earth. This clear vision can help us let go of the past without sorrow and regret. We can, instead, be filled with joy and excitement as we welcome the new ways. It is important that our attitude is joyful and open to the new. There is no possible way we can restore the old structures, and once we recognize the illusions upon which these structures were based, why would we want to? Finally, after centuries upon centuries of greed and violence, we can clearly see that they are useless, and, in fact, detrimental to our purpose on this material plane. Finally we can each connect with the truth of our existence on this planet. Finally we can break through the shroud of illusions that has surrounded earth life for so very long.

The most hopeful and joyous part is that each of us can experience this breakthrough for ourselves. We can *know*. We can make the deep inner connections which pierce the veil and bring us clarity and knowledge. We need not rely on anyone else to tell us. We can do this for ourselves.

As we welcome each day, we also welcome the new ways to earth, and we can give sincere thanks for the many blessings and gifts that are brought to us in this time of great change.

∞ ∞ ∞

The scope of the devastation and chaos during the great transformation may be unprecedented in earth's history. In any event, we must be prepared for such an eventuality. If a great number of us has undertaken personal transformations, then the upset during the time of great change may be lessened. If many of us have made solid inner preparations, then we can be calm and stable in the face of chaos. We can be comforters and helpers to those who are lost in sorrow, anguish, and grief. Some humans may panic to the point of insanity as they watch the old structures and the old way of life crumble all around them. We who are aware of the great significance of the time, we who have prepared to face this change, we must be the leaders. We must shower love and compassion to all who survive the transition and wish to begin anew. Our hearts must be open, the solace that we offer unending. We must never let ourselves feel burdened by this important role. We know we are not alone as we face each task, each situation. We have endless help from beyond the veil. This help is ever-present, always available. This is the reason we must cultivate conscious and direct communication through the veil to our spirit guides and helpers. If these connections are strong, we can access them at any time in any situation. Our guides are there, working with us and through us, helping us radiate love and compassion, helping us say and do what is appropriate for every circumstance. These direct connections to divine assistance lift away any burdens and nullify any tendencies toward martyrdom.

We who step forward to be leaders in this time do have great responsibilities, for our actions make the difference. We can, through our words, feelings, and actions, make this great transition a time of vision, of hope, and of joy. We can show others that humanity is indeed on the threshold of a huge evolutionary leap, and we can lead others to take this leap. We can, with the help of the time, change the world for the better.

∞ ∞ ∞

In times of great change, those of us who would lead all on earth to a new way of being must first be living this new way ourselves. Our example draws many to us, for we radiate love, compassion, kindness, and strength in times of chaos. We must make sure we have solidly adapted ourselves to this new way of being on earth. We must not falter under the pressure of intense changes in the outer world. We must make sure of our inner strength before we step into any leadership role.

The one way we can be certain that we have completely embraced the new ways of being on earth is to undergo a thorough personal transformation. The material in this book provides the information we need in order to do this. We are speaking here of changing the vibration of the entire body, mind, and spirit. We are speaking here of changing the makeup of the very cells of our bodies in order that we may hold at all times the higher vibration of love and compassion. This, of course, takes years of work, but every day of every year can be a joyous one. As we feel the light and love increase in our hearts, our minds, our bodies, we begin to know true joy. We are released slowly but surely from the illusions surrounding life on the material plane which keeps us locked in self-defeating patterns. We have a new vision of life on earth based on universal truth. We know this vision to be true because it comes to us from deep inside ourselves. As we strengthen our inner connections to universal truth, we see even more clearly how to proceed. We recognize each step as it needs to be taken. We feel secure within ourselves that our words and actions are appropriate.

The leaders who take the earth into the new cycle must be transformed so that other humans can see what is possible here on earth. All humans have the potential to undergo this personal transformation, to increase the vibration of their beings, to radiate light, love, compassion, and forgiveness.

We who choose to lead in this time must be impeccable in our actions. We must glow with light and love at all times. This can be achieved by changing the makeup of the body, mind, and spirit through constant attention and prayer. We can indeed reach a point where these desirable qualities are a solid part of our natures, and appropriate words and actions are our automatic responses in all situations.

Although this process of personal transformation takes years to complete, we must daily have a clear vision of who we wish to become. This vision must be a consistent one. We must, day after day, be striving toward the same goals. This book is here to assist all of us in doing so. We can begin by envisioning ourselves as radiant beings, completely lighted with the higher vibration of love. We can feel our connectedness to the universe and the strength this brings to us. We can feel a calm and a security we have never known before on the earth plane. We can feel joy.

∞ ∞ ∞

In times of great change, we must be ready. We must expect the unexpected in the outer world while relying on the links to universal truth within us. All is well when our inner connections are solid and strong. Every one of us who prepares for the transition, every one of us who would lead in these times must concentrate on cultivating strong inner connections. These connections can provide for us what the outer world cannot. We can receive comfort, support, and assistance. We can find peace when all around us is in turmoil. We can find answers to our questions and guidance as to how to proceed. We can receive a clear picture of the whys and wherefores of life on earth, a picture which disperses the veil surrounding material reality and shows us what is truly important as we live our earth lives.

As we can see, our access to these inner channels is extremely important, in fact essential, as we face these times of great change. We must begin now and work daily to improve our connections to these valuable inner channels. We can begin, as always, with a simple prayer that the connections within us to universal truth, love, and guidance be strengthened every day. Our daily meditation is also very important, for it is through deep meditation that we receive guidance, strength, and inner peace. Meditation aligns us with the core of universal truth within us. The benefits of meditation are numerous.

When the outer world confuses us and throws us off balance, we can use breathing to help clear ourselves, center ourselves, and tap into our inner core of strength. The balanced breath alone, performed slowly and deeply, can help align us and raise our vibrational level. As we proceed in strengthening our inner connections, we certainly find using the balanced breath very helpful. Let us also make use of powerful visualizations to assist us in delving even deeper into the rich inner worlds that are available to us.

∞ ∞ ∞

On earth there have always been problems with material resources. Humans have seen ownership of these resources as desirable. This desire has led to actions, sometimes violent actions, and disregard for the earth as well as for other humans. This cannot continue. The ways on earth must change. There may be nothing left to own, nothing left to desire, if we humans do not change our ways on earth.

The time is a crucial one. We are looking into the face of extinction, the extinction of many species on earth including humanity! Surely ownership, accumulation, and greed are not worth the annihilation of all humans as well as many other species from this planet.

Of course, our basic value system must change. Our motivation and our outlook must change. We are speaking of nothing less than a complete transformation of human consciousness. It is now time for this transformation to take place, or there may be nothing but a barren, ruined, lifeless planet with nothing on it worth owning, and, indeed, no one here to be owners.

We can begin only by changing ourselves. We must eliminate greed and violence from our own lives. Also, we must pray every day for the well-being of the planet and for the evolution of human consciousness.

There is much assistance coming to earth now from other realms. All over the globe opportunities for new awareness are being presented to everyone. Many are realizing the futility of this endless struggle for diminishing resources. Some are becoming sick of the violent ways. Peace is now greatly desired by many.

In order to turn the tide, we must use all our personal resources. We must allow and encourage the transformation to occur within ourselves. We must pray sincerely for others and for the earth. We must meditate on a regular basis so that we are calm, centered, and we take appropriate actions in all situations. We must use deep breathing, the alternate breath, the balanced breath, so that we raise our vibrational level and help raise the vibrations of all around us on earth.

∞ ∞ ∞

The turn of the century and the change of millennium bring a speeding up of events on earth. The earth herself is nearing a major turning point in her own cycles. In fact, numerous cycles are reaching points of climactic change. It is a very exciting and challenging time to be incarnated as a human on earth.

As we move through many lifetimes on this material plane as well as in other realms, we are naturally drawn to situations which provide the best opportunities for our evolution and growth. Therefore, we must realize that it is no accident that we are here now on earth to live and lead during this great transformation. The potential for our personal growth as well as for the evolution of humanity as a whole is tremendous in this time of great change. We must seize the opportunity and make the most of it. We must not let it pass us by!

The very reasons for our earthly existence and other mysteries of life are now being revealed to us humans. We all now have the ability to *know* why we are here on earth and what we must do to make the most of it. This knowledge may at first come from an outer source such as this book, but can always be verified by going to the core of truth deep within each of us. We need not rely on what others tell us, for we carry universal truths inside ourselves. We need only make and solidify our connections to these universal truths.

Once we are aware of the whys and wherefores of our existence on earth, once we *know* them to be true from our own inner knowledge, we must incorporate this knowledge into our daily actions on earth. We leave our old ways behind, and we move on to the new ways of being on earth. We reshape our values, we transform ourselves and our lives. We see clearly through the illusions surrounding life on earth to what is truly important as we live our earth lives. We leave greed and material gain behind for the true rewards that come with the evolution of our souls through our incarnations here on earth.

∞ ∞ ∞

On earth there are always challenges of a material nature. We humans must face survival upon this planet and all the complexities this entails. Being incarnated in a physical body on earth automatically brings material challenges, but we must not get so caught up in these challenges that we ignore our spiritual growth. The true purpose of our earth incarnations is to make progress in the evolution of our spirits. All the material challenges are simply tests to spur us on to further growth of our spirit selves. Many humans see the material challenges as an end in themselves. These people strive for material accumulation, and they do not see past this to the spiritual needs of humanity. Others include spiritual practices in their lives but still put material gain as a priority.

It is time for the illusion to be shattered. It is time for humanity as a whole to realize the true purpose of life on earth. It is time for all to see that material accumulation in the end amounts to nothing, whereas growth of the spirit offers true rewards which last far past our earth incarnations. None of us can take anything material with us when we leave our earth bodies, but we do take the results of our experiences here on earth. We can take spiritual enrichment with us when we move on from an earth incarnation.

All humans must begin to see past each single earth life, for we live many earth lives as well as many experiences on other planes. The process of soul evolution is a complex one, but we can begin to understand the basics. Once we grasp the true purpose for our lives on earth, we can begin to change our priorities, change our values, and change our lives.

The dawning of the new millennium brings the dawn of a new consciousness for humanity. Whereas before we have been asked to have faith, to believe, now we can *know* the truth for ourselves. We can *know* deep inside us the truth of the purpose of life on earth. This knowledge ushers in a new way of being on the material plane.

∞ ∞ ∞

There have always been mysteries surrounding life on earth. Now it is time for some of these mysteries to be resolved. The knowledge that is now flooding onto the earth plane is available to everyone. This knowledge makes it possible for humanity as a whole to adopt an entirely new outlook on earth life.

The first phenomenon to be ushered in by this knowledge is simply the ability for each individual human to connect with the truth by going within. Once we realize we can go within ourselves for verification rather than relying on the words of others, we feel very secure in the knowledge that we receive.

Next, we are able to see our current earth life in the wider context of the many existences we have experienced both on this planet and in other realms. With this vision comes the knowledge that our existence does not end with death on the earth plane. Death is merely a transition to another phase in another realm. Once we know this, we can lose our fear and our dread of death on the earth plane. This is a major mystery unraveled.

Also available to humans now through this knowledge is the purpose for our earthly incarnations. Much soul growth can occur on the earth plane through meeting and appropriately handling the material challenges that confront us. Once we view our material problems as forces which motivate us to grow in spirit, we can approach them with a new outlook. We can avoid being so caught up in these problems that we lose our perspective on our lives as a whole. We can get past any need to accumulate material goods for their own sake. We can eliminate greed and selfishness from our lives.

Once we grasp the greater purpose for our earth incarnations, we can begin to operate with a new set of values. Our old values based on material wealth and the prestige and power it brings crumble away. We now begin to value unconditional love and compassionate deeds. We see them as assets to the growth of our spirits, which is, after all, why we are incarnated on earth.

Once we accept love and compassion, forgiveness, and selflessness as desirable attributes, many undesirable aspects of earth life begin to fade away. Violence and strife, possessiveness, even hunger and illness can diminish and eventually be eliminated from the earth, once humanity embraces the new way of being.

This, of course, does not occur overnight. We are speaking here of a process of many years. However, we can see this major turnaround, this great transformation, within our lifetimes. Indeed, we are here to lead and to make certain that this transition is successful and complete. We can achieve much soul growth and greatly assist the earth and all who dwell upon her by undertaking this task.

We begin by opening ourselves to this knowledge and letting it alter and refine our values and our outlook. We can then embrace the new way of being on earth for ourselves.

∞ ∞ ∞

All over the globe, people are raising their personal vibrations and are tuning to the new ray of energy. The earth herself is increasing her vibration in accordance with her natural cycles. The time is ripe for change.

We who are aware of this time of transition, we who prepare, must do so in accordance not only with the natural cycles of the earth but also with universal truth and understanding. In order to prepare correctly and thoroughly, we must first make strong connections to the core of universal truth within us. This connection provides the insight and understanding we need. Through this connection we receive knowledge about the true meaning of our earth lives. Against this backdrop, our earthly challenges take on new shapes and colors, and we begin to see with new eyes. This knowledge of the universal truths that come from within provides a greater understanding than has ever before been available here on earth. Finally we *know* the truths about our earth lives, and we can act with confidence. We *know* we are proceeding correctly.

All preparations must begin with sincere prayer and a deep searching for our inner connection to truth and guidance. We must be patient, seek this connection every day, and it comes to us. We can help solidify this connection by continuously raising our personal vibrations through prayer, meditation, breathing, and visualizations.

Once we establish our inner connection to universal truth, we must nurture it by acting appropriately on the material plane. For many of us, this cannot be done overnight, for we hold many old habits and patterns based on our past illusions and misconceptions. Seeing through these illusions is the first step to changing our actions. As we make energetic progress in the new ways, our old patterns crumble and fall away. We slowly, steadily change ourselves day by day, act by act, cell by cell, until we have realized our own personal transformations. We must have patience and compassion with ourselves as we undergo this deep and thorough change. We must forgive our own shortcomings and continue on with the knowledge that we, indeed, do better as each day passes.

We can use visualization to break up and flush away unwanted patterns in our lives. Once we identify an inappropriate habit or reaction, we begin to watch ourselves as we do it. We can, during meditation or during some calm and quiet time, visualize ourselves acting differently, acting in accordance with our new knowledge. We see ourselves taking strong appropriate action in place of the unwanted pattern. We can put a shape and a color on that old habit and see it dissolve before our eyes. We see ourselves step forward with confidence, radiating with the inner light of our new connection to universal truth.

We must not let our past, our old ways, discourage us. We are changing every day. Every day is a new beginning, a chance to put into practice more and more of the new knowledge and the universal truths that are now available to us and to everyone on earth.

∞ ∞ ∞

As we approach the change in cycles for the earth and the great transformation for humanity, we must pay attention every day to the necessary preparations. We must allot some time in each day to focus on our inner changes so that we may be attuned to the outer changes on earth. If we are conscientious and adopt a daily ritual of meditation and prayer, we proceed steadily with our own personal transformations. Our personal transformations are necessary if we are to be prepared and ready to be of service as the great transformation occurs.

We find, as we continue day by day, that our awareness increases. We see and feel subtleties and nuances that we never noticed before. Our sensitivity to the needs of others increases, and we notice more ways we can be of service. Our entire outlook on our earth lives evolves to a new perspective, and this ushers in a new set of values. Once we begin conducting our lives by this new set of values, we are well on our way to making our personal transformations complete.

Our personal transformations include both inner work and outer work. Meditation, prayer, breathing, and visualization are our building blocks for all phases of our transformation and enlightenment. We need to do the inner work to maintain a strong, calm, and centered approach to the outer work. We must do the inner work to establish and maintain our connections to both universal truth and to guided assistance. We must then apply what we learn through these magnificent connections to our lives on the material plane. In this way, we assure that our personal transformations are thorough and complete.

We can use visualization to help us see ourselves in a new way. We can picture ourselves as lighted beings attuned to the holy energy of the universe. We can see ourselves radiating light and love onto the earth plane. We can see ourselves healing and serving others and the earth. We can feel ourselves filled with light and love and joy.

∞　∞　∞

The change in millennia brings a two-fold transition to earth. On the one hand, the planet is reaching a climax in her natural cycles; on the other, the human race is faced with a great challenge and a great opportunity. It is no accident that these two events coincide. In order for the transformation on earth to be thorough and complete, radical change must occur. There is no more radical change in the material realm than the actual shifting of the masses of the earth. These giant earth movements coupled with the new awareness now available to humanity set the stage for a new golden age on earth. It is, as we have said before, absolutely essential that the humans incarnated now deliberately and conscientiously establish this new way of being on earth. A sincere effort of will is needed by all who survive the major earth changes.

We who wish to do this work, we who wish to lead the way to this new way of being on earth must prepare ourselves in many ways. One of the most important ways is for us to establish personal links to the guided help that is available to us. Although we humans are the ones who have to make the actual major changes in our lives on earth, we have much assistance from beyond the material realm to help us do this. Once each of us connects with the most appropriate form of guidance, we can move forward with confidence. We know when we need to be where, and how we can best be of service in all situations.

Absolute sincerity, openness, and trust are needed in order to establish our connections to guided assistance. We must have patience and pray that the way may be opened for us.

Once the connection is made, we must honor it. We must interact with our guides with the utmost sincerity and respect. We must bathe all communications in light and love.

We can ask our guides anything. They tell us what is important for us to know. They can set us straight on any matters which may be confusing to us, but we must always listen with an open heart and mind, for some of the guided advice may be very surprising.

Our guides are entities, beings unto themselves. They are helping themselves through helping us. We are all evolving together. This is a great opportunity for all.

The psychic activity on the planet is increasing at a tremendous rate as we approach the great transition. Humans are teaming up with guided helpers in order to make this transformation successful and complete. We all must do our part. With guided assistance, we can know exactly what our part is and how best to proceed.

The universe is joyous and merciful. We find, as we prepare, that our new path is very fulfilling and suits our personal needs. As our values change, we find we do not need much of what we thought we needed. As we let go of the old ways, we are filled with love, light, joy, confidence, and a security we have never known before on earth. This is an exciting time, a time when the vibrations of the earth and the vibrations of all humanity are raised.

∞ ∞ ∞

We must honor our guides. We must consider our communication with our guides as sacred. We must have deep respect for our connections through the veil surrounding earthly reality. Most of all, we must surround all such contact with luminous light and love.

Our guides are beings who reside in another realm, a plane which is interrelated with earth. Our guides have access to information and to psychic powers which we do not. On the other hand, these spirit helpers cannot directly change anything on the earth plane. They can only help and guide us to make the needed changes.

For the first time in the history of the earth, we can see large-scale cooperation between beings in other realms and those of us incarnated on earth. This massive effort is needed to save the planet from destruction and to save the human race from extinction. The time is a crucial one. We must join forces with those who would aid us in bringing a new way of being to earth.

This union of spirit guides and humans is an excellent one. It brings hope and joy to the planet. With the combined talents and abilities of spirit helpers and humans, we have what is necessary to make seemingly impossible changes on earth.

Our spirit guides offer us much knowledge and wisdom. We can ask them whatever we wish about our earth lives. We can receive guidance in any area. Because of the state of their existence in spirit form, these guides have access to universal knowledge and truth. We now, through our inner connections to these spirit helpers, also have this access. We must honor and respect these connections, for they are extremely valuable.

Our relationship with our guides is a two-way street. We can also serve our spirit helpers by effecting change in our personal lives and on the planet. Our guides need to see the assistance they give us manifest here on earth through our actions. They help us with our growth, and we, through applying the guidance they provide to our earth lives, assist them in their evolution.

∞ ∞ ∞

Every day we must take some quiet time to go deep within ourselves to find the calm. Daily visits to our inner center of peace are essential as events in the outer material world become more tumultuous. Focusing inward for a few moments each day also maintains a healthy and operational connection to our spirit guides and to our core of universal truth. Meditation is one of the most useful and beneficial practices we can learn.

It is best if we adopt a routine which includes daily meditation and prayer. We must regard meditation and prayer as spiritual food so that our day is not complete without them. Meditation and prayer nourish us and nourish our connections to our spirit helpers and to the universal truth within us.

We must plan our days just enough so that we are not interrupted or disturbed as we seek the peace within. We must see to it that others around us are aware of the importance of these practices to us. As our awareness and our psychic sensitivity increase, we see that not only do we find the opportunity to take this quiet time every day no matter what is happening, but also we are refreshed and rejuvenated by it.

One danger that we must be aware of is becoming too busy to take this quiet time. The energy and the inspiration we receive in our lives from meditation and prayer often lead us to take on a great number of projects. We see many ways we can be of service to others and are inspired to take action. Helping others is excellent, and it is a natural result of our ongoing personal transformations. Indeed, serving others is essential to a complete and successful transition on earth. We must, however, balance the time we spend acting and interacting on the outer material plane with the time we need to go within ourselves for rejuvenation and spiritual nourishment. We must honor both the inner and outer realms and find a daily balance which works for each of us. If we sometimes have difficulty maintaining this balance, our spirit guides can help us.

∞ ∞ ∞

Each time there has been a major change on earth, there has been a major shift in the social structure. The cycles for major earth changes are huge from our human perspective. These major shifts in the earth's surface occur at intervals of several thousand years, and when they do occur, they often destroy most historical records and traces of society. This is why many of us humans live our lives blissfully unaware of the regular cycle of these major earth changes.

It is time for us to become aware of these great cycles of the earth, for we are nearing another period of climactic change. This time we can not only be prepared, we can also use the transformational power of this time to affect great change in society.

It is time for the social structure built on the false values of greed and material gain to crumble. It is time for humans to stop plundering the earth and each other for every bit of material wealth. With the help of the natural earth cycles of great change, we can establish a new set of values and a new way of being on earth.

Major earth changes bring chaos and destruction, but they also bring a cleansing and a clearing process which is much needed on this planet. For the first time in the history of the earth, we have the opportunity to work with these great changes to effect a major evolutionary step for humanity.

We must not overlook the assistance we are receiving from beyond the earth plane. This help is now flooding the material realm through telepathic contact from spirit guides to humans. We are well into a period of intense preparation, for we must be ready for the great transformation. With our knowledge and skills, and with the help from our guides, we can work with the physical earth changes to promote incredibly positive changes in the human psyche. This is no small task. It is a big step for life on this planet. It is up to us to prepare thoroughly and then follow through with every breath we take and every ounce of strength we have. We must remember that we have constant guidance and assistance in all we do.

∞ ∞ ∞

A century ago, life was very different on this planet. One century from now, life may be many times more altered. Society and all life on earth must necessarily be dramatically different following the great transformation. At this point in time, we can only begin to imagine the incredible changes that may occur for humanity and for the planet.

Great movements of the earth's surface happen at regular though very long intervals. Many of us incarnated now on earth may see these great movements in our lifetimes. Certainly these giant shifts in the earth's surface necessitate major changes in all life on the planet. If these physical earth changes are coupled with the evolutionary leap now possible for humans, life on earth must, within the span of one century, be entirely different from the way we now know it.

It is up to those of us now alive on earth to make these changes very positive and constructive ones for humanity and for the planet. We are the ones who must make this evolutionary step occur. The responsibility is great. The possibility of failure does exist, if we do not pay attention, prepare, and follow through. Our thoughts, our feelings, our words and actions are all very important, for they affect the outcome of this transition.

If we wish this great transition to be successful and complete, we must begin now to prepare. We can begin by filling ourselves with light, love, joy, and thanks that this tremendous opportunity has been given to us. If we proceed correctly, sincerely, and thoroughly, we can take great steps in the evolution of our spirits as well as help the situation on earth.

All is favorable. All is in readiness for a positive and a successful transformation, but we are the ones who must make it happen in this material reality. Although we are the ones who must bring humanity successfully through this transition, we are not alone in our efforts. We have an immeasurable amount of help and guidance from beyond the earth plane. Our spirit helpers cannot change events on earth, but they can assist us with information so that we know the best ways to proceed. Our guides bring us knowledge and advice on anything and everything in this important time.

∞ ∞ ∞

Every once in a while there are spectacular events on earth. Some call these events miracles and see them as direct help from the Great Spirit. In reality, these events are most often spurred by a higher energy entering the earth plane from other realms.

Psychic phenomena are the result of increased telepathic awareness. Such awareness can consciously put us in touch with this energy entering the material realm from other planes. Such energy has always filtered through the veil surrounding earth reality, but never before has this energy been present in such great volume. The earth plane is literally being flooded with energy from beyond the veil.

This energy brings an increased vibration to the planet at this time. Our bodies and especially our minds are being activated in new ways which before now were considered very rare. Increased telepathic abilities are a direct result of this great influx of energy from beyond earth. With the increase in telepathy come information and knowledge that have never before been so widely available on earth. A great evolutionary step for humanity is now possible. We can, if we wish, enter a new golden age on earth.

We must, of course, tune to this energy now flooding the earth plane and allow ourselves to change accordingly. We start simply by raising our personal vibration through breathing, meditation, visualization, and prayer. If we open our hearts and minds and pray that we may make the best use of this incredible opportunity, we find we have much assistance in doing so. As our psychic abilities increase, we are able to receive more information and more guided help. Then, we can proceed even further in increasing our personal vibrations and changing ourselves.

Step by step, a little at a time, we open ourselves to a new way of being on earth. We proceed slowly and carefully, changing and refining ourselves a little every day. If we assimilate each step thoroughly and proceed with sincerity, we can be completely successful in achieving our personal transformations.

∞ ∞ ∞

The great transformation affects the billions of people on the earth. No one remains untouched. The changes are so deep and thorough that little, if any, of our former lifestyles remains. Once we grasp this fact and accept it, we may be more willing to begin now to let go of the trappings of this society. We may see the value of changing our lives now in preparation for the great transition.

Those of us who cling to the false values and material comforts of our present society are the ones who suffer the most during these great changes. We must begin now to see through the illusions that have been present for so long on earth. We must begin now to base our lives on the new set of values for the new cycle on this planet. If we do this, we automatically move to change our lives and undergo personal transformations.

Those of us who choose this path are the ones who help to usher in the new cycle, the new golden age on earth. We are the ones who lead the way through the chaos and destruction to a new way of being on earth. It is up to us to prepare ourselves and be ready to face this giant challenge. We have the opportunity to transcend much of our past karma and to be of great service to the planet. We must, however, prepare seriously, prepare thoroughly, and prepare daily to meet this challenge.

It is a great test for us to live in the present society which is crumbling and at the same time prepare for the new cycle on earth. We must constantly seek guidance as to how to proceed, for we certainly cannot ignore our present situations. Sometimes it may be extremely difficult for us to apply our new values and our new vision to our present circumstances, but we must. This is how we manifest positive change on earth.

We must remember that every time we face a difficult situation, we can ask for help. There exists a multitude of entities on nearby planes whose purpose it is to guide us. They are always near and ready to help us move toward the new way of being on earth.

∞ ∞ ∞

Personal transformation is the first goal of those of us who would lead in the time of great change. We must, however, never lose sight of the greater good that we can do, and must do, on the earth plane. As we proceed with our personal transformations, we automatically change the way we act and interact on earth. Eventually our focus shifts from personal inner work to helping and serving others, but this occurs only after many years. It is important for us to realize that each time we selflessly serve others on the earth plane, we help solidify the inner changes we are making. In fact, our personal transformations must manifest in our deeds here on earth.

We must have patience with ourselves as we make these personal changes. We cannot push ourselves to go too fast, or we do not properly assimilate these changes. The new knowledge and information, the new light, must be absorbed into each of the cells of our bodies. This process takes years, so we must also have perseverance. We must not be discouraged when old habits and old patterns prompt us to react unsuitably. Getting upset with ourselves only enforces our negative feelings and prolongs the time needed to make the changes. Instead, we must try to detach ourselves from the habit, pattern, or inappropriate action. We see ourselves doing it. We accept the fact that we are doing it. We express our desire to change.

Loving ourselves as we are and also as the lighted beings we can become is essential. Love must permeate every aspect of our lives in order for our personal transformation to be complete. We can use visualizations every day to increase the light and love in our lives. We simply surround any trouble, any problem, any dark corner of our lives with brilliant golden light. We infuse any problem area with the luminescent light of love. We can use the same simple visualization if we are upset with ourselves or absolutely anything in our lives. Love is the highest vibration. We can accomplish much by surrounding all we do with love.

∞ ∞ ∞

The present is each breath we take. With each breath we can continually change our way of being. The combination of visualization and breathing is a powerful tool for personal change. We can use visualization with the out-breath to clear ourselves of our old ways, habits, and patterns. We can use visualization with the in-breath to infuse our entire beings with the light and love of the new ways on earth.

We can tailor this visualization and breath combination to what we need at the moment. We can be very general or extremely specific. Of course, we first must know how we wish ourselves to change. We must identify, at least in general, what we wish to bring in. It is advisable to always breathe in bright luminescent light, especially white or gold. If we need to draw more love into our beings, we can use brilliant pink. For healing we can visualize bright blue or emerald green. We are, after all, transforming ourselves into luminous beings of light and love. We can use the darker, murkier colors for what we wish to breathe out. Whatever we wish to rid from our beings, we identify it and associate an appropriate color with it.

For example, suppose we choose to rid ourselves of fear of failure, and we visualize this fear as battleship gray. We also wish to bring more confidence and joy into our beings, and we visualize these attributes as warm brilliant gold. We then simply take a few moments each day and see ourselves breathing out the dull gray and breathing in the luminescent gold. If we quiet ourselves first, and take long, slow, deep breaths, the exercise is even more effective.

It also helps if we see ourselves as luminous beings. If we picture ourselves as filled with brilliant light which radiates from us, we change more thoroughly and more quickly. We can use our minds along with our breath to alter the very makeup of our cells. We can change ourselves slowly, steadily, and completely.

∞ ∞ ∞

As the ages pass, humanity evolves. This evolution has for the most part been very gradual. However, in the twentieth century, we have seen a speeding up in the process of evolution. We are, as a species, gearing up for a great evolutionary leap.

We must realize that the outcome of this giant step for humanity is not guaranteed. The potential is there for a positive outcome, but a negative result is also possible. The positive possibilities include new awareness and knowledge which reach beyond this limited material realm. Also, we may be able to activate more of the brain including the area which is used for psychic abilities such as telepathy. After this evolutionary leap or transformation, we may see our lives on earth in a new way, and we may operate with a new set of values. It is very exciting to think about the changes we can see in ourselves and others in our lifetime!

As we have mentioned, this positive outcome does not occur automatically on its own. We must seize the opportunity to make it happen. The more of us who work toward this end, the better are our chances of achieving this positive result.

The negative possibilities must be stated, for they show the incredible importance of this time. It is probably no surprise that humanity faces extinction on this planet. The end of the human race is a possibility, but this need not be so. We must, however, pay attention to the lessons of the time in order to avoid this catastrophe and to facilitate a positive outcome to this great transition.

The lessons of the time are many. We must each conscientiously undergo thorough personal transformations in order for the human race to evolve in a positive way. We must pay attention daily to our inner connections so that they become strong and unshakable in times of trial and chaos. We must reorganize our value systems and our lives in accordance with the new information and knowledge now flooding the earth plane from beyond the veil. Every day we must fill ourselves and our lives with light and love.

∞ ∞ ∞

All life upon this planet is magical, sacred, and is filled with the spirit-in-all-things. We must view the earth and all upon her with new respect. We must cherish all we take from the earth and use it wisely. We must be thankful that the earth provides us with such bounty. We must return what we can to the earth with appreciation.

The earth has been thoughtlessly plundered and raped for centuries. The results of such unconcerned greed are now pushing humanity to the brink of extinction. The benevolent universe is offering us an opportunity to turn the tide. We can, if we wish, save the beauty and abundance of this planet, as well as humanity's place here. We must, however, take this opportunity seriously and begin by transforming our own lives.

We can, every day, notice what we use and how we use it. We can, with thought and preparation, eliminate waste from our lives. We can offer heartfelt thanks for everything we take from the earth to sustain us. This is no small task. We must give up our lifestyles built on comfort and convenience for lives built on integrity and respect for the earth.

It is advisable to begin now for several reasons. We must begin to make our personal transformations immediately if we are to make use of this opportunity. Transforming ourselves and our lives takes years to accomplish, and life on earth as we know it is nearing its end. We need to have adopted a new way of being upon this planet by the time the great changes come to earth. Only in this way do we save ourselves and preserve humanity's place on earth. We must realize that the lifestyles based on wealth, comfort, and extravagance cannot possibly survive the great transition on earth. Therefore, we must begin now to change our lives before we are forced to. Also, most importantly, our personal transformations and preparations set the stage for an entirely new way of being on the planet once the great transition has occurred. We can survive and establish new blessed ways upon the earth.

The new way of being on earth includes much respect for the planet and for our ancestors who understood the earth and used her wisely. We must begin over and establish a thankful and sacred relationship with the earth. If we do not, we may reside here no longer. This is given.

Preparing for the great transition necessitates such a complete personal transformation that we must change ourselves down to our cellular makeup. Those of us who willingly undertake such monumental personal change are blessed and guided. We could not possibly know exactly how we need to prepare as individuals without guided help from beyond the veil. With this guided help, we receive all the knowledge and information we need to complete our personal transformations and to prepare for the great changes on earth. If we ar sincere in all we do, if we are consistent in our desire to change for the good of the planet and all humanity, we receive all the assistance and protection we need.

∞ ∞ ∞

Only once in many centuries do we have an opportunity like the one we have in this time. In fact, never before has this particular powerful combination of forces been present on earth for the potential benefit of humanity. We must not waste this precious gift bestowed upon us by the benevolent universe. We must make maximum use of this opportunity, and that is why this book is being written.

Those of us who make the commitment to change and who follow through conscientiously and sincerely are truly blessed and guided. Those of us who now seriously undertake our personal transformations and continue with perseverance and dedication are the ones who step forward as leaders in the time of great change. We need many leaders. We need many who are prepared and ready to serve.

We are preparing to be facilitators on this planet. Our words and actions can guide humanity to a new way of being on earth. Our survival depends upon our evolution to this new way of being. Our leadership in this important time of change serves all humanity. We also serve the earth and those who help us from beyond the veil. We are the essential link between the old ways and the new way of being on earth.

The stage is set. The gifts are given. The opportunity is there. Now it is up to us to learn, to prepare, to change. We must begin by transforming ourselves and our own lives, for only then are we ready to lead others.

A glorious golden age for this planet is within our reach. We can help usher in this new golden age and this new way of being. We must, however, be willing to leave the old ways behind and adopt the new ways *now* in our own lives. We must be willing to focus daily on changing ourselves and our lives. The benefits are great for ourselves, for humanity, and for the earth.

∞ ∞ ∞

In the new earth cycle, the peacemakers are the leaders. War is scorned and seen as undesirable. Violence falls away with the old structures, as we learn to transform our anger and frustration. In the new golden age on earth, peace and tranquility reign.

We who would lead in this new time must educate everyone in the ways of peace. We must teach that true peace resides within each of us. The violence that we experience now on the earth plane is our emotions and desires pushed into physical action. We must realize that our emotions, even our feelings of anger and hatred, are valuable. We must learn and then teach others how to transform our lower emotions into powerful higher vibrations which then can be used in many positive ways. We can change our lives, the lives of others, and life on this planet with such knowledge.

Once we have experienced transforming our base emotions to high-frequency vibrations, we grasp the significance of all emotions on this material plane. Our emotions have color and form, and we can use visualization, along with other tools, to change the actual content of our feelings. In leading such visualization exercises, we must emphasize that we always work to raise the vibrations associated with our emotions. The forms we visualize must become lighter, the colors brighter and more luminescent.

Sometimes when the emotions we are working with are very intense and overwhelming, we must begin with deep-breathing exercises before we use the visualization techniques. Each situation is a little different. We must tune to what is appropriate and what is needed. With patience and love in our hearts, we can open the new ways to many.

This transformation of our emotional energies is one of the first major teachings we undertake. We can help people change their lives for the better by showing them how to identify their emotions and then transform them into the higher vibrations of love and compassion. We can teach peace.

∞ ∞ ∞

Blessed are those of us who would lead in the time of great change. We transform ourselves that we may help transform life on earth. We increase our personal vibrations that we may radiate light and love on all who surround us and on everything we do.

Dedication, perseverance, and sincerity are essential for those of us who would step forward as leaders. Our preparation takes many years. Our transformation must be thorough and complete. We must begin now if we are to be ready, yet it is never too late for anyone to begin. The day we awake and pray that we may change in accordance with the holy laws of the universe is the day we begin. Each day is an opportunity to take another step, however small, toward our new enlightened state of being. With each breath we take, we can change more cells in our bodies so that we can hold within us the higher vibration of light and love. There has never been a more hopeful or a more challenging time for the human race.

The responsibilities of those of us who would lead are great indeed, for we must be compassionate and generous. We must be willing to serve everyone we meet. We must employ our skills and talents, whatever they may be, to help others in every way we can. Selfless service must be the cornerstone of our existence here on earth.

The more we empty ourselves of our own selfish desires, the more we can fill ourselves with universal truth and knowledge. Our abilities to teach and heal others increase. We become stronger. Our personal vibrations increase so that we radiate warmth, peace, light, and love. Others can see by our example that we humans can indeed achieve peace of mind and harmony upon the earth. There is much joy in this realization.

We can usher in a new way of being on this planet, but we must dedicate ourselves totally to this end. We must be willing to focus every day on the changes we need to make. We must first transform ourselves and our own lives.

∞ ∞ ∞

In times of great change, the leaders make the difference between positive transformation and foolhardy disaster. We who would lead must be strong, centered, calm, and ready to face the chaos and confusion that come with rapid change. We can and we must prepare. Even though we cannot know the specific challenges we may face, we can still prepare ourselves thoroughly for this great transition.

The people who are seen as leaders are the ones who are balanced and joyful, compassionate and giving. Those of us who are prepared for the great changes have already let go of the old structures of civilization, so we can rejoice and help others. The light that radiates from us and the joy that we exude as we undertake each task draw others to us. When all the old ways are crumbling, we do not panic but embrace the great changes. We see through the destruction to a new way of being on earth. We welcome the great transition, and we can teach others to adjust and to welcome it, too.

When all that is secure and familiar falls away in the face of change, people cry and panic and reach out for help. We can serve many in these times of transition. We begin by offering comfort and solace. We feed and nurse those who are in need. Soon the hearts and minds of those we help are open, and we can instruct them in the new way of being on this planet.

Many leaders are needed, for this great transition affects every area on earth. Those of us who undertake this calling are truly blessed and are guided and helped by many who dwell beyond the veil surrounding the earth plane. This path of preparation is serious and calls for true dedication, yet it is also joyful and filled with light. Once we set forth on this journey of preparation, we must relax, take it slowly and steadily, and persevere. We can know in our hearts how much we are needed and how important this work is to the survival of humanity. Many from both sides of the veil are joining together in light and love to help bring about a new peaceful way of being on earth.

∞ ∞ ∞

A very different kind of leader must step forward in the time of great change. These new leaders must be teachers and healers. The leaders of the old structures of society pass away. No longer do doctors, lawyers, politicians, and businessmen control our fate. We turn away from those whose motivation is material gain and seek those who can help heal the earth for the benefit of all.

The new leaders do not use fancy rhetoric, for their deeds speak for them. Their selflessness shines through everything they do. They are magnets, drawing others to them with their higher vibration. These new leaders are gentle, loving, and most of all compassionate. They approach every situation with an understanding based on knowledge of universal truths. Their vision pierces the illusion surrounding life on earth. They clearly see a new way of being on this planet, and they conduct themselves according to this new way. Others gather around adopting the new values and this new way of being on earth. As changes come more quickly to this material realm, more and more humans abandon the old ways and seek the teachings of these new leaders.

The new leaders must be impeccable in their conduct. Every thought, word, and action must be geared toward serving and healing the earth and all upon her. This intense dedication and selflessness can come only through complete personal transformation. This means raising the vibration of the entire body, in fact, changing every cell in the body. This process, of course, takes years. This book is written to address and to facilitate this process.

Those of us who would lead in the time of great transition must be willing to undertake the years of preparation which are necessary. This is a joyful task filled with knowledge, light, and love. We are guided and helped by many who wish to see a successful transformation occur on the earth plane. We receive many benefits which are unavailable on any other path we might choose. In learning to teach others, we gain much knowledge for ourselves. In learning to heal others, we learn to heal ourselves. Through contact with spirit guides, we gain a sense of security not experienced before on earth. Through practice, we strengthen ourselves and align ourselves even more closely with the new ways.

Once we accept the fact that life on earth is changing, and indeed must change, then we look to the new ways. Once we see that the old structures are disintegrating, we can embrace the new values and build upon them. Once we understand that a successful transition to a new way of being on earth assures not only our evolution but also our survival, we work toward it.

∞ ∞ ∞

In times of great change when much is in chaos in the outer world, we must trust our inner connections to universal truth. These connections bring us stability and peace of mind when all around us is in confusion. It is very important for us to develop and strengthen these inner links so that we feel secure about using them at any time.

Meditation and prayer are the two major practices that we can use to help us make and solidify these inner connections. All guidance comes through these deep inner channels, as well as our knowledge of universal truths. Our daily prayers for the strengthening of these inner channels are heard and honored. Our daily meditation helps us develop the practice of going deep within ourselves and listening for guidance, knowledge, and truth. Once we can quiet and center ourselves in meditation, we are well on our way to activating these important inner links.

For those of us who choose to lead during and after the great transition, our inner connections are our source of information and inspiration. It is through these sacred inner links that we receive guidance from all those dwelling on nearby realms who wish to help us. We can obtain assistance for any situation; we can ask for any information; we can receive guided help at any time through our inner connections. Therefore, we must cherish and nurture them. We must hold them as great and honored gifts. We must remember to give thanks not only for the knowledge and assistance we receive, but also for the actual sacred connections themselves.

Tapping these important inner resources is absolutely essential for both our leadership roles and for our survival. There are many whose joyful duty it is to help us from beyond the earth plane. We dare not face this great transformation without their blessed guidance.

∞ ∞ ∞

The small, the weak, the gentle finally come into their own on the earth plane. The new values establish gentle and compassionate behavior as the most respected and revered. The new values also set modesty and selflessness as highly desirable attributes. Peace can spread over the entire earth when such values as these are in place.

In order to establish these values, we must adopt them and live them ourselves. We influence others by our example. We need not spend our energies and waste our voices on disclaiming the values of the past, for they crumble away on their own. As leaders in this new time, we simply live the new values every day with every breath. When others come to us and ask us, we then speak of the new way of being on earth.

Many who placed much value on profit and material gain are humbled and are disoriented by the fast-moving events of the great transition. Many humans are afloat with no base, no security, nothing to strive for, as the great changes proceed. Everything that they have worked for all their lives evaporates in the face of the great transformation. Disoriented and confused, these people seek answers; they seek help.

We who are the new leaders are there. We are prepared and we are ready to serve. We bring comfort and love to those who grieve over what has been lost. We need not lecture on the uselessness of clinging to the false values of the past. We need only radiate the joy of the new golden age, and others join in our enthusiasm. We need only serve with light and love in our hearts, and others flock to us and wish to join us. When so much of the old order is in ruin and decay, we stand out because we are calm, centered, loving, joyful, and we are willing to help anyone and everyone.

When others come to us and ask us, then we teach the new values and share our vision of the new way of being on earth. Others then willingly adopt these new values as their own and begin living the new way.

Section Six

Vision for the New Time

An eagle flies over the coastline. It is a new coastline. The map of the world has changed. Great sections of the earth's crust have sunk and other sections have risen up from the ocean floor. The climates and the weather patterns have also changed. The flora and the fauna readily adjust. Humanity must also adapt.

These tremendous changes come to earth in a regular cyclic pattern of thousands of years. Each time this great physical transition occurs, it ushers in a new phase for the planet. Each time these great changes come, there are some humans who know in advance and prepare.

There are many factors that are very different this time as we face a great transformation on earth. The planet is much more populated than ever before. There is also widespread technology, whereas before such advancements were located in only a few areas. The destruction of the earth's atmosphere and the pollution of her land and waters are also unprecedented. Unfortunately, the great earth changes cannot heal all these wounds. Many centuries must pass during which we hold a new reverence for this planet before the damages can be repaired.

The transition itself is critical. Those of us who know in advance are guided to appropriate places. We must pray and use visualizations during the changes not only to help assure our own safety, but to help the earth herself bury or somehow isolate the most lethal spots until long-term healing can occur. This was accomplished before, during the last great transition, but on a much smaller scale.

The technology that survives must be revamped and used for service not profit. Our entire way of living on this planet must change if humanity is to use this plane for learning and evolution. All the mistakes that have been made in this civilization come to an intense climax. We must face them and be willing to completely change our way of being on earth. We have this opportunity.

∞ ∞ ∞

Every day we must pray for a successful transition on earth. The great transformation must be in our hearts and minds as we go about our daily activities on the material plane. We must be mindful of the great changes as we approach everything we do. Those of us who take these words to heart are the ones who prepare by changing our lives and by undertaking our personal transformations.

The great transformation necessitates the collapse of the old structures of society. We must remove ourselves as much as we can from these old ways, while still remaining active and involved on the earth plane. This is not always easy to do, and we may sometimes have some difficult choices to make. We cannot, however, compromise our new path or our new values. We must remain steadfast as we move to slowly and steadily change ourselves and our lives. We must not deviate from the new direction to which we have dedicated ourselves, even if it means refusing a job or losing a friend. For whatever we have to forfeit or leave behind, we fill our lives with so much more as we proceed on our new path to personal transformation. As our needs and our values change, we find that our lives become lighter and more joyful. We find that what we now need and what we now value come to us. Our fears, our insecurities, our old lives pass away as we further refine ourselves and our lives.

The old values and the old ways do still tug at us from time to time as we move forward. We may be tempted by money or by someone's promises. We can see through these empty enticements. We hold the knowledge of the great transition within us. Every day this knowledge becomes embedded in more of our cells. We see clearly that it is time for the old ways to pass. We smile and let nothing deter us from the changes we have decided to make. At any difficult juncture, we need only pray for strength and guidance, and we receive all the help we need. We are blessed upon this path.

∞ ∞ ∞

Those who walk the earth in the time after the great transition hold in every cell in their bodies a new respect for this planet. Everything in nature is seen as a sacred treasure entrusted to our care. This new view of our relationship to the planet and all upon her is a cornerstone for the new way of being on earth.

Compassion for all that live upon the planet is an important part of our new approach. Love and compassion flowing from us make all the difference as we establish new foundations for life on earth. If society is built upon compassion and respect for each other and the earth, then truly a golden age for humanity is the result.

The great transition shakes and crumbles all the old structures that have existed for centuries on earth. We have the opportunity through thorough preparation and readiness to build a new society from the rubble of the old. We must be very clear about what we are doing, but this can be easily accomplished if we have first completed our own personal transformations. We then have this new way of being already living in every cell in our bodies. We automatically conduct ourselves in accordance with the new values. Many of us also have direct communication through the veil between the earth realm and other realms. We therefore have access to any guidance we might need when faced with rebuilding order here on earth. Detailed assistance is available to us in this important and sacred time. It is, after all, up to those of us who spent years in preparation for leadership during the great transition to also help establish the new way of being on earth. This is the most important part of all we have prepared for.

We have undertaken a sacred trust. We must follow through to completion. Once we have truly established the new values and the new ways on earth, we can smile and feel much joy in our hearts, for then we have helped humanity take the most essential evolutionary step.

∞ ∞ ∞

Memory is a part of life on earth, but we must learn to have memory without longing. If we long for that which has passed away, we diminish the energy we have for the present. In the times of great change as well as in the time following the great transition, we must focus as much of our energies as we can on establishing a new way of being on earth. Although there may be certain people, places, or things that we miss from the old time before the change, we must not let our memories stir deep longing for that which is gone. We must be able to let go of the past and hold joy in our hearts for the present.

We humans who are alive on earth during the time of the great transformation have a special task. We must always speak of the past while holding a vision of the future. The generations that follow us remember nothing of the old structures and rely on us to tell them the story of the old ways and the great transition. When we speak of the times before the great changes, we must not speak with longing or yearning in our voices. We must remember that our emotions are powerful, and such spoken longing can possibly undermine the new structures we are working to construct. We must emotionally leave the past behind in order to focus on the needs of the present.

If we find we are yearning for some aspect of the past, we can use a visualization exercise to identify the feeling, detach ourselves from it, and change it. When we realize we are longing for something, we picture it. We pour all of our yearning into the picture in our mind. We attempt to empty ourselves of longing by pouring it all into the visualization. Once we have done this, then we begin to spin bands of brilliant pink, gold, and white light around the picture until it is a sphere of whirling luminescent light. Now we take this sparkling sphere of joy and light into our hearts if we need it, or we send it out to help the present energies on the earth plane.

∞ ∞ ∞

Apocalypse is a word that many fear. It is a word that brings to mind devastation, destruction, and ruin. It is a fact that ruin and decay are a part of the natural cycles present in the material world. Without destruction there would be no constructive change. When the time comes in one of the great cycles on earth for major change, then great destruction must first occur to clear the way. It is the way of the world.

We must, as we prepare to face the great transition, look beyond the time of chaos and ruin. The time of destruction is temporary but necessary. We must hold joy in our hearts as we look to the time when peace and tranquility return to the earth plane. It is difficult to show joy when all around us in the outer world is crumbling, but we can hold joy within us. On the inside, we can be calm, centered, strong, and joyful. On the outside we must be flexible, gentle, loving, and most of all compassionate. Many around us may be distraught and filled with fear. Calm, compassionate, loving words and actions can bring much comfort to those we encounter.

The most helpful approach during this apocalyptic time is letting go. We must relax and release the past while all the time holding within us the assurance of a bright future built on new values. Many may clutch and cling to that which is decaying, for they feel they are losing all they have worked for and built. Their old values based on material gain must crumble and pass away along with their possessions. This may be devastating to some, and they may close themselves to the possibility of a new life without wealth and power based on profit.

Yet there is a new energy afoot, and it is present and available to all on earth. Even in the time of the most turbulent chaos, this new energy shines. We can tune to this new energy now in preparation. It can strengthen us and guide us through the most upsetting times. We can then assist and serve others who suffer greatly from the apocalypse.

∞ ∞ ∞

The light that shines now upon the earth from beyond the veil is one of healing love. As we face the time of destruction and chaos, we can tune ourselves to this healing loving light. The new ray of light is very strong and is there for any of us who wish to see it, feel it, and bring it into our bodies.

This same ray brings new awareness to those of us who are open to it. The knowledge that is now entering the earth plane with this ray is here to both awaken and heal. Once we grasp the universal truths that are being made evident, we automatically begin to align ourselves with them and with the healing process which is so needed now on earth.

To make the best use of this precious gift, we must be able to quiet ourselves and bring this healing ray of light and love into our bodies. We can see this ray enter the top of our heads, flow down our spines, and flow out the bottom of our feet then traveling deep into the earth which now also needs great healing. This ray is luminous and bright and contains many colors. We can, through visualization, emphasize one color or another, choosing whichever we need for our personal healing and transformation.

When we do this exercise, we must be conscious that we are tuning to a glorious gift which has been given now to help us and the earth. We must be aware that we are healing and aligning the planet as well as ourselves. We begin by standing, feet slightly spread. We center ourselves in whatever way suits us, through breathing, chanting, singing, or prayer. We will ourselves and our bodies to be open to this blessed ray. We visualize the ray, whether it be multicolored or the color we choose to emphasize, pouring down through the top of the head, down the throat, down the spine, down the legs, out through the arches of the feet penetrating deep into the earth. We see this loving, healing light go directly to the core of the earth. In this way, we align ourselves with universal truth, and we bring healing light and love to ourselves and to the earth.

∞ ∞ ∞

As the ages come and go, humanity as a whole faces distinct problems and challenges. We are evolving not only individually but also as a species. What is unique about this time is the speed at which our evolution is occurring. We have come to a point in our development where a great leap is possible. This is due to several factors. We have increased our scientific and technological awareness over the last century. This in and of itself has brought many challenges to humanity. Because of our highly developed technology, we and many other species are facing extinction. We must, in fact, make a leap in consciousness simply to save ourselves.

Beyond this situation, the earth herself is ready for an evolutionary change. The balance on the planet can be restored only through major earth movements including shifts in the earth's crust. This, of course, affects all life on the planet and adds to the potential for an evolutionary leap for humanity. If the possibility of extinction alone does not force this step, the addition of major earth changes certainly does.

We also have at this time the introduction of new energy from beyond the earth plane. This new ray of energy is a gift to the earth and to humanity. This ray is filled with light, love, and knowledge. This new energy does not change the situation on earth by itself, but instead brings an opportunity for us humans to increase our awareness and understanding so that we can make appropriate changes and evolve. It is up to us to open ourselves to the gifts of knowledge and enlightenment that this new ray of energy brings and to put them to use on earth.

Through the combination of factors, humanity can make an incredible evolutionary leap within the span of our lifetimes. We can begin to function in an entirely new way, a way which is beneficial to us, to the planet, and to all upon the planet. Change is a part of all natural cycles. Rapid change presents a unique situation, for we must be prepared to respond correctly in order to make the most of such a time. We have assistance from the earth and from forces beyond the earth as we face this challenge.

∞ ∞ ∞

In all the ages past, there has never been a time to match the extraordinary circumstances we have today. All is in place, all is in readiness for the great transformation. The unique combination of forces present provides both an incredible opportunity and a formidable challenge.

The day comes to every one of us humans alive on earth when each of us realizes deep in our gut that major change is afoot. This galloping change is leading us rapidly away from the past and into a chaotic and uncertain future. Once we truly grasp that we cannot maintain the old ways with which we are familiar, then we turn to the task of adapting, adjusting, and seeking order in the new time.

Those of us who have spent time preparing for this transformation are the ones who are ready to build new structures in the ashes of the old civilization. Once the deterioration and destruction of the old ways are complete, we must be ready to step forward with peace, order, and a new way of being on earth.

Chaos and confusion weigh heavy on the heart. Those who survive the destruction of the current civilization long for stability. We who are prepared can bring this and more. The potential for what we can accomplish in this time is far greater than we are able to imagine. With the help of spirit guides and angels, we can begin to envision a new world, and we can begin to build it.

We begin with the universal truths that we hold in the core of our beings. We begin by helping everyone discover and know these truths. Once everyone vibrates to these universal truths, new values emerge, and we begin to build a new way of being based on these new values.

Calm, peace, and joy radiate from us, so that our vibrations alone bring comfort and assurance to those who are distraught. We can, by living this new way of being based on the new values, set an example which is then eagerly followed by all who seek to bring stability out of chaos.

∞ ∞ ∞

Time is a concept which is relative to earthly reality. Once we step beyond the boundaries of the material realm, time does not apply in the same way. If we could view the situation on earth from beyond the veil, we would see a planet and her inhabitants reaching a climactic condition. We would see that major change is inevitable.

Earth is garnering much attention now from those who exist in other realms. There are those who have chosen to watch over and assist the earth and all upon her now in this time of great change. Channels of communication are opening between these discarnate beings and those on earth who wish to serve. We humans may not possess the powers or have access to the information that these spirit beings do, but we can communicate with them and ask for their guidance and help.

The situation on earth is so critical now that many powerful spirit beings are gathered around, watching events on the planet, offering their assistance. For every one of us humans who awakens and wishes to serve the earth at this time, there are many spirit guides ready and willing to help. The contact and the energy exchanged between the material realm and other realms are increasing at an amazing rate. Knowledge and guided assistance from beyond the veil are now widely available to those on earth who are open and wish to receive them.

There are, of course, prerequisites for establishing contact and receiving help. We must be open, sincere, and willing to use all knowledge and assistance in selfless ways on the earth plane. If we were to use spirit guide contact for material gain or other selfish purposes, we would increase our negative karma. We would eventually lose our links to our guides, were we to continue on this path. If, however, we approach such contact with respect, if we honor our guides and pledge to selflessly serve the earth and all upon her, then we can receive an abundance of help from our spirit friends. We can learn much about the universe and about this climactic time on earth from our spirit friends.

∞ ∞ ∞

A light in times of darkness, comfort in times of chaos, these and more we can be through preparation and perseverance. We can be calm, stable, and secure within ourselves, and then we can reach out to others who are distraught. We must, however, begin to prepare now, and we must continue our preparations thoroughly and systematically.

As we prepare, let us envision ourselves every day as filled with brilliant light. The more we picture ourselves as bright, luminescent beings, the more light and love we can hold in our bodies. The more light and love we hold in our bodies, the higher our vibration. The more consistently we vibrate at a higher rate, the more complete our personal transformations become, and the sooner they are accomplished.

Of course we need to employ more than just this visualization to further our personal transformations, but this vision of ourselves as lighted, luminescent beings is very important. If we see ourselves in this way as we move through each day, we become more accustomed to a higher rate of vibration. The new cells in our bodies which we manufacture each day hold a higher vibration, and so we change. We move slowly, steadily, day by day, changing our cells and increasing our vibrations. Consistency and perseverance are essential, as is sincerity of intent.

Each day we must cleanse ourselves of desire for self-gain. We become more magnetic and more powerful as we progress in our personal transformations, so we must be aware of the dangers. If we use our increased powers for personal profit, we are causing incredible damage to ourselves in the face of universal karma. We then lose much more than we have gained.

We can use prayer on a daily basis to help keep ourselves aligned with what is right. If we pray every day that we be cleared of desire for personal gain, we are heard and we are helped. If we are sincere as we undertake these changes, we are blessed and guided every day.

∞ ∞ ∞

It is useless to try to stop change or hold on to the past. We must take the first step, which is to willingly open ourselves to the future and to the new ways it brings. Once we do this, we can begin to prepare. We do not forget the past. We do, however, let it go and allow ourselves to move into the flow of the time, which propels us toward a new way of being. We must learn from the time and take advantage of the many gifts and opportunities that are available to us.

As we proceed with our personal transformations, we find it becomes easier and easier to let go of the past along with any grief, regret, or longing we might feel. Each day we breathe in the brilliant light of the new ways and exhale the residue of the past. In this way, we slowly, steadily change the makeup of our very beings, so that the new ways become a very part of us. This procedure takes daily attention, but it is worth every moment we spend.

There is danger during times of great change that we may become paralyzed with grief over the loss of the old civilization which is passing away. We must realize from the first that we cannot stop its disintegration nor can we bring it back. We must let it go and move on. There are procedures we can follow to alleviate any sadness or longing for the past which may hamper our own progress. It is important that we do not get bogged down with sadness over the loss of all the old familiar ways. We must, from the start, adopt the attitude that, while we remember what has gone before, we are moving to establish a new way of being for the good of the earth and all who dwell upon her. Once we set this in our hearts and minds, we can use the following exercise to strengthen this outlook and to alleviate any pain and longing associated with letting go of that with which we have been familiar for so long. This exercise is especially useful if we find we are holding grief, remorse, sadness, or longing within us.

We begin by focusing on these feelings, by actually seeing them inside us. We picture these emotions as a particular color such as dark gray. We feel how heavy, how leaden they are. Crying may help us focus on and feel these emotions. We then visualize a brilliant white star about one foot above our heads. We take the time to see it clearly as it shines luminescent and bright. Now we breathe in this brilliant white light, pulling it down through the top of our heads, down along the spine so that we become lighted. We then breathe out the heavy gray emotions. As we take each in-breath, we see ourselves becoming brighter and more luminescent. As we exhale, we see the dark gray lift and move out of our bodies. We continue until the dark gray emotions have dissipated and we are completely filled with light.

∞ ∞ ∞

It is very important in times of great change to see the joy in every part of our lives. When events are moving quickly, there is often much uncertainty. We may feel insecure, and we find little stability in the material realm. By taking each day one at a time and by living in the present without grief for the past or fear for the future, we can find much joy within us and all around us. We must simply look for it and be open to it.

Joy is essential. We must bring as much joy as we can to our lives and to the planet, for the new ways on earth are to be based on love, compassion, selfless service, and joy. We can find joy in the beauty of the planet and in the reality that the earth is moving to heal herself. As disruptive as earth changes may be, they bring a new cycle, new ways, and great healing energy to this planet. In this there is much joy!

We can find joy within ourselves. We need only relax and journey to our inner center of peace, calm, and universal truth. There we find a wellspring of joy and love, for we are vibrating in harmony with the universe. It is very beneficial for us to connect with this peaceful, joyous place within us on a daily basis. The joy we find deep within us can then flow out from us to others and to the earth. Our joyous vibration can be like a salve to those around us who are depressed, fearful, and distraught.

There is much joy in our connections through the veil surrounding earth. The knowledge that we humans have assistance and guidance from those who dwell beyond the earth plane is very reassuring. Those entities who have chosen to dwell in realms associated with the earth are there specifically to help us. Their superior knowledge and telepathic talents can be employed to assist us every day. We can ask these spirit guides anything we wish, and we can request assistance with everything we do. Our connections with these spirit helpers are filled with love and joy. We can feel this exquisite joy every time we communicate with these spirit friends. The fact that we no longer have to face any problem alone is joyous in and of itself. As we grow to know our spirit companions, we develop rich friendships and a deep love for them. They in turn love and assist us. There could be no more joyous association than this! Our spirit guides walk with us and help us through every minute of every day if we so wish. We can feel security, support, and nurturing love from our spirit helpers, and in turn we help them by returning their love and by establishing on earth the new ways of love, compassion, selfless service, and joy.

Between the beauty of the earth, the love and assistance from our spirit companions, and our own inner connection to universal truth and harmony, we can experience joy every day of our earth lives. There is no more important time to allow the joy and love to flow through us out to others and onto the earth plane.

∞ ∞ ∞

People of the earth must unite in sending love to the planet in this perilous time. We may, at times, think that we do not know what to do to help the worsening situation on earth. We must then remember that sending love to the earth, either individually or in groups, is very beneficial.

Love is the great healer. As the planet moves to heal herself, she needs much love. Instead of expending our energies worrying about the disastrous consequences of various situations, we can use our energies, we can use our hearts and minds, to channel love to the planet.

Every day, let each one of us take a moment or two to pray for the earth and to send love to her. The continuation of this material realm as a home to humans depends upon the well-being of the earth. Our daily prayers, thoughts, and emotions are of much assistance to the earth in this time. We must visualize healing love energy surrounding the globe and also penetrating to her core.

Here is a suggested visualization which, when used with prayer, is a very powerful tool for helping the earth. This can be done any time, anywhere. Begin with a simple prayer for the well-being of the earth. Following this, visualize a glowing sphere of luminescent golden light in our heart area. Stay with the visualization until the golden sphere is tremendously bright. As we see this sphere, let us also feel deep love and reverence for the planet. Now watch the sphere expand until it encircles us. See it continue to grow until it engulfs all around us. Now the brilliant sphere expands rapidly until we see it encircling the entire planet. We must make sure as we picture this that the sphere of golden light glows incredibly bright. We see the golden light not only surround the earth, but also permeate the planet to her core. In this way, we take the love in our hearts for the earth and send it to every cubic inch of the planet. If we could manage to do this prayer and visualization each day, we would be connecting ourselves with the planet, and, most importantly, we would be helping her in this time of change.

∞ ∞ ∞

It has been thousands of years since the last set of great changes on earth. The earth is ripe and ready for a giant transformation. We, too, must be ready with every fiber of our beings. This is a serious commitment, one we must make with sincerity. If we proceed with dedication and perseverance, we receive everything we need to prepare ourselves and to help others prepare.

We must be consistent in our intent. We must approach this work with a selfless attitude. Daily renewal of purpose is helpful here. If we connect each day with our inner center, and through our centers to the purpose of selfless service, then we achieve consistency in our intent. We must not be fooled. Empty words are useless. We must be sincere in our hearts. We must experience this sincerity with such feeling that it overspreads our entire bodies. Our intent is all-important. We must rid ourselves of selfishness in all we do, for if we allow selfishness and self-importance to creep into our hearts and minds, we are no longer aligned with the universal truth. We lose the way. Preparations for selfish reasons are worthless. They do not hold true.

The only way we can be secure upon our path is by clearing ourselves daily of selfishness and self-importance. We must hold steadily to our true purpose of selfless service to the earth and to all who dwell upon her. We must sincerely align ourselves each day with this purpose. This daily rededication is an essential part of all preparations for the great transformation.

Again, it must be emphasized that we must *feel* the sincerity. We must mean it with our hearts. Evoking this emotion of sincerity on a daily basis is one of the most powerful tools we have to keep us on the path of proper preparation. We are never lead astray if we truly wish to serve others. We are blessed with protection and guidance as long as our intent is sincere.

If we can begin our day every day with a brief prayer that we may be cleared of selfish ways, we are on the right track. If we could add a simple visualization that evokes the feeling of sincerity, we proceed steadily on the path. We need only take a moment and one deep breath. We visualize a pink sphere glowing in our hearts. We see it glow brighter as we feel love. We could feel this love for the earth, or for another person, or for a pet, or a place. The important part is that we feel the emotion of love in our hearts. Once we feel this and see the luminescent pink sphere glowing even more brilliantly, we rededicate ourselves to a selfless approach to all we do. We see the bright pink sphere expand until it engulfs us, and we feel the love and sincerity of purpose overspread us as well. Every cell in our bodies feels the love and sincerity.

∞ ∞ ∞

Every day presents an opportunity to take another step on the path of preparation for the great transition. Of course, daily awareness is very important. If we are conscious every day of our need to prepare, then we more readily recognize opportunities when they arise. Every time we serve others with love in our hearts, we move forward on the path. Every time we send love and healing energy to the earth, we help prepare the way for a positive transformation. Every time we feel joy when we think of the great changes, we make changes within ourselves.

We must take advantage of the quiet moments that each day offers. We use these moments for prayer, for meditation, for visualization, and for breathing. Even a few moments spent in this way each day are helpful.

Thinking about the great transformation every day helps us see areas of our lives that we wish to change. If we refine ourselves and our lives a little each day, we move steadily forward in our preparations.

Our inner knowledge assures us that these great changes are inevitable. We therefore live each day with an eye to this great transition. This approach helps us recognize situations that are opportunities for us to further prepare ourselves. We must employ our psychic tools every day to move forward with this preparation. Even if we take only one moment or do one deed that furthers our preparations, we move steadily forward.

Daily attention is necessary because we are constantly changing the cells in our bodies. We wish to every day hold more of the vibration of these changes within our very beings. This conscious changing of the makeup of our bodies is an important part of all preparations because we must evolve in harmony with the times. The very best way we can be prepared is to hold the imprint of the change to a new way of being in every cell in our bodies.

∞ ∞ ∞

Every day as we move closer to the great transition, we must set our lives in order. We must examine every detail of our lives with an eye to the new way of being on earth. We must slowly and systematically clear away all in ourselves and our lives that tie us to the old order. We immediately replace all that we clear away with the new values, the new way of being. We approach this process step by step, day by day. We must be thorough. We must keep at it.

We must also remember to be kind and gentle with ourselves. Gentleness is a much more effective persuader than force. We must love ourselves as lighted beings every step of the way. We need not become distraught over our weaknesses and failings. We must have patience with ourselves, for we cannot accomplish personal transformation in a day, in a month, or even in a year. This process is slow. It is best if we proceed slowly and thoroughly. Each change we make must be completely assimilated by our beings. Steady progress is more important than the speed at which we move.

From the start, let us see this process as joyful rather than arduous. We are, after all, preparing ourselves for a glorious new way of existence on planet earth. The new way of being is so superior to anything we humans are familiar with that it is difficult for us to imagine all the benefits. Our personal transformations are the first step in a giant evolutionary leap for humanity. It is time for us to make this leap. Let us join together and prepare.

Let us see ourselves and our lives with new eyes. May we see clearly all that we need to change. Let us be joyful as we sever our ties to the old structures and as we clear away those aspects of ourselves that hinder our progress. Each day if we recognize something we need to change or if we make one small alteration in our lives, we are doing well.

∞ ∞ ∞

The sun and the planets in this solar system are but a tiny speck in the vast universe. So, also, the human experience on earth is but one of a myriad of experiences available in the universe. When we see our earth lives in this perspective, we can more easily look beyond our day-to-day stresses and problems. It is important that we maintain such a perspective because we, as humans incarnated on planet earth, have only so much time and energy. We must learn how best to use this time and energy.

This is a crucial time for earth and for humanity. If we do not pay attention to what is important now, we may lose the earth experience for all time. Therefore, let us focus on the priorities presented by this time of transition. Let us allow the trivial troubles in our daily lives to be dwarfed by the great challenges now facing humanity as a whole. Let us not exhaust ourselves on the inconsequential problems which pass in a day, a week, or a month. Let us instead place our emphasis on the challenge facing all humanity and the planet brought by this time of transition.

Of course we must deal with our daily troubles, but let us do so with humor and with this greater perspective in mind. Our day-to-day problems shrink to their proper size in our lives when we place them against the backdrop of the great universal challenge now facing humanity. If we get too caught up in our daily stresses, we exhaust ourselves on trivial matters, and we have little if any energy to deal with those areas which are really important.

Let us focus now on what our priorities must be in this time of great change on earth. First, we must connect every day with an awareness of this crucial time. We must, on a daily basis, see this giant challenge now facing humanity. This alone changes our lives, for we more readily recognize what is important and deserving of our time and energy and what is not.

Next, we begin adapting ourselves and our lives so that we are prepared to meet this great challenge. This process of personal transformation also takes daily attention, and we must make sure that we set aside time every day to address this priority. Our paths to this personal transformation necessarily differ, but daily attention is essential no matter how we proceed.

Prayer is extremely important, for we humans, and the earth as well, need the prayers of many in this critical time. Let us ask in our prayers that this great transformation on earth be positive and successful, and that we humans enter upon a new way of being on earth.

Let us use visualizations to send love and healing energy to the planet and to all humans upon it. We need much love and healing in this time. Let us use cleansing breath to clear us of all hindrances to this new way of being. Let us quiet ourselves in daily meditation that we may connect with the core of universal truth within each of us.

∞ ∞ ∞

Our emotions are valuable. The combination of our emotions and our intent is a powerful key to our progress. Our emotions, however, are volatile. They come; they go; they change. We must learn to work with our feelings to accomplish what we wish.

For instance, we have already outlined how to transmute emotions of a low vibration, such as anger, to emotions of a high vibration, such as compassion. This is important work for those of us on the path of preparation. We are not speaking of control of our feelings, but of recognition, understanding, and transformation of our emotions.

It is very important to let emotions flow. We cannot work with our feelings unless we recognize them and experience them. This is the first step to all work with emotions; we experience feeling. Then we can identify the emotion or emotions. Then we can proceed to focus on the feeling, transmute it if we wish, or perhaps send the emotion to a certain person or place.

Much can be accomplished through this work with our emotions. This work can change our lives many times over for the better! We must begin by seeing every feeling as valuable, for each emotion has the potential of bringing love, joy, or compassion to someone.

Sending the emotion out to someone or perhaps to the earth is the very last step in this work. We must first fully experience and identify the feeling, and, if necessary, transmute the emotion to a higher vibrational level. Here is where the element of intent must be mentioned. Intent is directly linked to our karma. What we intend with our actions and our emotions is as important as the actual result. If we mean well, but our practice falls short due to inexperience, we are still on the right track. If, however, we intend harm of any kind, we are seriously complicating our own karmic situation.

We must, then, intend beneficial results from all our emotional work. If we experience the lower emotions such as anger, frustration, and the like, we must willfully transmute them to a higher vibration before we send these feelings out to anyone.

∞ ∞ ∞

In this crucial time, it is very important that we keep love alive in every aspect of our lives. We can begin with a deep love for the planet. It is extremely beneficial for the earth and for ourselves if we connect with this love every day.

When we speak here of experiencing love, we speak of experiencing with our minds, our hearts, and, indeed, with our entire bodies. Many of us have had the sensation of being overwhelmed by feelings so that even our extremities are involved in the outpouring of emotion. Once we grasp how important and powerful our emotions are, we also realize the value of being able to contact our feelings and evoke them at will.

The most valuable emotions are love and compassion. We must, in our preparations for the great transformation, learn to transmute our lower emotions to the higher vibrational level of love and compassion. We must also learn to evoke love on a daily basis. There are many ways we can do this, and we each need to find a suitable method. Often love flows from us when we pray. Prayer is an excellent place to start. Prayers for those whom we deeply love readily call up the emotion in our body-mind. We must allow this love to flow through every fiber of our beings and then out onto the earth plane.

For some of us, love flows strongly when we meditate and connect with the core of universal truth within us. Gratitude for our connections to our spirit helpers often evokes love. When we feel love and compassion for our spirit guides, we must allow this love to permeate every cell in our bodies as well as flow out to the spirit companions. It is a cleansing and invigorating feeling to experience overwhelming love.

Visualization and breathing are often useful tools for increasing the love in our lives. We can begin by thinking about someone or something that we love very much. Let us then see this love as a sphere of luminescent pink light in our hearts. We focus on our feelings of love and see them in that sphere. Next we add breath. As we breathe in, we see this brilliant pink sphere grow a little, and we also feel the love energy increase. We can picture a beam of white light entering the top of our heads. We can breathe in and pull this bright white light into our hearts, which increases the size and brilliance of the pink sphere. On the out-breath, we see this pink sphere in our hearts glow brighter. We continue this in a relaxed manner, allowing the sphere to grow and brighten with the breath. We see the sphere and the love it holds reach up into our throats and deep into our abdomens. We then see it grow to include our heads and our knees. We continue until our entire bodies are encircled by this brilliant pink sphere of light and love. We feel every cell in our bodies vibrate and tingle with this all-pervasive love.

∞ ∞ ∞

Some humans may see the great transformation as some sort of punishment. In fact, the earth moves to rebalance and heal herself. During these tumultuous days, we humans do face much personal karma. We, of course, experience karmic situations throughout our lives, but these intensely chaotic circumstances bring us incredible challenges and opportunities. We may, during these times, move to balance ourselves by working out our karma.

It is important that we enter these times of transition with the proper attitude. If we view the great changes as an opportunity to rebalance the energies of the planet as well as our own lives, then we meet every challenge with enthusiasm. If we see the great transformation as a time when we can neutralize negative karma from many past lifetimes, we gladly face any test.

We must, however, be ready. If we enter these times unprepared, we may falter and end up producing more problems and more negative karma for ourselves. It is true that these times are severe, and the challenges are immense, but we have been given all we need to successfully deal with every challenging situation.

We begin with awareness of the oncoming transition. We take a deep breath and accept the responsibility of preparing to meet both our personal and the planetary challenges. We pray that we may be strong, centered, and thoroughly prepared for every situation. We pray that we may clear away our past negative karma through selfless service on the earth plane at this time.

There are many facets of preparation for the great transition, but none so important as preparation of our attitude. We must enter these times with a very positive and joyful mindset. We must connect with this positive approach on a daily basis. We must see the destruction of this material society as a deep-cleansing process that is essential for the survival of humans upon this planet. We must be filled with joy at the prospect of helping humanity establish a new way of being on earth.

We can also feel elated about the potential for clearing our personal karma. Mistakes of many lifetimes can be rectified through our actions during this time of great change. By approaching every day, every person, every situation with unconditional love, compassion, and selfless service, we evaporate our past negative karma. There are numerous opportunities for us to help others during the great transition, but we must be prepared. This book addresses all basic aspects of this preparation.

The earth is ready for the most dramatic change she has experienced for thousands of years, and so must we be. We must be willing to completely transform ourselves and our lives. The reality is that our lives change anyway, so we might as well accept the changes and seek ways we can make the best of them. This is what this preparation is all about. We joyfully seize the opportunity brought by this time of great change to improve ourselves and all life on this planet.

Section Seven
Beginning Again

The poles of the earth and much of the landmass shift. This brings the climax of the great transition. Once this has occurred, everything on earth begins to settle down, and we who remain begin to rebuild.

We must know how to proceed. Part of our preparations is ample forethought about the new way of being on earth and how we are to establish this new way. If we have been correct and thorough in all our actions to this point, we move easily on to this new plateau.

The transformation brings great cleansing to the planet and to humanity. The rate of vibration of the earth and all upon her is raised. Those of us who survive the many rapid changes are ready for the new ways. We have little thought of bringing back any semblance of the old order. We have moved far beyond any longing for the past and its trappings. This is as it should be, for we must be thoroughly dedicated to establishing the new way of being on earth.

We need not wonder how to begin, for our actions during the great changes have already made a beginning. We have practiced selfless service and approached all situations with love and compassion. We hold in our hearts a new reverence for the earth. We approach our earth incarnations with new knowledge. We have here all we need to establish the new way of being on the material plane.

We must continue to set an example with all our words and actions. It is extremely important that we continue to stay connected to the core of universal truth within us, as calm settles once again upon the earth. Our guides and spirit helpers are ready to help us with any details of the rebuilding process. We must put this new way of being into words so that we can properly teach the children. We have guided help with all our tasks during this important time. We can look to this time with joy in our hearts, for the true flowering of the human spirit comes to pass in these days.

∞ ∞ ∞

In the end, the results of the great transformation depend on how we humans handle it. Our actions and our reactions determine whether we come through the tumult and chaos ready to begin a joyful new way of life on earth, or, indeed, whether we make it through at all.

This is a crucial turning point for humanity. We must recognize this and accept the responsibility. The karma of the ages is focused on this climactic time. We must prepare not only to face the great transformation, but also to transform ourselves in accordance with the time.

All is well when we turn within for guidance. We humans are not asked to face this critical change alone. We must become aware of all the help we have available, and we must ask with humility and respect that we be connected with this help. Many who have at one time been incarnated here on earth are available to us now as guides and helpers. These spirit entities are duty-bound to assist us in any way they can. They are working on their own evolution by helping us. We must make many strong connections with our spirit helpers, for their guidance is extremely valuable to us in this time.

If we see the larger picture, if we see both incarnate and discarnate souls joining together to bring about a positive, successful transition on earth, then we can feel hope and joy. We humans can receive both comfort and confidence through our connections with our spirit guides. Our guides have access to much information which they are willing to share with us in order to help us. We must develop clear communications with our spirit helpers in order to receive all the knowledge and assistance that they are offering to us.

We need them now, and they need us, for those in spirit cannot directly affect change on earth. We humans must do this. They help us and guide us, and we take specific actions on the material plane. This bond between the spiritual and material worlds is sacred and must be nourished with care.

∞ ∞ ∞

All is well upon the earth even during the days of destruction and chaos, for it is during these times that the earth is healing. We humans must remain open and must not judge the events of the time. What may on the surface appear to be disastrous occurrences may, in fact, be cleansing and healing processes.

We must always trust the universe, especially when we are in the midst of chaos. We must remember the earth is moving to rebalance her energies. We can help speed the process along by doing two things: we can pray daily for the complete and thorough healing of the planet; we can send love and healing energy to the earth using our tools of breathing and visualization. These practices are very helpful, especially if they are undertaken by many humans during this time of transition.

Of course much is lost as these great changes occur, but the old order and the old ways must be swept away. We must be prepared to let go. In fact, we can be filled with joy and gratitude that this much-needed cleansing, this great transformation, has come to earth.

Once the earth settles down and all is calm and quiet, we must not waste a moment reflecting on what is lost and gone. If we find ourselves thinking about the past or longing for what is gone, we must take a deep breath and let these thoughts and feelings flow out and away. Our energies during this sparkling time after the transition must be focused on the new way of being on earth. There is much to do, and we must be ready to move ahead.

Our guides are very important to us during this time of rebuilding. They can provide us with much-needed information on health and healing, on energy sources, on food and cultivation, and much more. In fact, we can turn to our spirit helpers for guidance on any matter, as we work day by day to establish a new structure for society on earth. This period of rebuilding is an extremely sacred time. All of our preparations throughout the many years lead up to this time. We who prepare and step forward as leaders during the great transition now face our greatest task. We must now establish the new values and the new ways firmly on earth. Our work sets the basic structure which lasts for thousands of years. We must have both vision and practicality as we proceed.

If we have reached this point, we have prepared ourselves well. We need, however, to continue to rededicate ourselves daily to the task at hand. We need to pray every day that we are proceeding correctly. Even in this quiet aftermath, we must pray for guided help. In fact, this may be the most important time of all for spirit guides and humans to work together. Our guides are ready and eager to provide us with all the information we need to establish the new way of being on earth. This is a joyous time when there is a new balance between the material and the spiritual on earth.

∞ ∞ ∞

The new millennium brings new hope for humanity and for the earth. The planet and all upon her are truly blessed in this time of great change. The spiritual movement that is now afoot is the most widespread ever in the earth's history, for it includes all peoples, all religions, all countries, and all races. The gifts that are given now to humanity are available to everyone incarnated on this planet. The knowledge of these gifts and the wonder that they bring are making their way around the globe.

Of course these gifts are perceived somewhat differently by the people of various cultures and religions, but these gifts all stem from the same source, the new ray of energy now entering earth. This new ray brings an opening between the earth realm and other realms through which much communication and knowledge may flow. Humanity now has access to universal truth and knowledge. We now also can consciously connect with spirit guides and helpers who dwell on nearby planes. These gifts carry incredible potential, but it is up to us to recognize this potential and make use of it.

These gifts are here to help us prepare for the great transition, move through the time of change with joy and love, and establish a new way of being on earth once all has become quiet again. If we use these gifts properly with honor and respect, they serve us well and become an intrinsic part of the new culture, the new way of being.

We must begin now by giving thanks for these gifts and the opportunities they bring. We must cherish this new energy and all the knowledge and guidance that comes with it. We must make these gifts a part of ourselves and our daily lives, so that we carry them with us through the great transition into the new time. Indeed, these gifts are here now to help us make this transformation successfully and move to a new way of being. These gifts are our salvation. Let us offer heartfelt thanks that we have been so blessed.

∞ ∞ ∞

The highest vibration we can hold on earth is love. Love and compassion, understanding, and forgiveness are the cornerstones of the new way of being on earth. All of the new values stem from these attributes. As we move to the other side of the great transformation, we incorporate the new values into everything we do.

The importance of this time cannot be emphasized enough, for we are laying the groundwork for a new society which may exist for several thousand years. We would be surprised and awed by the far-reaching effects of our decisions and actions during this time of rebuilding following the great changes. We must begin now to envision the new ways and the new values manifest on earth. We must move to make them an integral part of our lives through our own personal transformations. This is the best and the most effective way to proceed because these new ways and values become a part of us, of our very beings. It is then very natural for us to rebuild and restructure everything based on these new ways and values.

This is why we must begin now to change our cellular makeup so that we can hold the higher vibrations of love and compassion within our bodies at all times. We humans have the opportunity to take giant steps, to evolve to a higher state of being, but we must consciously prepare and willfully move in this direction.

All is well when we vibrate with love and bring more love onto the earth plane through our words and actions. In the time following the great transition, we can make this highest vibration of love the standard for all life on earth. We can make compassion, forgiveness, and understanding the norm for society. We can set selfless service as the basis for all actions. This is not only possible; this is as it should be in this new time. We are the ones who, with the help of our spirit guides, can establish this new way of being on earth.

∞ ∞ ∞

We humans as a whole feel and act differently after the great transition because we evolve to a higher state of being. The rate at which our bodies vibrate is higher. Our cells hold a higher vibration.

We are alive at a very extraordinary time because we are the ones who make this transition physically, mentally, emotionally, and spiritually. It is up to us to carry it off. The future of humanity depends on how well we accomplish this task. The time is right. Many gifts have been given to us to help us take this evolutionary step, but we are the ones who must do it.

Every day we need to bring more love into our lives and into our bodies. The vibration of love is the highest and most beneficial vibration of all, and love is what we need the most on earth now. The importance of increasing the love in our lives cannot be overemphasized. We need to employ many tools to bring more love into our daily lives and onto earth at this time.

This book is here to help guide us to this end. We have already outlined several ways to increase the love around us and within us. We have shown how we can take any emotion, even intense anger, and transmute it into love. We have spoken of ways to generate more love using visualization and breathing. We must each find ways to bring more love into our bodies, our lives, and onto the earth every day.

In the quiet of meditation we can use brilliant pink light to open ourselves to more love. Simply see the beautiful pink light wash over us in luminescent waves. Breathe in as the wave crests within us; breathe out as it flows out into the area around us. This exercise is relaxing and it also raises our personal vibration.

Once we begin operating from this higher vibration of love, we see our lives evolve, and we see ourselves evolve, also. Connecting on a daily basis with this highest of all earthly emotions is essential if we are to successfully move through the transition to a new way of being.

∞ ∞ ∞

Love is the basis for the new way of being on earth. This is simple, straightforward, and true. Love in all forms is the highest vibration we can experience on earth. In the new time following the great transition, we evolve to a state where we can radiate unconditional love in any situation by using our will. This highly evolved state is possible only after we complete our own personal transformations, but it is real and attainable by all who wish it and work toward it. This new state of being is no longer reserved for yogis and gurus, but is now available to everyone. The times dictate that humanity must evolve in this way in order to survive.

Instead of focusing on what we wish to eliminate from life on earth, such as violence and greed, we focus on what we wish life to be and what we wish to become. The old values and old ways fall away by themselves. If we move forward toward this new way of being just a little every day, we in time transform ourselves and our lives.

We must begin by believing that this evolved state of being can be obtained by everyone. Of course, this path takes sincerity, patience, and perseverance, but the time is right for many of us humans to take this giant step. Those of us who wish to see new values and a new way of life on earth must begin by transforming ourselves. Once we have raised our personal vibrations so that we radiate love and compassion and eliminate the lower vibrations from our energy fields, we evolve to this new state.

We must be very thorough as we move ourselves to this new way of being. We must continually identify the old patterns and old ways and the lower vibrations they hold. Once we recognize these lower ways, we must not hesitate to transform these lower vibrations to the higher vibrations of love, understanding, compassion, and forgiveness. This book offers many tools to help us do this.

Through this continuous process of consciously raising our personal vibrations, we slowly and steadily transform ourselves. The evolutionary leap comes when this higher vibration becomes constant in our bodies and in our lives. This does take many years to achieve, but it is possible and indeed necessary. We move into a state of being in which the very cells of our bodies have been transformed in order to hold these higher vibrations. We no longer have to identify and transmute those thoughts, emotions, or actions which hold the lower vibrations, for they bounce off of us and fall away.

Of course we must continue to renew ourselves daily through prayer, meditation, breathing, and visualization. By this time, these practices have become an integral part of our everyday lives. We have transformed ourselves, with the help of our guides, to beings of the highest order who literally radiate light and love. We can begin now by seeing ourselves as these luminescent beings and by believing in our hearts that we can make this evolutionary transformation. We must move toward the new ways if humanity is to survive at all on earth.

∞ ∞ ∞

After the great transformation, we humans are operating on a higher vibratory level. Our psychic connections play an important role in setting up new structures for society. We humans used our telepathic links to our guides to help us prepare for the transition. These communications continued to be strengthened during the great changes. Now, in the aftermath, we make these psychic connections a part of our lives and a part of the new way of being on earth.

Direct contact with the ancestors and with our helpers who dwell beyond the veil surrounding earth is a valuable resource. We cannot approach life on this planet in an arrogant way when we have such communications. We realize how much we do not know. We approach the ancestors and spirit guides with humility and respect. We honor them and thank them for the knowledge and the guidance they bring. This attitude of sincerity, gratitude, honor, and respect must be the basis for all contact with our ancestors and spirit guides. This must be firmly established if we are to integrate such communications into our daily lives on earth.

As we set up new structures for society, as we teach the new values to our children, let us honor our psychic links and make these connections a part of this process. We can, of course, seek help from our spirit guides as we do this. Our guides have access to knowledge and information beyond our earthly resources. The ancestors possess the wisdom of the ages, which they gladly share. Let us nurture these psychic connections and establish them as a normal part of our earth lives. We must view life on earth in new ways in this new time. We must be open to the bonding between our spirit helpers and ourselves. Humans and spirit guides can approach earth life together, as a team, in fact. Humans and spirit guides work together not only to establish the new ways on earth but also to continue the blessed evolution of the planet and all who incarnate on the earth plane.

∞ ∞ ∞

Were we to jump from this moment ahead into the new time, we would be amazed at the differences, especially in how we feel. We can see ourselves in this new era as filled with peace, joy, love, and compassion. These feelings become the norm once we incorporate into our daily lives the process of transmuting our lower emotions to these higher vibrations. We humans learn the simple truth, that we do not have to be helplessly overcome by unwanted emotions such as sadness, grief, anger, or frustration. We can take these or any feelings and transform them into the higher vibratory rate held by love and compassion. This transmuting of emotions becomes standard practice as we begin the new time on earth.

Once we have learned this technique, our lives improve immensely. We begin each day with joy and continue through filled with compassion for others and love for the earth and for our lives here. Our very presence radiates such an uplifting vibration that others are drawn to us, and we are able to teach them the new ways.

Next, we might be surprised to note the incredible comfort and security we feel. We might think this is unlikely because humanity has just undergone a period of intense chaos and destruction, and little of the former way of life remains. Material security is seen in a different way in the new era. We humans embrace the truth that our real security comes from within. Our connections with our spirit guides reinforce this truth. No longer need we fret or worry about any challenge that earth life presents us. We can turn within and communicate with our worthy and knowledgeable helpers from beyond the veil. They provide comfort and love, as well as information to help us. The love in our lives increases through our contact with our spirit guides. Also, we no longer fear death, for we see it as our transition from an incarnated state to one of spirit where we live on to experience evolution in other realms in other ways.

∞ ∞ ∞

Everyone in the new era is on a new path. The very vibration of the earth herself is different, and humans, as well as all life on the earth, must adapt. Whatever little remains of the old time before the transition is seen in such a different light that nothing is as it was before the change. We humans, too, evolve and adapt to the time.

The ability to adjust and adapt to the great changes is an essential attribute for all life on earth. Part of our personal preparation is increasing our outer flexibility while remaining strong and centered within. There are several ways we can do this. We must, of course, be able to let go of the old ways as they crumble and fall away. We must take deep breaths and let the old ways pass away with ease. Instead of feeling grief or loss, we feel joy at the prospect of the new way of being. This ability to joyfully let go is an important first step in increasing our ability to adapt to the times.

The more we strengthen our inner connections to universal truth and love, the more we strengthen our links to guided help, the more centered and stable we are within. We can remain unshaken by tumultuous outer events if we are strong and balanced inside ourselves. Our links to universal truth help us keep a proper perspective on all the great changes that surround us. We know it is time and we welcome the changes. We see them as healing and balancing for the earth. Our links to our spirit guides provide much knowledge and information to help us adjust and adapt. Our guides can assist us with the details of adjusting our lives on earth to suit the new era. Our spirit helpers are a tremendous resource to us as we continually adapt to the changes on earth. They can help us with any aspect, any phase of our readjustment. We need only request their assistance with sincerity. Our daily prayers that we may flow with the times also assure us of any help we may need.

∞ ∞ ∞

After the calm has returned to the earth, every day is a day of rejoicing. We honor the earth and all upon her in new ways. Instead of being overcome by grief for what has been lost, we are filled with gratitude for the bounty that we find around us. We see the earth with new eyes, and we approach her with new values, new reverence, and new respect.

With the help of our spirit guides and those humans who successfully survive the great transition, we find all we need to rebuild life on earth in an entirely new way. Our resourcefulness during this time is abundant.

The very first step we must take, along with those steps necessary for our basic survival, is to establish a circle of reverence. The precise details of this circle can be decided upon by the individuals who participate, but the purpose is as follows: to honor the planet, to give thanks for all the earth offers us, and to generate deep love for the earth. Song and prayer are both helpful to this end, and visualizations can also be used. It is essential that we establish this new reverence for the planet as the basis for the new culture and the new society which is to grow out of this time of rebuilding.

We must also value love and compassion above all else, and we must express these attributes daily to all those around us no matter what they do. We do not always need to speak, but we can use visualization along with our emotions to communicate love and compassion. Words can at times be misconstrued, but love, unconditional love, is always understood, at least emotionally.

Here we have the basics for the new ways on earth: reverence for the planet and love and compassion for each other. We humans can evolve to a place where these new ways are the norm, and all the violence and greed, self-pity, and suffering so prevalent in the society that is passing no longer exist among humans on earth.

∞ ∞ ∞

All is well in the universe and all is well on earth in the aftermath of the great transition. Unlike previous times when few were prepared for disaster, many have the opportunity to prepare and survive these climactic changes. Part of this preparation is receiving a clear vision of life on earth following the great transformation. We can use this vision to guide us as we undergo our personal transformations and ready ourselves for the great changes on the planet.

Our guides, our spirit helpers, our inner connections to universal truth provide the knowledge and information we need to formulate a vivid picture of the new way of being on earth. We must see this vision clearly in our minds and hold it in our hearts as we proceed with all preparations. We do not need to take the time to envision the details of life in the new era. We must go forward with the knowledge that we receive exactly what we need when we need it on the material plane. We need to fix instead upon the new value system, the new attitude, the new behavior that humans must adopt in the new time. The new way of being on earth necessitates that humans maintain a higher personal vibration. We must raise the energy level in our bodies so that we consistently operate from the heart chakra and above. The lower vibrations are tolerated only in that they power the way to the higher energy centers in the body. In other words, we become a new type of human, one that is inspired to act from the higher vibrations of love and compassion rather than from the lower energy centers in the body which activate power, greed, lust, and violence.

We must begin by believing that we can become such evolved human beings. We must envision the new ways clearly. If we begin to see ourselves as lighted beings, if we see ourselves as connected to universal truth and love, we have already begun to move toward this reality. We must see this; we must feel this; we must make this vision a part of our daily lives.

∞ ∞ ∞

The wild times during the great transition are fleeting. During this chaotic period, every action, every word, every deed is important. Indeed, the very survival of humanity upon this planet depends upon our thorough preparation leading to and our actions during the great transformation.

No less important is the period immediately following the intense changes, for in the calm following the chaos, we humans are to begin again upon the planet. Careful deliberation and solid connections to the core of universal truth within each of us are essential. We cannot drift aimlessly through this time. We must step forward with determination and purpose if we are to establish the new way of being upon the earth.

We must see the truth of the time. This is the beginning of a giant new cycle which lasts for thousands of years. We are laying the foundation for this great new era, therefore much depends upon us and what we choose to do. The very destiny of humanity is in our hands. This is a great responsibility. We need not feel fear in the face of this challenge, for we are the joyful recipients of much guidance, knowledge, light, and love during this period of rebuilding. Our spirit helpers come even closer, aiding us with every detail of the new ways that we can and we must establish. Those who help us from beyond the earth realm have been waiting for the opportunity to assist us in this way. Much good can be accomplished through cooperation between our spirit helpers and ourselves. Working together, we can achieve many amazing things.

We must begin now thinking about this important time after the transition. We must prepare ourselves, not only for the time of great change and chaos, but also for the time of calm which follows. We must know exactly how to proceed, and with the help of our guides along with the thorough preparations we have made, we do.

As we prepare ourselves for the time of rebuilding, let us begin by embracing the new values which set the foundation for the new era. Reverence and respect for the earth and everything upon her are first in our hearts and minds, along with love and compassion for each other. We must also step forward in selfless service every day in every way we can manage, for this is the way of the new cycle. Our loving attention to the needs of the earth and the needs of each other is basic to the new way of being. Our expanded psychic awareness, our connections through the veil are encouraged and honored. Indeed, our communications with those beyond the earth plane become an established part of the new structure of society.

Nothing must be left to chance as we set the foundation for the new way of being on earth. Every word, every act, every gathering, every ceremony must be filled with the highest vibrations of reverence, love, and compassion.

∞ ∞ ∞

After the great transition, there is much for us to do. Those of us who have prepared for this important time must step forward and lead. We must be prepared for every eventuality in that we must remain resourceful and adaptable. We must not waiver, however, when establishing the new structure for society. The new values must be clear and held in the hearts and minds of all. It is up to us to lovingly bring the new way of being to everyone on earth.

There are several procedures we can use to go about doing this. The first and perhaps most effective is to set an example for others with our words and actions. Indeed, we must apply the new ways to every aspect of our own lives. Our calm, centered, loving approach to all we do draws others to us. We are magnets, attracting others with our high vibration of love and compassion. Many then observe our ways and adopt them.

If we are to lead in this new time, we must be ready to be very active and to selflessly serve others at all times. We must, of course, keep ourselves well and do what we need to for our own health and well-being so that we have inexhaustible energy to help others. As leaders, we must be out among the people, serving and helping in every way we can. This is another very effective method we can use to establish the new way of being on earth. By directly helping and serving others, we touch them with the new ways. Others then automatically turn to us for advice and for answers. Once others turn to us and ask us, we know what to say. We tell them of the new ways.

In this time following the great changes, people want to reestablish order. We must make sure that, as we rebuild the structure of human society, we do so on a firm foundation of universal truth and love. The earth and all upon her have been shaken to the core. At last we humans can be in direct contact with that core of universal truth within each of us. We, as leaders in this new time, must encourage everyone to connect with this inner truth and to nourish this connection. If we say and do that which is verified by each person's inner connection to universal truth, we all embrace the new way of being without doubt, without fear.

We must be ready to endlessly teach and heal. As we approach each individual, we must give the person our complete attention. We can then sense, perhaps with the help of our guides, how best to serve and to communicate the new way of being. Individual attention is another very effective approach to spreading the new ways. Humans, in this virgin time following the clean sweep of the great transition, are searching for calm, order, and structure. We can provide exactly what is needed if we are properly and thoroughly prepared. We must first undergo our own personal transformations so that we totally accept and embrace the new way of being on earth.

∞ ∞ ∞

Such beauty as the earth presents must be respected and revered. We must breathe in this beauty and offer deep thanks from our hearts. In the new era, the earth sustains us and nurtures us. We must also feel gratitude for the bounty the earth offers so that we may survive.

In the new times following the great transition, our relationship with the planet must be markedly different from what it has been in past centuries. Instead of taking and taking from the earth, we must also give. We must seek a balance between what we take and use to sustain our existence in this realm and what we return to the planet physically and emotionally. We can give to the earth physically by cultivating properly and planting trees. We can give to the earth emotionally by daily expressing our love and thanks for the beauty and the bounty we receive. We can pray for the well-being of the planet, as well as use visualization to send gratitude and love to the very core of the planet.

This new relationship with the earth is similar to the one between our native ancestors and nature, but more evolved. The early peoples upon this planet had great reverence and respect for the earth and built rituals and religions around their relationship with her. We need to return to this deep reverence for the earth, but take it even farther. We can use our inner connections to universal truth, our psychic connections through the veil to guide us in all matters concerning our relationships with the planet. Before we undertake any action that alters or somehow affects the earth, we must ask if it might upset the balance. Even tilling and gardening must be approached with the utmost respect.

We must interact with the planet for our own survival. In the new time, we must return to the earth as much as we take from her. This balance is essential to the new way of being on earth. We must, each day, connect with the earth in a deep and loving way. Our new approach and attitude toward the planet usher in a time of great harmony on earth.

∞ ∞ ∞

In the new times, it is up to us to bring joy into every aspect of our lives. This is more easily done at this time than ever before on earth because of the increased vibration of the planet and all upon her. Joy is a healing and invigorating emotion, one which we cannot have too much of as we begin to rebuild after the transition.

All is well when we incorporate the feeling of joy into our daily practices as well as our group ceremonies. The knowledge of the universe newly showered upon us in these times inspires much joyful emotion. Our constant contact through the veil to our spirit helpers evokes intense gratitude and joy. All we need to do is to call to mind these gifts, and we can bring joyful feelings into our personal meditation or to a gathering of many.

Joy, along with love, compassion, and forgiveness, is the emotion that we wish to have fill our lives in the new era. Taking a few moments each day to allow the joy of the universe to flow through us is extremely beneficial. Joy, like love, is an emotion of the highest vibration. It cleanses and energizes both the physical and etheric bodies. When we feel joy, we are connecting with the truth of the benevolent universe. When we call up the emotion of joy in ourselves, we must let it flow freely through us and out to others.

One very effective way to connect with joyful feelings on a regular basis is for us to have a special spot that we find incredibly beautiful. When we visit this place, we are overcome by the beauty, and this inspires joy. We can use breathing, specifically deep balanced breath, to increase the joy within us and help it reach every part of our bodies. Sometimes tears spill from our eyes as we are overwhelmed by these intense joyful feelings.

Now that our hearts and minds are open to universal truth and knowledge, now that we are connected through our own inner links to all the help and guidance we need, now that we have survived the great transition and begun a new way of life on earth, we have much reason for joy.

∞ ∞ ∞

Every day in the period of calm which follows the great transition we take another step in rebuilding the structure of society. We must be very aware of what we are doing during this time. The new structure must be built on values and practices that promote the new way of being on earth. We must consciously imbue all aspects of our lives with the new way of being. Then, as the new structure of society evolves, all is in harmony with the new ways.

Helping and serving each other must be at the very heart of the new structure. Whether we interact with family, friends, neighbors, or strangers, we must always be ready and willing, in fact eager, to serve. This type of bonding with others through selfless service is one of the cornerstones of the new golden age for humanity.

Of course, we must also respect and care for ourselves. We continually seek a balance between our outer work, serving others, and our inner work, nourishing and revitalizing ourselves. Each day has a place for both. We must honor the time each of us takes for our inner journeys. We must support and encourage each other to take the needed time every day. We know how important this time and space is for us, so we must allow others and, in fact, help them make a place for these inner connections.

At the same time we must encourage group work. The gatherings could be for spiritual ceremonies using prayer and visualization, or they could be for actual physical work such as building shelters, or both. These gatherings must be filled to overflowing with joy and love. We who organize these groups can make sure this occurs by radiating a warm and loving approach to all who participate. We can bring song, chanting, poetry, even theater to these gatherings to emphasize love, compassion for others, and selfless service for all. We must be inventive and allow our spirit guides to help us, for much of what we establish now lives on for centuries as the structure and the rituals of the new golden age.

∞ ∞ ∞

Joy is manifest upon the earth in the time of calm following the great transition. Humanity stands in awe of the power of heaven and earth. There is widespread respect and reverence for all of nature and abundant compassion for all humans. We must seize the mood of this time and apply it to the new structure of society we are building.

We who survive the great transformation, we who live on to rebuild society in the new era, we must be properly prepared and ready to move forward as soon as the calm settles in. We must not waste any time or leave any regrouping to chance. Strong, solid leadership is essential in this sacred and tender time following the great changes. We know what we must do, and we step forward without hesitation.

At first, many are preoccupied with meeting their own material needs for survival. As we gather in groups to assist each other in obtaining food, shelter, and clothing, let us also include matters of the spirit. In this new time, humanity must recognize that attention to our spiritual needs is equally as important as tending to our material needs. The society in this new era must be based on a balance of material and spiritual concerns. This balance, this harmony between the material and the spiritual, sets the basis for the new golden age on earth.

In these early gatherings, let us make sure that our spirits as well as our bodies are nourished. Let us join together in song and in prayer. Let us use chanting and visualization to feed our spirit selves. Just as we share food, let us share compassion and love. These first circles of survivors set the basic tone for the society that is to follow. Let us never lose sight of how important these gatherings are. Let us pray every day for help and guidance. Let us make sure that these first groups congregate in light and love, and that all that is needed for a new way of being on earth is included.

∞ ∞ ∞

All is well on planet earth. A feeling of well-being spreads over the globe following the great transition. Much that is associated with the low vibrations has been cleansed away. We stand on the earth in a sparkling new time, the very beginning of a great new cycle.

Those of us who experience the transition from the old society to the new way of being on earth stand as the very cornerstones of the new time. We have witnessed the transformation both of ourselves and of the planet. This experience has earned us a place as wise leaders, as sages, as elders. We have helped carry humanity through the time of great chaos and change, and now we stand ready to serve in the new time. We must step forward and do so.

Our greatest task as we enter this new phase for both the earth and humanity is to teach. The new values, the new ways must be taught to all humans, especially the children. We must be thorough and exact. We must be very perceptive and able to recognize any bits or pieces left from the old society. It is our duty to transform these leftovers into whatever is appropriate for the new era. Once the children born in the new time grow to become leaders, the new ways are firmly established on earth.

Our responsibility is tremendous. We have, however, incarnated on earth at this time to face and to undertake these great challenges, for it is up to us to not only transform ourselves and prepare for the great transition, but also to set up the new structures after the changes have taken place. Once again, a reminder: we have endless guidance and assistance from beyond the veil. We are a part of a great partnership that includes spirit entities from other realms as well as us humans. We are joining together to accomplish something that this planet, this plane of existence, has never seen before. We are the ones who experience the great changes and live on to establish a new way of being on earth.

∞ ∞ ∞

All is well after the great transition because the earth has shaken off the lower vibrations which have entrapped humanity for centuries. The earth herself has greatly increased her vibratory rate, and so have we humans who have survived. All is in readiness for us to establish a new way of being on this planet.

First, it is essential for us to pray daily that we may be guided step by step in this task of immense importance. Second, we must use visualization and breathing to fill ourselves every day with joy, love, compassion, and forgiveness. This helps us keep the correct attitude as we approach this important work. The third step is to continue our daily meditation as a way to connect ourselves with the guidance we need in this new time. By now, the channels of communication between our spirit guides and ourselves are strong and clear. Our guides have helped us prepare for the great changes; then they helped us during the time of chaos and destruction; now they stand ready to help us establish the new ways on earth. It is up to us, however, to find the quiet space in each day to go within, connect with our inner center, and listen for the guidance that these spirit helpers provide.

This time of rebuilding is the most precious and sacred time of all. We must not neglect our responsibilities for even one day. We must realize that every thought, every word, every emotion, every action is significant, for we are making an imprint which remains for centuries to come. If we begin each day with a sincere prayer that we go forward in light and love and accomplish what needs to be done that day, we are blessed and guided. If we take the time to quiet ourselves and listen, if we conscientiously center ourselves and look, we recognize the guideposts, and we proceed correctly. This time of calm following the chaos is peaceful and serene and must be regarded with reverence and respect. This is the new era. We must step into it with love in our hearts and a deep desire to serve.

∞ ∞ ∞

All is well upon the earth after the great transition. Many problems which plagued the planet before the great changes are solved naturally as the earth undergoes deep healing.

Other problems and challenges must be faced by those of us who survive. There are certain challenges that are uniquely human and must be solved by those of us who begin again following the great transformation. We are dealing with the karma of humanity. There is much that we can do to balance our personal karma as well as the karma of all humanity in this new time. We must be aware of the significance of this time in the evolution of humans. We must be aware of the incredible importance of the task before us.

We have much help. The earth herself has set the stage by vibrating at such a high rate that those humans who do not adapt by raising their personal vibrations do not survive. We must, in the time of calm following the great changes, move to stabilize this high rate of vibration within ourselves and others. In this way, we assure that we operate from the higher energy centers in our bodies. Our actions on the earth plane are then motivated by and filled with love, compassion, understanding, and forgiveness. We use the now familiar tools of meditation, prayer, visualization, and breathing to firmly establish this higher vibratory rate in ourselves and others. We incorporate these sacred tools into the fabric of daily life in the new era.

We also step forward each day in selfless service. We nourish, heal, and care for each other as all settles into the calm following the chaos. This, too, must become accepted as the standard for all human behavior on earth in the new time. Those of us who have prepared ourselves thoroughly as leaders set a tireless example and teach others of the necessity of this selfless approach. We, as visionaries and teachers, spread the new knowledge of the universe and of life on earth through our pictures, our stories, our deeds. We can paint a picture of a glorious golden age, which others then also see, and we can all fulfill.

∞ ∞ ∞

In the new era, the new golden age for humanity, we who are leaders must do all we can to establish a solid structure for society. This means setting standards for daily routines as well as yearly ceremonies. The same basics must be emphasized in all interactions, whether they be personal communications with spirit guides or social intercourse with a large gathering of humans. These important basic modes of behavior include sincerity of heart, an open-minded approach, a joyful attitude, and compassionate, loving feelings, words, and actions. These can all be encouraged and cultivated by those of us who would lead in this new time. Our actions set the example for many; our words, our teachings help others understand the incredible importance of such blessed behavior in this new era.

We must remember how valuable and helpful our spirit guides can be, for our guides have talents and resources beyond those we have access to on earth. Our guides have helped us prepare for the transition; they have stood by us to guide and protect us during the chaos and upheaval; now they step forward in light and love to assist us in establishing a new way of being on earth. This is the most important part of the entire experience because what we set up in this new time is the foundation for all civilization for hundreds and hundreds of years. Our spirit guides have been waiting. They are ready to help. They know what we need. We must trust them and listen carefully to their suggestions and then find ways to apply their advice to life on earth. Our guides have pledged to help us in every way they can. We must do our part: we must be open; we must take the time to listen; we must pray that we hear clearly; we must pray that we have the strength, the courage, the perseverance to implement this guided assistance; we must manifest this divine guidance on the physical plane with our own words and actions. It is a huge task, to be sure, but one we are capable of handling.

Our guides have a superior understanding of the universe. They possess knowledge beyond that which we have on earth. They are willing, in fact anxious, to use their wisdom and their talents to help us in this time. We must admit we cannot accomplish what needs to be done without their help. On the other hand, our guides cannot directly affect changes on the earth plane. *We* must do this. It is evident that a partnership is needed between humanity and those spirit entities who have pledged to guide and assist us. We need only wish for this partnership, ask for it, pray for it, and it is ours.

Now it is up to all of us who read this book to step forward and change our lives. We must seek out our spirit guides. We must seek what is appropriate for our personal transformations. We must prepare ourselves for the great transition and for the new way of being that we establish on earth. Let us rejoice at this prospect and fill ourselves with joy, gladness, light, and love.

Appendix

The balanced breath is the most basic of all breathing exercises. Begin by sitting quietly and drawing attention to the breath. Watch the breath go in and out, and notice which parts of the body move along with the breathing. Now simply apply a count or a rhythm to both the in-breath and the out-breath. For example, use the count of three. Breathe in: one, two, three; breathe out: one, two, three. This ensures the in-breath and the out-breath are equal or balanced. The final step is to add a pause after both the in-breath and the out-breath. Breathe in: one, two, three; hold the breath: one, two, three; breathe out: one, two, three; hold: one, two three. This exercise helps to balance the energies in the body, as well as quiet the mind. A rhythm, a part of a song, a short saying could all be substituted for the count. Choose something that, when it is repeated, brings both balance and joy.

The alternate breath is used to quiet and center both the physical and the etheric bodies. Begin by sitting quietly. Breathe in and out at a regular rate, drawing attention to the breath. Now take the thumb of the right hand and place it against the right side of the nose, closing off the right nostril. Breathe in slowly through the left nostril, drawing the breath deep into the abdomen. Next, take the index and middle finger of the right hand and place them against the left side of the nose, closing off the left nostril. Lift off the thumb from the right nostril at the same time. Breathe out through the right nostril. Keeping the index and middle finger in place, breathe in deeply through the right nostril. Then close off the right nostril with the thumb, lifting the two fingers from the left side of the nose. Breathe out through the left nostril. Keeping the thumb in place, breathe in through the left nostril deeply and easily. Then replace the index and middle finger on the left side of the nose, lifting the thumb from the right. Breathe out through the right nostril, then in again through the right. Switch and breathe out through the left, then in through the left. Continue until the bodies' energies are drawn to center.

The alternate breath and the balanced breath may be combined simply by adding a count or a rhythm to the alternate breath procedure. The pause used in the balanced breath may also apply in the alternate breath method. For example: breathe in through the right nostril for a count of three; pause or hold for a count of three; breathe out through the left for a count of three; hold for a count of three; then breathe in through the left nostril for a count of three; hold for a count of three; breathe out through the right, one, two, three and so on.

∞ ∞ ∞

My name is Darci Stillwater. I am currently a resident spirit entity on a plane that is closely associated with earth. My dwelling here and my work here are both linked with earthly existence in a way that it is now time for humans to understand.

I am a spirit guide. It is my joyful duty to assist and serve my friend and companion Annie in any way I can. In doing so, I help both Annie and myself move forward in the evolution of our souls.

I have experienced many human lifetimes. This time I, along with many others, have chosen to serve the earth as a spirit guide. It is from this position I feel I can do the most to help the planet and all upon her in this crucial period of change. By residing in this associated realm, I have access to the knowledge of the vast workings of the universe. My skills for tapping the incredible resources available on this plane are highly developed. I have worked diligently to achieve this honored position, and I intend to use all my talents, skills, and resources to the very best of my ability to serve the earth and all upon her.

My association with Annie is blessed and unique. We have been paired in many lifetimes. Our karma is deeply intertwined. We chose to serve the earth together but from seemingly separate realms. Annie, of course, is incarnated as a human, and I have chosen a position as a spirit guide. We entered this situation with the intention of working together. We are pleased to say that our work has begun, and this book is the first result of our blessed relationship.

It is important for those who read this to understand that thoughts, words, visions, and feelings can all flow easily between the earth plane and this realm where spirit helpers reside. Much can be shared by humans and their spirit companions. The door is now open for much contact and communication between the earth realm and this spirit plane. My association with Annie is only one pairing of many that already exist, and there is the potential for many more. In fact, every human alive today has the ability and the opportunity to connect with appropriate spirit helpers.

The bonds between humans and the spirit guides who help them can be vibrant and strong. We spirit entities can become a real and active part of life on earth through our close links with individual humans. Indeed, it is time for those incarnated on earth to team up with those dwelling on this spirit plane for the betterment of all. It is through such teamwork between spirit guides and humans that the earth can not only survive the great changes but also evolve into a wondrous new realm of peace, love, compassion, and understanding. Much needs to be done. We begin by simply reaching out to each other through the veil surrounding earth. It is time for us to find each other and join together in love.

In the realm where I currently reside, there are many challenges. These challenges are quite different from those that humans face on earth. We in this realm work constantly to develop and refine our telepathic skills. We are also continuously examined by those master guides who teach us. Our knowledge of the workings of the universe must be thorough and exact. We must possess patience and forgiveness, compassion and unconditional love in such great amounts as are unimaginable now on earth. We must operate with the highest integrity in all we do. Only when we meet these criteria and more are we allowed to step forward and make contact with humans as spirit guides. When humans receive contact from spirit guides, they must realize that the spirit entities approaching them as guides have undergone thorough and rigorous training and have reached a certain plateau of honor. We spirit helpers are well qualified to assist humans and the earth at this time.

I, myself, have spent much time in preparation. My skills are such that the master guides selected me for this project, the writing of *The Dawn Book*. In selecting me, the master guides also chose Annie, for we are a pair. We each entered our respective realms with the wish, the goal of working together on a project such as this book. It took a great deal of time, preparation, and personal growth for us each to be ready, to connect, and to begin working together. This has now occurred, and I must take this opportunity to express my happiness, my joy at the bond that has formed between us.

The relationship between a human and a spirit guide is sacred. This relationship possesses some familiar attributes which also exist in human-to-human interactions. The greatest and most all-pervasive of these is love. Love knows no boundaries between realms and can flow strongly and easily between humans and spirit guides. Shared intimacy, comfort, security, and understanding exist in human-spirit guide relations as they do in human-to-human relations.

There are advantages which human-spirit guide relationships possess that human-to-human interactions do not. Since we spirit guides are detached from the day-to-day struggles of the material plane, we can assist humans greatly.

We can offer a universal perspective on earth life, along with knowledge and resources otherwise unavailable to humans. We are also always prepared and ready to help our human friends in any way we can. No matter where a human might be or when a human might call out for assistance, we spirit guides can be there instantly with comfort, suggestions, information, and love. There is no more special, more supportive, or more profound a relationship than the one between a human and a spirit guide.

As I mentioned before, Annie and I each entered our respective realms with an eye to working together. From the beginning of my instruction on this spirit guide plane, I was placed under the tutelage of the master guide Arcillis. He and the other master guides have for a long time been preparing the material contained in this book. The masters have always known about this great transformation now coming to earth, and they have been offering thorough instruction to all spirit guides on how we may best serve the earth and help humans during this transition.

Once the master guides were satisfied that I had completed all of the instruction that is now basic to spirit guide work, I was further educated specifically for this project. All of the material found here in *The Dawn Book* has been prepared by Arcillis and other master guides, and then given to me for final organization. It was my joyful duty to transmit this information, sentence by sentence, page by page, to Annie. She then wrote it down and is making the material available to all humans.

My bond with Annie is strong and filled with light and love. We wish to continue working together in service to the earth and for the good of all who dwell upon her.

∞ ∞ ∞

My name is Annie. I was born in the US to a Yankee mother and a Scottish immigrant father in the late 1940s.

Throughout my childhood, I was sure of only two things: I was extremely sensitive to the people and situations which surrounded me, and I was a seeker, always restless, but I did not know why. My nature is such that I allowed my feelings and my intuition to guide me. Rather than making hard, fast, rational decisions on what career would bring the most profit and material security, I allowed my heart to steer me to studying art and literature. Although it was not financially easy for my family, I received a full college education.

The first few years following my graduation were spent traveling around the country and the world with my musician husband. The continuous interaction with people from other countries brought me a wider perspective and a more tolerant outlook. Throughout this period, I was concentrating on photography and constantly studying the world around me through the camera lens.

I can see myself, a young woman in my early twenties, seated with my husband in a late-night deli in New York City after one of his performances. As we waited for the subway home, we were discussing his precognitive dreams. I was baffled. How could someone dream something that had not yet happened? I shall never forget how he turned to me and said, "Do you think that this," he motioned at the scene around us, "is all there is? Do you think that what we can see, hear, and touch is all there is in the universe?" I was dumbfounded and sat there motionless as my mind seemed to zoom into uncharted territory. From that moment on, I wanted to know what else there is besides this earthly existence. I began my studies by reading everything I could find by and about Edgar Cayce.

After the break-up of this marriage, my intuition led me to a new group of friends. I was working as a designer at a knitting mill, sitting day after day at a drawing board listening to FM radio. This is 1972 when FM was progressive and just coming into its own. I needed new friends, and the music drew me to introducing myself to radio people. Women announcers were very rare in those days, and I was fortunate to befriend one of the few women DJs on the air. She was beautiful, mystical, and continued my education by introducing me to the world of unseen energies. She taught me that the food we cook is only as beneficial as the enɾ gy we put into preparing it; she showed me how to use the I Ching; she drew up my natal astrology chart, which, when I saw it, stunned me with its familiarity. This thrust me into a deep and intensive study of astrology, and soon after my radio friends left the area, which radio people often do, I, too, became a DJ on a nearby college station. This is when I realized that I had a voice. Not just a voice to express myself, but I had a voice that suited the airwaves with its timbre and tone. Within two years, I was a professional announcer with a full-time on-air position. My study of astrology and my participation in some form of radio continues to this day. The constantly changing face of the media makes any radio job unstable and insecure. I managed to stay employed as a full-time radio announcer off and on for twenty years, but I had to change stations several times to do this. My search for agreeable employment led me to the state of Maine where I fell in love with the wild frontier beauty of the area. My intuition told me I was home. The mountains, the coastline, the lakes, and forests all called me to stay.

At midlife, I found myself in rural Maine, unemployed and burdened with a painful back injury. It was as if life had stopped me in my tracks. I looked back on what I had accomplished and I was dissatisfied. Had I wasted my time and energy studying art and writing and putting all those years into radio? These were some of the darkest days of my life. I spent most of my time in isolation. Even though I had meditated regularly for over fifteen years, I found it difficult to meditate now because of the pain. I tried doctor after doctor with little success.

Four months into the injury, I experienced a breakthrough which has changed my life. I felt Darci's presence very close to me, and I began to hear him speak to me. At first I thought

I had finally gone over the edge and lost all grasp on reality, but Darci was patient. He remained close and comforted me. My long walks to help my back turned into opportunities for long conversations with my beloved spirit companion. A friend gave me a copy of *Companions in Spirit* by Leah Maggie Garfield and Jack Grant. Darci suggested that I read the book carefully and learn the guided meditation outlined within it. I learned this chakra-cleansing meditation and gained confidence in my ability to communicate through the veil. In fact, the very first time I used this form of meditation, it was not Darci, but another guide who immediately stepped forward to help me with my health problems.

My outlook changed dramatically. Now I feel joy and love all around me. My guides bring me comfort and security, which I have never been able to find in this material realm. The first four months of spirit guide contact were still rough because my body was not used to operating on this frequency. I worked very hard at untying the knots in my third and fourth chakras so that my energy would flow more smoothly. I prayed and practiced yoga and meditation daily.

Three months into this new way of life brought Christmas 1989. By this time, I was comfortable with the chakra cleansing meditation, and Christmas week I practiced every day. On the winter solstice, Darci and I pledged to work together. The simple ceremony was attended by several from the spirit realm. The weather had been bitter cold for weeks, but on Christmas Day the temperature moderated enough for a walk outdoors. I remember I had cried that morning because I was overwhelmed by the cruelty and violence on earth. On this walk, I was contacted by the master guide Arcillis. The channel was very clear. I could hear his voice very distinctly. He told me all on earth will change, and he asked me if I wanted to be a leader in the new time. He asked me if I would write this book. He gave me specific instructions, that I should rise each day at dawn, ground and clear myself, and meet with Darci, who would convey the information to me sentence by sentence.

This is how I came to know Darci and to telepathically transcribe the information in this book. Now I see that all I have experienced in this lifetime, all the skills I have developed, have brought me to this point. Now I am filled with joy at the opportunity to step forward and serve.

Education of a Guardian Angel, the story of how Darci became a spirit guide and how he began his work with Annie, is now available from the author, from bookstores worldwide, and from Ozark Mountain Publishing, http://www.ozarkmt.com.

About the Author

Annie Stillwater Gray is a writer, a mystic, an astrologer, a public speaker, a teacher, an audio and visual artist, a healer, a singer-songwriter, and a media veteran. She has been on the air every year since 1974 and currently has her own syndicated radio program, The General Store Variety Show, now in its 15th year. Annie has studied Integrated Energy Therapy, Reiki, and Bach Flower Remedies. She has been helping people consciously connect with their Spirit Guides since 1989. Annie received a BFA from Boston University in graphic arts and writing. She creates songs and designs all the CD covers and publicity for her bands. At the date this book is released, her band is the western quintet Merry-Go-Roundup.

Books by Annie Stillwater Gray

Education of a Guardian Angel
Published by: Ozark Mountain Publishing

The Dawn Book
Published by: Ozark Mountain Publishing

For more information about any of the above titles, soon to be released titles, or other items in our catalog, write, phone or visit our website:

Ozark Mountain Publishing, LLC
PO Box 754, Huntsville, AR 72740
479-738-2348/800-935-0045
www.ozarkmt.com

If you liked this book, you might also like:

Holiday In Heaven
by Aron Abrahamsen
Between Death & Life
by Dolores Cannon
We Are the Creators
by L.R. Sumpter
The Essenes – Children of the Light
by Stuart Wilson and Joanna Prentis
Ask Your Inner Voice
by James Wawro
A Funny Thing Happened on the Way to Heaven
by Grant Pealer
The Healing Christ
by Robert Winterhalter

For more information about any of the above titles, soon to be released titles,
or other items in our catalog, write, phone or visit our website:
Ozark Mountain Publishing, LLC
PO Box 754, Huntsville, AR 72740
479-738-2348
www.ozarkmt.com

Other Books By Ozark Mountain Publishing, LLC

Dolores Cannon
A Soul Remembers Hiroshima
Between Death and Life
Conversations with Nostradamus,
    Volume I, II, III
The Convoluted Universe -Book One,
    Two, Three, Four, Five
The Custodians
Five Lives Remembered
Jesus and the Essenes
Keepers of the Garden
Legacy from the Stars
The Legend of Starcrash
The Search for Hidden Sacred Knowledge
They Walked with Jesus
The Three Waves of Volunteers and the
    New Earth
Aron Abrahamsen
Holiday in Heaven
Out of the Archives – Earth Changes
Justine Alessi & M. E. McMillan
Rebirth of the Oracle
Kathryn/Patrick Andries
Naked In Public
Kathryn Andries
The Big Desire
Dream Doctor
Soul Choices: Six Paths to Find Your Life
    Purpose
Soul Choices: Six Paths to Fulfilling
    Relationships
Tom Arbino
You Were Destined to be Together
Rev. Keith Bender
The Despiritualized Church
O.T. Bonnett, M.D./Greg Satre
Reincarnation: The View from Eternity
What I Learned After Medical School
Why Healing Happens
Julia Cannon
Soul Speak – The Language of Your Body
Ronald Chapman
Seeing True
Albert Cheung
The Emperor's Stargate
Jack Churchward
Lifting the Veil on the Lost Continent of Mu
The Stone Tablets of Mu
Sherri Cortland
Guide Group Fridays
Raising Our Vibrations for the New Age
Spiritual Tool Box
Windows of Opportunity
Cinnamon Crow
Chakra Zodiac Healing Oracle
Teen Oracle
Michael Dennis
Morning Coffee with God

God's Many Mansions
Claire Doyle Beland
Luck Doesn't Happen by Chance
Jodi Felice
The Enchanted Garden
Max Flindt/Otto Binder
Mankind: Children of the Stars
Arun & Sunanda Gandhi
The Forgotten Woman
Maiya & Geoff Gray-Cobb
Angels -The Guardians of Your Destiny
Seeds of the Soul
Julia Hanson
Awakening To Your Creation
Donald L. Hicks
The Divinity Factor
Anita Holmes
Twidders
Antoinette Lee Howard
Journey Through Fear
Vara Humphreys
The Science of Knowledge
Victoria Hunt
Kiss the Wind
James H. Kent
Past Life Memories As A Confederate
    Soldier
Mandeep Khera
Why?
Dorothy Leon
Is Jehovah An E.T
Mary Letorney
Discover The Universe Within You
Sture Lönnerstrand
I Have Lived Before
Irene Lucas
Thirty Miracles in Thirty Days
Susan Mack & Natalia Krawetz
My Teachers Wear Fur Coats
Patrick McNamara
Beauty and the Priest
Maureen McGill
Baby It's You
Maureen McGill & Nola Davis
Live From the Other Side
Henry Michaelson
And Jesus Said – A Conversation
Dennis Milner
Kosmos
Guy Needler
Avoiding Karma
Beyond the Source – Book 1, Book 2
The History of God
The Origin Speaks
James Nussbaumer
The Master of Everything
Sherry O'Brian
Peaks and Valleys

Other Books By Ozark Mountain Publishing, LLC

Riet Okken
The Liberating Power of Emotions
John Panella
The Gnostic Papers
Victor Parachin
Sit a Bit
Nikki Pattillo
A Spiritual Evolution
Children of the Stars
Rev. Grant H. Pealer
A Funny Thing Happened on the
    Way to Heaven
Worlds Beyond Death
Karen Peebles
The Other Side of Suicide
Victoria Pendragon
Feng Shui from the Inside, Out
Sleep Magic
Michael Perlin
Fantastic Adventures in Metaphysics
Walter Pullen
Evolution of the Spirit
Christine Ramos, RN
A Journey Into Being
Debra Rayburn
Let's Get Natural With Herbs
Charmian Redwood
A New Earth Rising
Coming Home to Lemuria
David Rivinus
Always Dreaming
Briceida Ryan
The Ultimate Dictionary of Dream
    Language
M. Don Schorn
Elder Gods of Antiquity
Legacy of the Elder Gods

Gardens of the Elder Gods
Reincarnation...Stepping Stones of Life
Garnet Schulhauser
Dancing Forever with Spirit
Dancing on a Stamp
Annie Stillwater Gray
Education of a Guardian Angel
The Dawn Book
Blair Styra
Don't Change the Channel
Natalie Sudman
Application of Impossible Things
L.R. Sumpter
We Are the Creators
Dee Wallace/Jarrad Hewett
The Big E
Dee Wallace
Conscious Creation
James Wawro
Ask Your Inner Voice
Janie Wells
Payment for Passage
Dennis Wheatley/ Maria Wheatley
The Essential Dowsing Guide
Jacquelyn Wiersma
The Zodiac Recipe
Sherry Wilde
The Forgotten Promise
Stuart Wilson & Joanna Prentis
Atlantis and the New Consciousness
Beyond Limitations
The Essenes -Children of the Light
The Magdalene Version
Power of the Magdalene
Robert Winterhalter
The Healing Christ

For more information about any of the above titles, soon to be released titles,
or other items in our catalog, write, phone or visit our website:
PO Box 754, Huntsville, AR 72740
479-738-2348/800-935-0045
www.ozarkmt.com